ASSISTIVE TECHNOLOGY
FOR YOUNG CHILDREN WITH DISABILITIES

Assistive Technology for Young Children with Disabilities

A Guide to Family-Centered Services

Sharon Lesar Judge
& Howard P. Parette

EDITORS

BROOK
LINE
BOOKS

ISBN 1-57129-051-6

Library of Congress Cataloging-In-Publication Data
Assistive technology for young children with disabilities : a guide to
    family-centered services / Sharon Lesar Judge & Howard P. Parette,
    editors.
        p.   cm.
    Includes bibliographical references and index.
    ISBN 1-57129-051-6 (pbk.)
    1. Handicapped children--Services for.   2. Preschool children-
-Services for.   3. Self-help devices for the disabled.   I. Judge,
Sharon Lesar.   II. Parette, Howard P.
HV888.A84   1998
362.4'0483'083--dc21   98-39363
                                                             CIP

Cover design, book design and typography by Erica L. Schultz.

Printed in USA
10 9 8 7 6 5 4 3 2 1

Published by
BROOKLINE BOOKS
P.O. Box 1047
Cambridge, Massachusetts 02238
Order toll-free: 1-800-666-BOOK

CONTENTS

Preface

The power of assistive technology to enable infants and young children to participate in family, school, and community activities is becoming widely recognized. Unfortunately, in this time of rapid technological development, many inherent challenges and barriers still remain. For example, some devices may be so sophisticated that the family finds them too frustrating and complicated to use. Other devices may be simple to operate, but finding and paying for them can be difficult for families. Inadequate training and inappropriate application of device strategies are increasingly becoming a concern of professionals. In addition, limited family involvement during assistive technology decision-making may result in limited device use by the child and family. These issues, as well as the movement from child-focused to family-centered early intervention services, point to a need for a comprehensive resource guide that can answer professionals' *and* families' questions about the various issues related to assistive technology services and devices.

This book is meant to assist professionals, parents, therapists, and anyone else involved with young children in the selection and use of appropriate assistive technology that promotes a child's overall development and has a positive impact on the entire family. It provides a blueprint for developing and implementing family-centered, culturally sensitive assistive technology practices. It is our hope that this book will enable more young children with disabilities to gain access to the technology that is truly assistive to their lives.

Chapter 1 provides an overview of assistive technologies and services, the issues and challenges facing the field, possible solutions to those challenges, and a framework for accessing and matching assistive devices to children with disabilities by using a family-centered approach. This chapter is important in terms of understanding the challenges as well as moving toward solutions to those challenges. Chapters 2-4 provide practical information and strategies related to the assistive technology applications that can be used by young children with disabilities. These chapters provide the reader with concrete ideas, activities, frameworks, and resources related to best practices in early childhood development and intervention.

Chapter 5 focuses on issues related to family-centered assistive technology decision-making. With careful consideration of child, family, and device features and service system variables, the assistive technology decision-making process should result in the selection of assistive technology devices that can improve the quality of life for many young children with disabilities and their families. Direct attention to families' expectations, needs, and perspectives is provided in Chapter 6; important concepts of family systems theory are discussed in the context of assistive technology interventions, along with specific information on how assistive technology devices and services affect the family. Chapter 7 explores cultural and ethnic influences and their relationship to assistive technology service delivery. With each individual child and family, cultural issues arise that must be examined in light of a wide range of considerations related to acculturation, developmental expectations, social influences, and life experiences. This chapter carefully explores the process of assistive technology decision-making from a more culture-sensitive perspective. Chapter 8 provides a conceptual framework for designing effective inservice training. Chapter 9 closes the book with our perspectives on the continuing challenges in assistive technology. The appendices are useful guides to assistive technology resources and equipment.

We believe readers in search of information on family-centered assistive technology assessment and intervention practices for young children will find the contents of this book timely and thorough. We acknowledge that no volume can fully explore the rapid developments in assistive technology; but we are confident that this volume, supported by continuing related literature, will help families receive more responsive and appropriate assistive technology services.

ACKNOWLEDGMENTS

Many individuals have given of their time and their knowledge to make this book possible. I would like to acknowledge those who were directly involved in the writing. I thank Phil Parette, my co-editor, for his obvious contributions to the book. Without his enthusiasm, encouragement, and collaborative nature, this book would not have been possible. I also extend my sincere appreciation to all of the authors who contributed chapters to this book. They were magnificent in producing chapters of top quality under bothersome conditions (i.e., my nagging). They have been a marvelous group to work with, and I have come away from this project with some new and talented colleagues. I owe much appreciation to Ms. Charlotte Duncan, whose careful editing and feedback has been invaluable. Finally, I would like to thank Dr. Milt Budoff at Brookline Books for his continual support and belief in the book.

I am especially grateful to my family and friends, whose tolerance and support have enabled my professional perspectives to develop and be documented. I especially want to thank my son Colin, whose sudden appearance delayed the completion of this book, but whose presence has helped me maintain a healthy perspective on what is important in life. *—Sharon Lesar Judge*

In addition to the acknowledgments noted above, I would like to express appreciation to Patty Riches and her family for their support of this effort. Their willingness to allow me the freedom to pursue a career has not been without sacrifice, and this gift on their part has contributed mightily to my ability to participate in this professional endeavor. *—Phil Parette*

Contributors

Dianne H. Angelo, Ph.D., Department of Communication Disorders and Special Education, 3A Navy Hall, Bloomsbury University, Bloomsbury, PA 17815

Mary Beth Bruder, Ph.D., Department of Pediatrics, Division of Child and Family Studies, University of Connecticut Health Center, 263 Farmington Avenue, Dowling North, MC-6222, Farmington, CT 06030

Patricia L. Hutinger, Ed.D., Macomb Projects, College of Education and Human Services, 27 Horrabin Hall, Western Illinois University, Macomb, IL 61455

Joyce Johanson, M.S., Macomb Projects, College of Education and Human Services, 27 Horrabin Hall, Western Illinois University, Macomb, IL 61455

Sharon Lesar Judge, Ph.D., Assistant Professor, University of Tennessee, 331 Claxton Addition, Knoxville, TN 37996-3400

Elizabeth Lahm, Ph.D., Department of Special Education and Rehabilitation Counseling, University of Kentucky, 229 Taylor Education Building, Lexington, KY 40506-0001

Howard P. Parette, Jr., Ed.D., Professor, Southeast Missouri State University, One University Plaza, Cape Girardeau, MO 63701-4799

Lois Symington, M.S., East Tennessee Technology Access Center, 4918 North Broadway, Knoxville, TN 37918

Alice Wershing, M.Ed., East Tennessee Technology Access Center, 4918 North Broadway, Knoxville, TN 37918

CHAPTER ONE

Providing Access to Assistive Technology for Young Children and Families

Sharon Lesar Judge
The University of Tennessee, Knoxville

Assistive technology is increasingly being used by young children with disabilities to enhance their quality of life. The recent advances made in the development of assistive technology has allowed infants as young as 3 months to interact with computers, 18-month-old children to use simple vocal output aids, and 3-year-old children to use sophisticated vocal output systems for intentional speech (Behrmann, Jones, & Wilds, 1989; Butler, 1988; Campbell, McGregor, & Nasik, 1994; Male, 1997). The assistive technology devices available are as diverse as the needs and characteristics of the children and families who benefit from them.

With the assistance of technology, young children with disabilities can experience more success in exploring the world around them; in communicating their needs, desires, and discoveries to others; and in making choices about their world. However, assistive technology must be viewed as a means rather than an end in itself. As tools for playing, it provides a means for children to use adaptive switches to activate toys. As tools for learning, it provides a means for children with physical disabilities to learn independently by manipulating their environments. As tools for communicating, it provides a means for children unable to verbalize to interact with others by using augmentative and alternative communication devices (Behrmann et al., 1989). In addition, assistive technology can be used to facilitate inclusion of young children with disabilities into regular child care, preschool, or other educational environments as well as home and community activities and routines (Campbell et al., 1994; Spiegel-McGill, Zippiroli, & Mistrett, 1989).

Even with the thousands of commercially manufactured and homemade assistive technology devices currently available, professionals and parents continue to demand more access to technology. While the benefits of assistive technology for young children seem clear, the reality of funding shortages, bureaucratic barriers, and accessibility can be frustrating and discouraging both for families and for professionals alike (Male, 1997).

This chapter is intended to provide a framework for accessing assistive technology devices and services using a family-centered approach. The chapter begins with a brief overview of assistive technologies and services. This is followed by a review of the research literature that highlights the issues and challenges affecting assistive technology service delivery. Finally, the implications of that knowledge to improve the availability of assistive technology to young children with disabilities and their families is described.

Assistive Technology and Related Services

The impetus for the use of assistive technology evolves from the passage of Public Law (P.L.) 100-407, the *Technology-Related Assistance for Individuals with Disabilities Act* (Tech Act). This legislation was designed to enhance the availability and quality of assistive technology devices and services to all individuals, including very young children. The Tech Act defines assistive technology as "any item, piece of equipment, or product system, whether acquired commercially off the shelf, modified, or customized, that is used to increase, maintain, or improve functional capabilities of children with disabilities" [P.L. 100-407, 29 U.S.C. 2201, §3(1)]. Examples of assistive devices for young children include positioning and mobility devices, augmentative communication aids, computer applications, adaptive toys and games, and the entire range of medical technologies, such as apnea monitors, ventilators, and tracheotomy tubes.

This broad definition of assistive technology has now become universal for most federal, state, and local institutions and has wide implications for education. It now appears in every piece of legislation passed since 1988. Using this definition, assistive technology embraces all devices and equipment which can help young children with disabilities to develop and use their skills to the best of their potential.

Assistive technology devices can be divided into two categories: high-technology (or "high-tech") and low-technology (or "low-tech"). Low-tech devices are passive or simple with few moving parts, such as simple switches, head pointers, picture boards, or crutches (Mann & Lane, 1991). High-tech devices have greater complexity and may have an electronic component, such as computers, power wheelchairs, or augmentative and alternative communication (AAC) devices. The number of high-tech devices has increased dramatically in recent years. However, low-tech options are often used prior to high-tech devices since they tend to be less expensive in cost and easier to access. A low-tech device may have as much value as a high-tech one if families find the device has enhanced their children's functioning, independence, and quality of life. Table 1-1 (on the next page) shows examples of devices from both categories that might be useful for young children.

The Tech Act further defined assistive technology services as any service that directly assists a child with a disability in the selection, acquisition, or use of an assistive technology device. Furthermore, the amendments to Part H of the *Individuals with Disabilities Education Act* (IDEA) *of 1991* include the promotion of the use of assistive technology for children ages 0-3 years. The Final Regulations define

Table 1-1. *Examples of low- and high-technology devices*

Low-tech	High-tech
Communication boards	Augmentative communication devices (e.g., Touch Talker, Wolf, Dynavox)
Walkers	Powered mobility equipment
Simple switches	Electronic switches
Velcro closures	Computers and peripheral devices
Scanning devices	Alternative keyboards (e.g., TouchWindow, PowerPad, IntelliKeys)
Adaptive utensils	Robotic arm, electric feeder
Loop tape messages	Speech synthesizer
Battery-operated toys	Computer software

early intervention services to mean "services designed to meet the developmental needs of infants and toddlers" and selected in "collaboration with the parents." In the context of the Part H program, assistive technology devices and services are to be determined on an individualized basis as part of the development of the Individual Family Service Plan (IFSP). Assistive technology services to young children include:

- The evaluation of the needs of a child with a disability, including a functional evaluation of the child in the child's customary environment;
- Purchasing, leasing, or otherwise providing for the acquisition of assistive technology devices;
- Selecting, designing, fitting, customizing, adapting, applying, maintaining, repairing, or replacing assistive technology devices;
- Coordinating and using other therapies, interventions, or services with assistive technology devices;

* Training or technical assistance for a child with a disability or, if appropriate, that child's family; and
° Training or technical assistance for individuals who provide services to or are otherwise substantially involved in the major life functions of children with disabilities.

Federal laws such as IDEA require that assistive technology devices and services be provided to children with disabilities by the public agency (e.g., public school, early intervention program) serving them. With regard to assistive technology, IDEA provides that if a child with a disability requires assistive technology devices, services, or both, in order to receive a free and appropriate public education, the public agency must ensure that they are made available to the child, either as special education, related services, or supplementary aids and services. Thus, if assistive technology is identified as part of the child's IFSP or Individual Education Plan (IEP), the assistive technology, as well as the training in the use of it, must be provided by the public agency at *no cost to the parents.* Other legislative policies that encourage assistive technology use for young children are described in Appendix F (p. 268).

Issues and Challenges Affecting Assistive Technology Access

It is clear, in light of the recent legislation, that the concepts found in these mandates not only open new vistas for young children with disabilities but present new challenges for all professionals who provide services to young children. Professionals are now responsible for helping children and families select and acquire assistive technology devices as well as instructing them in their use. Because of these new initiatives, agencies that serve young children have recognized the need for assistive technology and struggle to meet the challenge in a manner that provides appropriate technology, trains professionals and families in the use of assistive technology, and demonstrates unique ways for families to access assistive technology in a timely and reasonable fashion. Inherent in these challenges is the pressing need for greater sensitivity to both family and cultural issues during the decision-making process. This is particularly important given the increasingly diverse service populations who will become recipients of early childhood special education services in the new millennium.

These recent developments in public policy emphasize the significant contribution assistive technology may provide for young children with disabilities. Although the intent of the legislative policies is to increase the knowledge of, access to, and utilization of assistive technology, many barriers and challenges remain. As individual states evaluate the effectiveness of their assistive technology projects, they have raised many critical issues related to the actual use of assistive technology by young children with disabilities. These include: (a) limited numbers of young children receiving assistive technology services and devices, (b) insufficient funding for purchasing or renting devices, (c) inappropriate matching of child to technology, and (d) substantial need for assistive technology training and public awareness for professionals and families (Behrmann, 1994; Hayward, Tashjian, & Wehman, 1995; Parette & VanBiervliet, 1991).

Limited Access to Assistive Technology

One of the biggest technology issues is the small number of young children with disabilities who receive assistive technology services and devices (Hayward et al., 1995; Parette & VanBiervliet, 1991; RESNA, 1989). This unmet demand for assistive technology may be due to several reasons. First, many Tech Act projects initially felt their primary responsibility was to "get the word out" concerning awareness of technology assistance. However, this resulted in a limited number of children being provided direct services due to insufficient funding available for direct provision of assistive technology to children and families. Knowing about technology but not being able to obtain it creates frustration for many families and professionals. It is unlikely that states will have substantial success in creating resource bases to ensure the delivery of devices and services to young children. Changes in public and private insurance policies will be necessary since the assistive technology budgets of public school systems and other agencies are inadequate to effectively administer the costs of services and devices.

Another explanation for limited access is the scarcity of trained professionals to identify, assess, and implement needed assistive technology for young children. Even though every state and U.S. territory has received funding through the Tech Act to provide assistive technology devices and services, many professionals, as well as parents of young children, are unfamiliar with assistive technologies and often do not know where to begin to look for needed services or assistance. Lesar (1998) found that 68% of early childhood special education teachers surveyed felt unprepared in the use of assistive technology. For these teachers, limited knowledge and usage of assistive technology prevented them from accessing and implementing assistive technology services and devices. Even when school districts and agencies have technology specialists, assessments are often backlogged, devices are improperly matched to individual children following incomplete assessments, one-shot training may be provided, and there is little follow-up due to time constraints and multiple tasks imposed on specialists (Lahm, 1996). As technology becomes more available for young children with disabilities, having trained staff available who can assess a family's needs and child's technological needs and help them support the use of a device is essential.

Funding

Funding problems in most states are still a critical barrier for many young children with disabilities. LaPlante, Hendershot, and Moss (1992) claim that more than 2.5 million Americans are still in need of assistive technology devices because they cannot afford them. Funding under the Special Education and the Tech Acts is available for supplying technology-related needs, but it is limited. Many states are struggling to determine how the intent of the legislation can be implemented with existing funding streams. Even with a variety of federal, state, and private insurance funding sources, funding options beyond those currently available are very much needed for young children to obtain assistive technology (Wallace, 1995). In addition, a lack of information about sources of funding for assistive technology is frequently reported by families of young children with disabilities and professionals (Parette, Hofmann, & VanBiervliet, 1994).

Related to funding resources is the difficulty of repairing, maintaining, and upgrading the devices as needs change (Hutinger, Johanson, & Stoneburner, 1996). Many agencies and school districts do not have a technology repair system or a technology specialist to determine the cause of the malfunctions. Funding of assistive technology needs should include upgrading, maintaining, and repairing equipment in a timely fashion.

Matching Needs of Child to Technology

Successful use of assistive technology requires team-based assessments that lead to identification of appropriate devices and services. This occurs when family members play an active role during the assessment process and assistive technology decision-making is a collaborative effort between family members and professionals. When family and child needs, preferences, abilities, and experiences are not considered in the assessment process, the choice of device will most likely lead to limited use (Allaire, Gressard, Blackman, & Hostler, 1991; Culp, Ambrosi, Berniger, & Mitchell, 1986) or abandonment (Parette & Angelo, 1996; Scherer, 1996).

Problems associated with abandonment or lack of implementation of assistive technology may be a direct outcome of ineffective assessment and intervention processes. While the field of early intervention has emphasized family involvement in *all* aspects of assessment and intervention, family involvement during assistive technology assessment has been limited (Parette & Angelo, 1996). For example, agencies providing assistive technology services may utilize traditional assessment methods involving a succession of professionals seeing a child in isolation of the family. The use of traditional assessments, including standardized tests, have been recently criticized for not providing relevant information to enhance the acquisition of functional skills of young children with disabilities (Linder, 1993). The results of a traditional assessment may lead to the recommendation of a device geared toward specific school tasks, as opposed to a tool to facilitate independent functioning of a child in multiple environments. Additionally, therapeutic assistive technology services (e.g., teaching a child to use a device) may be conducted in structured settings that do not reflect the natural conditions under which a child will be expected to use a device. The lack of family input in the assistive technology service delivery system may delay a child's progress in generalizing use of a device to natural settings. Finally, the outcomes of traditional assistive technology assessments may yield very isolated recommendations that may result in limited device use by the child and family. One way to increase appropriate assistive technology recommendations for young children is to develop assessment and intervention strategies that promote child and family competencies in the assistive technology decision-making process.

Another factor associated with technology abandonment is a failure to identify family needs, resources, and support as a component of the assessment process (Angelo, Jones, & Kokoska, 1995). IDEA recognizes the key role families play in the development of the young child, as reflected in language such as "family-centered" or "family-focused" care. This rethinking of family-centered intervention in assistive technology contrasts sharply with a traditional perspective in which the term "intervention" is generally defined either at the level of program involvement or in terms of the provision of a specific professional therapeutic or educational treatment. For example, many assistive devices that are acquired for young children with disabilities are viewed as something used in a school or clinical setting instead of devices that increase the independence and functioning of children across environments. It is also frequently assumed that only specialists have the necessary knowledge and experience to make decisions about appropriate devices for children to use. However, the child and family have unique expertise concerning their activities and goals and the environment in which they live. Failure to use this expertise may result in the failure of the device to meet the needs of the child and family, resulting in abandonment of the device.

Training and Public Awareness

The future of assistive technology will depend on the extent to which individuals who provide services to young children and their families have the knowledge and skills to access and use technology services. Since preservice training in assistive technology is often lacking, professionals who work with young children with disabilities need additional training to increase their technology competencies (Kinney & Blackhurst, 1987; Parette & VanBiervliet, 1991). Lack of technology training and technology support services has been reported as a barrier to implementing assistive technology services (Behrmann, 1994; Hutinger et al., 1996; Lesar, 1998). It is reasonable to assume that if teachers and other professionals in the field of early intervention have inadequate skills and knowledge about technologies, then they are failing to access and use assistive technology with infants and young children. Ongoing training and staff development is imperative in order for professionals to become and remain informed users of advancing technology.

In addition to training professionals, there is a need to provide family members with information about and access to technology, including products, information services, and training on technology use. Parent training should focus on their rights to request assistive technology devices and services from schools and agencies (Hayward et al., 1995). To ensure that the device has enough practical applications and is responsive to child and family needs, training should occur in the context of the family's daily life and natural routines. When training integrates the technology into the home and community, it will result in functional daily use of a device that promotes the child's overall development of independence in his or her environment.

Implications for Practice

Issues related to access to assistive technology for young children with disabilities and their families must be linked to best practices. The following describes a model for obtaining and using assistive technology devices and services for improving service delivery. The prevailing professional and legislative focus on family-centered interventions coupled with innovative developments and research on technology abandonment and acquisition of skills establishes a need to develop a family-centered model (Blackstone, 1994; Parette, 1991, 1994). Table 1-2 contrasts the professional-centered model of assistive technology service delivery with a family-centered model.

While many young children gain access to assistive technology, studies show rates of technology abandonment ranging from 8% to 75%, depending on the type of device (Scherer, 1996). This crisis of

Table 1-2. *Family-centered model for accessing assistive technology services*

Professional-centered model	Family-centered model
Professional assesses the child in a clinical setting in isolation of the family.	Family is involved in the delivery of assistive technology from the beginning and leads the team process that includes home, school, and other environments.
Professional determines child's needs and choices based on assessment results.	Family gives specific information about needs, preferences, abilities, and experiences.
Professional selects the device based on available resources or amount of training required for the child and professional to use the device.	Family receives an array of options and hands-on experiences prior to payment.
Professional determines if the device is appropriate for the child.	Family evaluates the appropriateness of the device to determine if the device fits their needs.
Professional teaches the child to use a device in a clinical or school setting.	Family receives training in use of the device across settings and activities.

technology abandonment happens for various reasons, ranging from children outgrowing particular assistive devices to professionals determining what they think is appropriate as opposed to listening to child and family preferences. Often the reason for abandonment is that the family has had little say in selecting the assistive device. Other major reasons for technology abandonment include: (a) lack of meaningful training on how to use the device and/or lack of ongoing team support; (b) sophistication of the device to the extent that it confuses the family, child, and professionals; (c) lack of access to and information about repair and maintenance; and (d) lack of motivation to use the device or do the task for which it is intended (Phillips & Zhao, 1993). Users of assistive technology view this dilemma as a service issue (Turner et al., 1995). As long as professionals fail to listen to families and continue to assume the responsibility for determining the child's needs and choices, devices may continue to be discarded subsequent to family dissatisfaction.

There are several strategies that professionals and families can employ to ensure access and prevent technology abandonment (Male, 1997; Parette, Hofmann, et al., 1994; Turner et al., 1995). The key to success in implementing any of these strategies is for professionals to empower families to capitalize on the technological options for their children. Using a family-centered approach, professionals will need to reassess their roles and responsibilities and develop effective help-giving behaviors and attitudes that promote family competencies and decision-making capabilities in all aspects of the selection and provision of assistive technology (Dunst, Trivette, & Deal, 1994). Table 1-3 presents strategies to guide families and professionals in overcoming some of the barriers they may confront in obtaining assistive technology.

Implementing the strategies outlined in Table 1-3 requires that parents and professionals develop advocacy skills. Many professionals and families decide that the funding options for assistive technology are too complicated, and they become discouraged and give up pursuing devices and services. It is important that professionals and families become familiar with the disability legislation. By understand-

Table 1-3. *Strategies for obtaining assistive technology*

- Clearly understand outcomes of using technology that reflects existing family needs, strengths, and resources (not intrusive to the family; can be used in natural environments).
- Request literature on assistive technology devices, ask questions, and suggest options for selections.
- Become familiar with key disability legislation.
- Obtain a comprehensive technology evaluation, using a team approach. Family input is necessary if technology is to succeed over time.
- Talk with other parents, professionals, and others involved in service delivery to young children with disabilities about their experiences in using specific types of technology (child space, use, and maintenance issues; comfort level; training).
- Borrow or loan assistive devices for trial use prior to ordering. Families should be able to borrow and try out the technology before a purchase is made.
- Ensure appropriate supports and technical assistance be available to the family and service providers to effectively use technology (training, funding, maintenance).
- Identify a funding advocate familiar with sources of funding and skillful in assisting parents in justifying need for the device.
- Obtain information on the reliability and cost of maintenance and repair of device.
- Get information about the longevity of the device and how it can be adapted or exchanged when it is no longer in use for the child.

ing the disability legislation and adopting self-advocacy skills, their success for acquiring assistive technology will be greatly enhanced.

Many programs offer a short-term loan program whereby children and their families can try out the recommended technology. Assistive devices can be borrowed for a trial period so the family can access the technology over an extended period of time and use it during actual home and school routines. Often manufacturers offer rental options for extended evaluation and trial implementation, with rental fees credited toward the purchase price of the device.

Many states have established assistive technology centers or resource programs; these can be located by contacting a state department of special education or early childhood education division. In other states, technological resources are available through Alliance for Technology Access (ATA) Centers. The Alliance works in partnership with technology vendors, families, professionals, and persons with disabilities to provide the latest information about available products and services. A number of organizations are devoted to supporting the use of computers and assistive technology with young children. Most are listed in the annual *Resource Directory* published by Closing the Gap, Inc. Closing the Gap offers workshops, consultations, an annual international conference, and the most up-to-date reports available on technology uses in special education for children. Table 1-4 lists some of the resources available for finding more information about assistive technology for young children.

Concluding Comments

Despite financial problems and other barriers to acquiring assistive technology, use of devices has increased dramatically for young children with disabilities over the past decade. These increases may be due to increased public awareness; reduced costs of technology; and improved designs that make devices lighter, smaller, easier to use, and more adaptable. Nevertheless, considerable unmet demand for assistive technology still remains. We hope that the issues discussed in this book will provide a better framework for accessing and matching assistive devices to children with disabilities by using a family-centered approach.

Table 1-4. *Resources related to technology and children with disabilities*

Alliance for Technology Access
2175 East Francisco Blvd, Suite L
San Rafael, CA 94901
(415) 455-4575
email: atainfo@ataccess.org
http://www.ataccess.org

IBM Special Needs Systems
11400 Burnet Road
Internal Zip 9448
Austin, TX 78758
(800) 426-4832
http://www.austin.ibm.com/sns

American Foundation for the Blind Technology Center
11 Penn Plaza, Suite 300
New York, NY 10001
(212) 502-7642
email: afbinfo@afb.org
http://www.igc.apc.org/afb/

Macomb Projects
27 Horrabin Hall
Western Illinois University
Macomb, IL 61455
(309) 298-1634
email: TL-Carley@wiu.edu
http://www.wiu.edu/users/mimacp/wiu

Apple Computer, Inc.
Worldwide Disability Solutions Group
20525 Mariani Avenue
Cupertino, CA 95014
(800) 600-7808
http://www2.apple.com/disability/disability_home.html

National Center to Improve Practice (NCIP)
55 Chapel Street
Newton, MA 02158-1060
(617) 969-7100
email: ncip@edc.org
http://www.edc.org/FSC/NCIP

Closing the Gap
P.O. Box 68
Henderson, MN 56044
(507) 248-3294
email: info@closingthegap.com
http://www.closingthegap.com

RESNA: Association for the Advancement of Rehabilitation Technology
1700 N. Moore Street, Suite 1540
Arlington, VA 22209-1903
(703) 524-6686
email: natloffice@resna.org
http://www.resna.org/resna/reshome.htm

Council for Exceptional Children (CEC)
1920 Association Drive
Reston, VA 22091
(800) 345-8320
email: cec@cec.sped.org
http://www.cec.sped.org

Trace R & D Center
S-151 Waisman Center
1500 Highland Avenue
Madison, WI 53705
(608) 262-6966
email: info@trace.wisc.edu
http://trace.wisc.edu/

CHAPTER TWO

Assistive Technology Applications for Play, Mobility, Communication, and Learning for Young Children With Disabilities

Sharon Lesar Judge
The University of Tennessee, Knoxville

Elizabeth A. Lahm
University of Kentucky

The power of assistive technology is becoming widely recognized. Young children who are unable to communicate effectively, are physically challenged, or have severe disabilities are learning to use a wide range of assistive devices to participate more fully in life and in the learning process. Assistive technology can serve as the window that enables a child to have greater independence and more active involvement in play. The various types of assistive devices permit infants and young children with disabilities to move around their environments, speak and communicate with others, and participate in developmentally appropriate activities that might not be possible without technology (Campbell, McGregor, & Nasik, 1994).

Several studies have shown that young children with severe and profound disabilities can learn from contingency experiences through the use of assistive technology (Brinker & Lewis, 1982; Daniels, Sparling, Reilly, & Humphry, 1995; Sullivan & Lewis, 1990, 1993). Results from these studies suggest that activities with adapted computer systems, switch-interface devices, and switch-activated toys provide the important nonsocial character of contingency learning that is not easily experienced by children with disabilities who rely on social interaction with adults for most learning (Daniels et al., 1995). Contingency-learning experiences give young children with severe disabilities an initial step toward using more sophisticated types of technology for such functional skills as communication, mobility, or play (Campbell et al., 1994).

Assistive technology offers young children with disabilities a set of tools to assist in achieving developmental goals while interacting with objects, materials, adults, and other children in their environments. Through the use of technology, young children with disabilities may be able to participate independently in activities such as building with blocks, working puzzles, drawing, or making music. Assistive devices enable young children to play, speak, or move around their environment to facilitate physical and social inclusion in educational settings as well as in home and community activities and routines (Behrmann, Jones, & Wilds, 1989; Mistrett, Raimondi, & Barnett, 1990; Spiegel-McGill, Zippiroli, & Mistrett, 1989). Therefore, a greater emphasis on assistive technology should be incorporated into early childhood special education, since technology expands a child's options and independence (Hutinger, 1987; Hutinger, Robinson, & Clark, 1990; McCormick, 1987; Reed & Bowser, 1991; Spiegel-McGill et al., 1989; Sullivan & Lewis, 1990).

This chapter reviews assistive technology applications that can be used by young children with disabilities to enhance play, learning, communication, and mobility. We begin with a brief overview of the forms of play and describe how technology can be adapted to enhance play and learning environments. The next section contains a discussion of the issues related to augmentative and alternative communication (AAC) and technology-enhanced language development. This is followed by a description of the various types of assistive devices used for positioning and mobility. Finally, issues and future directions in assistive technology applications will be discussed. The software, AAC devices, and computer peripherals referred to in this chapter are listed in Appendices A–C (pp. 253-263).

Assistive Technology as a Tool to Enhance Play and Learning

Envision a preschool classroom with 15 children during center time. Some children are playing with miniature kitchen articles, baking a cake for baby's birthday. Two children are on the mat playing cars, crashing their vehicles into a block. A few are trying to build with blocks in the same area and are having a difficult time. Others are staging a war of dinosaurs, while some are coloring at the table. Everyone is busy doing something. Most are chatting away to themselves, their friends, or the teacher.

Now walk into the noncategorical special education preschool classroom. The same activity centers are in this room, but it is much quieter. A few children are either busy in the kitchen, playing with toy figures, or working with puzzles. Two children are on the mat with toys placed around them, but the toys have been bumped out of reach, and they cannot move closer to retrieve the desired play items. One child is in a wheelchair, which has been positioned in the kitchen area. A spatula and a pan have been placed on his tray, but he spends his time watching the others. About half of the children are verbalizing as they play. One or two try to catch the teacher's attention to show their accomplishments. Overall, the room is quiet, appears less busy, and feels like a less fun place to be.

In the first room, the level of play is intense, and language is being used to complement their play. This group of children is having fun. The second classroom also shows individuals at play; however, their play is less active and intense. Language is not used to facilitate play or social interactions. Some children are not involved in play at all.

If play is the "work" of children and the vehicle for gaining basic knowledge about their world, the second classroom of children will achieve far less than the first. To be most beneficial, play must be highly interactive, both physically and cognitively. A major role of the special educator in early childhood education is to adapt the play environment so all children can participate in high-quality play activities. "Failing to address these problems leaves children to learn in less normal, less useful, and more dependent ways" (Wolery, Strain, & Bailey, 1992, p. 102). Technology can be used to facilitate play and enhance the play environment for children with disabilities.

Forms of Play

Not until the turn of the century was play recognized as an important component in the development of young children. Some of the early classic theories provided a rationale for play through the perspective of their theory. For example, "play gives the active child an acceptable outlet" is from the "surplus energy theory"; and "they learn through their play" comes from the "practice theory" (Almy, Monighan, Scales, & Van Hoorn, 1984, p. 2). More recent psychodynamic theories express play as opportunities for children to "work out emotional conflicts." Piaget (1962) introduced the idea that play is crucial to cognitive development and develops in stages. Other theorists describe play as important in evolution and development, as a personality trait, and as performance (Almy et al., 1984). Today, play is seen as a critical component of early special education, both as a teaching context and as an end in itself (Cook, Tessier, & Klein, 1992). In both contexts, play facilitates language, cognitive and social skill* development, and general learning and literacy (Davidson, 1996).

Young children generally engage in three forms of play: sensorimo-

---

* A classic theory describes play in terms of its social character: *isolate play,* or playing alone; *parallel play,* or children playing alongside each other without social interaction; and *cooperative play,* where the children play interactively.

tor, symbolic, and game play (Sheiman, 1986). The level of social and cognitive complexity of play increases with the age of the child, shifting from predominantly sensorimotor play in infancy to predominantly game play in the primary grades. *Sensorimotor* play is characterized as functional, with motor actions dominant. Exploration and practice are also necessary to master an activity (Cook et al., 1992).

Symbolic or pretend play shows the relinquishing of reality to allow imagination to alter the roles and objects in the play situation. One object is used to represent another in dramatic and constructive play. Preschool classrooms provide opportunities for symbolic play through their homemaking, grocery store, and dress-up centers. Using pretend and representative objects, children play out familiar roles, such as baking, shopping, and other family routines. Cognitive, social, and language development are critical elements of symbolic play (Davidson, 1996).

Game play is characterized by the engagement of two or more people in an activity with a common theme. For example, one theme in Duck Duck Goose is tag, which sets the stage for learning turn-taking skills. In this stage of early game play, the teacher frequently orchestrates the activity by directing the required behavior. As the student grows older, these skills are expected to transfer to more complex, interdependent forms of game play.

Technology in Sensorimotor Play

For children with limited motor ability, technology can play a crucial role in adapting play environments. Battery-operated toys controlled by switches are often used to establish an understanding of cause and effect (e.g., when a switch is pressed, a toy fireman climbs the ladder). The broad range of switches available commercially makes it possible to use a simple switch with almost any child. With proper switch selection and switch mounting, most children can activate battery-operated toys to achieve interaction with their environment. Developing this skill is especially useful when school and service agency budgets are constrained.

The general types of actions most likely to be useful with infants and young children to activate a switch are listed in Table 2-1 below. Features of each type of switch are noted to assist in selecting the appropriate switch for each child. Several resources are available with instructions for making switches (Burkhart, 1985; Goossens' & Crain, 1992).

Toy selection for sensorimotor play demands a thoughtful process. Toys can be categorized according to their primary output modality: sound, music, motion/animation, travel or movement through space, and tactile. It is important to select toys that match the child's needs. Some children are startled by loud noises or abrupt movements. Children with sensory impairments need toys that capitalize on their alternate sensory abilities. Age-appropriateness of toys is also very important. A lack of motor ability does not mean the child lacks the cognitive ability to use toys.

When using switches with adapted toys, adults must be careful not to become fixated at the cause and effect level of interaction. It is easy to satiate a child on cause and effect interactions, especially with a limited library of toys. Understanding cause and effect is a founda-

Table 2-1. *Types of actions required for activating switches*

Action	Response requirements	
Touch	Any contact with the switch surface	
Pressure	Pressure applied to the switch surface	
Pneumatic	Air pressure change from a sip or puff	
Squeeze	Air pressure change from a squeeze	
Travel or movement	*Pass through*	Any movement through a specified plane
	Proportional	Movement results in proportional control
Neural or muscle	Contraction or relaxation of a part of the body	
Pull	Pull part of the switch away from another part	
Light	Movement of a body part with a light mounted on it; used to point	

tion skill required of more advanced skills. The teacher must construct the learning environment so as to elicit these more advanced skills. Cause-and-effect skills can be used to teach early communication, choice-making, sharing, and other skills.

Switch use at the sensorimotor play level does not have to be limited to battery-operated toys. Use of switches with functional environmental objects, such as tape players, fans, and lights, introduces the child to control of the living environment. Special switch interfaces can be purchased to provide a safe connection to electrical devices. Although these interfaces allow connection to virtually any electrical device, consideration for age-appropriateness of devices is a must. Typically young children are not allowed to activate most electrical devices, though items such as room lights, television, and radio are often within reach. However, introducing control of these items to young children with physical disabilities will advance their knowledge of the world and their role in it.

A more difficult sensorimotor environment to create is one that allows the child to discover many objects and effects at their own free will. In an attempt to replicate the play environment of children without disabilities, numerous interactive objects could be placed within visual range of the child with a disability. Multiple switches could be arranged so the child, either intentionally or unintentionally, activates them. In such an environment, the child is at liberty to explore many stimuli and develop preferences. However, this type of environment is difficult to arrange for the child with limited movement. Recently a new Baby Babble Blanket that advances us toward this type of environment has become available commercially. The blanket is constructed with 12 pressure-sensitive switches embedded in it. An infant lying on the blanket accidentally activates a switch with minimal body movement. The switches activate tape recordings of the parents' voices, providing positive reinforcement for movement. A similar mat could be used with animated and sound objects. Over time, use of this assistive technology should enable the child to demonstrate a preference for some of the objects connected to these switches and selectively move his or her body to activate those preferred switches (Fell & Ferrier, 1994).

Computer software is available to help advance children's skill levels beyond switches paired to single objects. Software that encourages the use of scanning and choice-making aids children in moving from cause-and-effect learning to using switches to select from an array of possible responses. This type of interaction will be important later when children are introduced to instructional software that uses a moving cursor to scan choices, or to AAC devices that use scanning to move between communication options.

Technology in Symbolic Play

Using technology in pretend play is not as immediately obvious to adults or children as a play area filled with props. As with these props, however, pretend play can be taught by adults and peers (Davidson, 1996; Smilansky & Shefatya, 1990). Similarly, pretend play can be taught using assistive technology as a prop. Adults and peers can implement play training by commenting, modeling, and scaffolding play relative to each of the three components of symbolic play: acting out pretend roles, pretending the use of objects, and pretending the use of action.

Adults play six different roles in the pretend play of children:

1. *Observer.* Possibly the most important role is observer. Watching children play helps the teacher know the level of children's play and where and when to intercede with the play.
2. *Stage manager.* As stage manager, the teacher prepares the play environment by securing adequate space and managing the child's play activities. Themes and props are chosen according to their familiarity and the skill level of the children. More realistic props are needed for younger and less skilled children, and more open-ended props for older and more skilled children. Specific exploratory and direct teaching activities are conducted to help make the props familiar and expand the knowledge base of the children.

When using assistive technology to facilitate play, the role of stage manager becomes critical. The technology, such as the array of switch-operated toys or the computer software, becomes a component of the play environment. These must be selected and arranged to match the needs of one or more children.

3. *Player.* The teacher can also be a player or participant in the play. Knowing the level of social development of each child, the teacher can co-play, facilitating parallel, associative, and cooperative play, as needed by a specific child. For example, the teacher can pretend to be feeding a dog by pressing a switch connected to a battery-operated dog.

4. *Mediator.* As mediator, the teacher helps the children resolve conflicts that arise during play. Often, when two or more children are using a computer, conflicts arise about who should operate the mouse or what software to use.

5. *Interpreter.* As interpreter, the teacher helps children understand the comments or perspectives of others, which are often coming from an egocentric point of view. Sometimes a teacher might have to help children clarify their communication with each other when communication displays are used for different activities.

6. *Social director.* The final role of the teacher is social director. In this role, the teacher helps the children enter into play and select roles and encourages other children to join the play activity. These roles overlap, with one intervention serving multiple roles for different children (Davidson, 1996).

For children with physical disabilities who cannot interact with the physical world to meaningfully explore it, a technology-based play area that replicates the play area of other children is needed. The area should be thematically organized. For example, if the theme is the house, the props available should be household items, like a telephone, doorbell, lamps, dolls, radio, TV, and other relevant objects. Each of these items should be able to be controlled by using a single switch. If the child is nonverbal, a peer or adult could assume the role of the child's playmate, providing language and context to the child's actions.

For children who are ready for more symbolic props, software can be used to create a meaningful and engaging play environment. Several levels of programs are available. On a very basic level, programs such as the *Living Books* (Broderbund) provide electronic environments that children can explore. When used with the house theme, a child can participate in solitary, parallel, or associative play using *Silly, Noisy House* (Voyager). The teacher or a peer can enhance the child's play by providing a commentary while the child with the physical disability controls the object selection process. If needed, utility programs like *ClickIt!* (IntelliTools) can be used to make the program switch-accessible.

On a more advanced level, programs that allow children to construct a picture that is then used to develop a story are available. *Kid Pix* (Broderbund) is a good example of a program that has many props that can be used to construct a scene. Depending on the language level of the child, adults or peers could assist with developing the story around the picture. Some programs have the stories already constructed, and the child can choose the ending, like "Toy Store." This allows children the opportunity to play out different perceptions of the world.

The application of assistive technology to promote symbolic play with children with disabilities is not currently documented in the literature. However, symbolic play is well documented in the dramatic play literature. Therefore, if technology-based programs can be used as a dramatic play tool, it would follow that assistive technology can be used to teach symbolic play by providing children with limited abilities the opportunity to participate in activities that promote higher levels of social, cognitive, and language development.

Technology in Game Play

Technology can be used in game play by providing access to game pieces, spinners, dice, and other game materials. Children without the ability to manipulate the physical devices of various games are limited in opportunities to participate. The adapted computer interface for children can serve as the access tool for manipulating simulated games pieces. For example, a child with limited motor abilities can use a simple switch to activate a "spinner" for such games as Candy Land or other nontech games often found in programs for young children. Simple software game programs that introduce children to turn taking and cooperative play are precursors for the learning that leads to higher level game playing, such as that found in multiplayer Sega or Nintendo games. Table 2-2, below, lists different types of computer software appropriate for the three forms of play.

Table 2-2. *Software for three forms of play*

Form of Play	Title	Source
Sensorimotor	Interaction Games	R. J. Cooper
	Press to Play Series	Don Johnston
	McGee Series	Lawrence
	Silly Noisy House	Voyager
Symbolic	Blocks in Motion	Don Johnston
	Animals Coloring Books	IntelliTools
	Kid Pix	Broderbund
	Millie's Math House	Edmark
	Playroom	Broderbund
	Toy Store	Jokus
	Silly Noisy House	Voyager
Game	Turn Talking	R. J. Cooper
	Candy Land Adventure CD	Playskool

Assistive Technology to Enhance Learning

Assistive technology is not only a desirable addition to instruction and the learning process; it is now mandated by federal law to be incorporated into educational programs for children with disabilities when appropriate. Thus, it is necessary to examine ways to incorporate these technologies into the best practice approaches of early childhood special education.

In general, play in the early childhood curriculum is described as opportunities for children to follow their own inclinations; and they do not need to be asked to follow the structure or routine imposed by the teacher. Some aspects of play in which computers and other technologies are particularly effective include: (a) intrinsic motivation, (b) attention to means and not ends, (c) freedom from external rules or limitations on practice, and (d) active engagement (Almy et al., 1984).

When computers are used with young children with disabilities, they are nonjudgmental and infinitely patient, allow children to explore or practice at their own pace, and never tire of repeating the same activity or story. These characteristics make computer-based instruction a natural strategy for instruction of young children. There are many opportunities within the preschool curriculum to naturally include computer-based instruction to capitalize on its potential benefits.

Theme-Based Learning

Typical early childhood classrooms incorporate a variety of activities throughout the school day. One common model is to use a theme for a week or longer as a context for many developmental activities. For example, "animals" might be used as a theme for the context in which the teacher conducts group and individual play activities, fine and gross motor activities, as well as literacy activities. The abundance of early learning computer programs available that provide exposure to an array of animals gives the teacher the flexibility of focusing the theme in several different ways (e.g., by animal habitat—pet, zoo, farm; by category of animal—mammal, reptile, bird). There are software programs that specifically teach the information about and recognition of animals. Other software programs use animal characters to teach other concepts, such as numbers. Still others tell animal stories or present animal pictures to be colored. A range of software programs is also available for other unit areas, including body parts, nursery rhymes, school, family, community helpers, foods, transportation, and seasons. Early childhood classrooms are rich with non-computer materials that can supplement any theme. The following section describes how technology can be infused into an animal thematic unit throughout various classroom activities.

Free play. Free play periods can include computer centers set up with programs that complement a current instructional theme. For example, these five programs might be available, each on a different day: *Talking Animals* (Orange Cherry Street), *McGee Visits Katie's Farm* (Lawrence), *Camelephant* (Jokus), *The Tortoise and the Hare* (Broderbund), and *The Three Little Pigs* (Milliken). These programs use different input devices, can be run alone or used cooperatively with a friend, and enable children with a variety of ability levels to participate. They provide children with a choice during free play time while introducing additional experiences with the animal theme.

Morning circle. Common activities during circle time include taking attendance (i.e., learning and recognizing written and spoken names), calendar (discussing days of the week, seasons, and holidays), show and tell (possibly related to the animal unit), and general announcements for the day or week. During circle time, the adult has the opportunity to introduce a new software program related to the theme. Attendance might be taken using a talking *SpeakEasy* with each child's picture on it. This provides the nonverbal child the same opportunity to say his or her name during roll call. A special theme song, such as "Old MacDonald's Farm," might be sung with the assistance of the computer. Some days the computer may be used to assist with singing, while on other days an adapted "Tape-A-Mike" might be used to capture the children's independent or group performances. The preceding examples of assistive technology can bring a new meaning to participation in the language-intensive activities of circle time.

Planned activities. All children need some direct instruction in order to efficiently achieve new skills; consequently, some classroom programming is devoted to more structured, planned activities. Some children may work on cause-and-effect skills by using battery-operated animals. Others might work on specific vocabulary-building activities related to the animal theme using computer software, such as the animal category of *First Words* (Laureate). Structured instruction may also focus on developing early number concepts for some children. Software programs that use animals for number skill development include *Mighty Math Zoo Zillions* (Edmark), *Playroom* (Broderbund), and *Millie's Math House* (Edmark).

Snack. All children enjoy snack time. This activity provides an opportunity for children to have additional fun with animals and technology. Animal crackers, decorated cookies, or cereals with animal promotion characters may be used. A *Wolf* voice output AAC device could be programmed to pronounce specific names of snacks and then used by the children to make requests. A cup of milk might be paired with a picture of a cow. The device may also have simple "yes" and "no" responses for responding to table talk during snack or a response for requesting "more" when additional food is desired.

Story time. There are numerous literacy skills that can be addressed by assistive technology during story time. Some are similar to the "reading aloud" activity that most teachers perform daily. Software programs like *Mr. Right's Animal Farm* (Powerhouse Entertainment) provide digital narration of stories but also provide the child the opportunity to control the pace of the story. The child can control the number of times a page can be repeated, allowing him or her to independently engage in the activity. The software also enables the child to have the story repeated over and over as many times as desired.

The teacher may choose to use the traditional printed book to read to the whole class and use assistive technology later to supplement that activity. The children can participate in the story by commenting on the pictures and sharing their thoughts. As an extension of the activity, one or more children can "re-read" the story again on the computer. Some software allows children to rearrange the ending of the story in different ways. Two examples of animal stories are *Explore-a-Story: The Three Little Pigs* (Learningways) and *The Ugly Duckling* (Milliken). Other software, such as *Kid Pix* (Broderbund), allows children to create their own animal stories by using tools to draw or to stamp pictures of animals on a page and then verbally record their stories about the pictures by using the microphone feature. These stories can be printed out and used to decorate the room or sent home to share with parents. Other software, such as Pelican's *Big Book* series, allows children to generate their own stories and then print them out in large, poster-sized colored books that can be used for story time.

Centers. The focus of center activities may be more on group activities rather than the independent activities during planned instruction. There are several software programs that introduce children to game playing through turn taking. For example, *The Playroom* (Broderbund) presents children with a mouse house in which children roll the dice and advance around the game board.

Each of the preceding examples illustrates the use of assistive technology across the curriculum when using an animal thematic unit. The individual objectives of the children can be addressed through a variety of on- and off-computer tasks. The computer is only one medium for presenting learning materials to children. It can assist in providing young children with multimodal learning opportunities to meet their unique needs. It can also assist in providing access to learning materials to some children who cannot access standard print and manipulative materials.

Augmentative and Alternative Communication (AAC) and Early Childhood

AAC devices have created options and opportunities for young children to develop communication abilities, overcome communication problems, and provide a link between them and their daily life experiences. Young children may use AAC devices to support (augment) or replace (alternate) a child's means of communication. Young children who have limited oral communication abilities may need to rely more heavily on these techniques, while for others it simply supplements and clarifies speech or is a transitional language that facilitates the later development of speech (Burkhart, 1993).

An increasing number of young children are using AAC devices as a means for communicating (Behrmann et al., 1989; Butler, 1989). Interestingly, several studies suggest that children using AAC systems do not demonstrate the range of strategies and techniques necessary for facilitating communicative competence in daily interactions (Goossens', Crain, & Elder, 1994). For example, Light, Collier, and Parnes (1985) found that only a small percentage of preschoolers in their study initiated communication using their communication boards, and only a small percentage of the vocabulary available on the board was actually used. In another study, Harris (1982) found that children using AAC systems tended to communicate predominantly with adults in the classroom and less frequently with peers. In addition, training and use of AAC devices tend to occur in isolated therapy settings rather than natural settings that occur throughout the day (Hutinger, 1996; Parette & Angelo, 1996).

These findings suggest that the manner in which professionals design and train AAC systems for young children in large part determines the way in which they will be used to impact their environment (Goossens' et al., 1994). Many factors should be considered to ensure the success of AAC systems in promoting children's language development and production of speech. These include access methods; output methods; and strategies that promote frequent, interactive, and generative use of AAC (Behrmann et al., 1989; Burkhart,

1993; Goossens' et al., 1994). Each of these factors will be addressed in the following sections to promote child and family competencies in AAC.

Access Methods

The access method is how the child will interface with or use the device. The method of accessing a device depends on the selection technique required and the display format of the assistive device. Appropriate decisions concerning the type of selection technique and display format are crucial for the child's success in using an AAC system. The type of AAC device selected for a particular child is based upon the child's ability to quickly access sufficient vocabulary with minimal effort. Usually the child's motor abilities rather than linguistic and cognitive abilities serve as the deciding factor in determining the access methods needed by the child. As will be discussed further in Chapter 5, a team composed of professionals and family members should evaluate over a period of time the most efficient access method for a child. Young children may initially need a more direct access method that purposely minimizes the cognitive and linguistic requirements of the child. However, when these same children demonstrate a basic understanding of communicative interaction when using the device, a more sophisticated access method or a series of different access methods can be used to address communicative needs for a particular activity.

Selection technique. There are two primary methods of access: *direct selection* and *scanning*. With direct selection methods, the child points directly to the desired target. At the most basic level, a child points directly with a finger, hand, eye gaze, fist, or any other body part. Sometimes a pointing aid, such as a headstick or mouthstick, may be required to improve the pointing process. Other indirect methods of direct selection include the use of a light pointer, optical head pointer, joystick, and switches (Glennen, 1992). Some examples of low-cost direct selection devices include a communication board, pocket picture holder, eye-point display frame, and communication vest.

Scanning is an indirect access method that requires less motor ability but higher cognitive and attending skills. Scanning is any technique or aid in which picture or symbol items are presented to the child visually or aurally and the child selects his or her choice by activating some type of switch. Some examples of low-cost scanning devices include loop tapes, rotary scanners, sequential scanners, and clock communicators.

The simplest form of scanning is item-by-item scanning. Using this strategy, the child activates a switch that presents each item, one at a time, until the desired selection is reached. Once the item is presented, a child can either use a second switch to select the item, activate the same switch for a longer time to select it, or pause for a preset length of time to allow the device to select the item. Some children begin with this method since it maintains their attention longer through active involvement and, thus, minimizes the time spent waiting (Burkhart, 1993).

Scanning speeds can be increased by presenting items in groups (row-column scanning or group-item scanning) or automatically. With row-column scanning, the communication aid scans by row until the child activates a switch when a desired row is identified. At that point, each item in the row is presented; and the child activates her switch again to select an individual item within the row. With automatic scanning, the child activates the switch to start the device and then waits while each item is presented. When the desired item is reached, the child activates his or her switch to select the item.

Whenever possible, direct selection techniques should be used with young children because they are faster and cognitively easier to learn than scanning. Infants as young as 9 months of age learn to reach and point to get what they want (Owens, 1988). Children who function below a 4-year-old age level have difficulty learning to use scanning methods because of the attention and higher cognitive skills required throughout the scanning process (Glennen, 1992).

Display format. Communication devices present information in the forms of real objects, photographs, line drawings, detailed pictures, colored symbols, letters, or words. Information can be represented using a variety of display formats that can be grouped either as static or dynamic displays. In a static display, the order and placement of the pictures or symbols remain the same. A static communication aid might have an overlay of pictures attached to a surface that needs to be changed manually—for example, by turning the pages of a communication book or changing the overlays on a communication board. In contrast, a dynamic symbol display can constantly change picture or symbol arrays electronically. This allows the child access to a large set of vocabulary items. There are commercially available communication symbol displays that can be used in a wide range of activities and with a variety of devices (see Goossens' et al., 1994; King-DeBaun, 1990, 1993, 1994). In addition, software programs are available to assist in display development, for example, *Boardmaker* and *The Communication Board-Builder* (Mayer-Johnson) and *Overlay Maker* (IntelliTools).

There are a number of alternative input options available for young children to access computer software. *IntelliKeys, TouchWindow,* and *Concept Keyboard* are just some of the products available for children to interface with a computer without using a mouse. Some products, such as *Discover:Board* and *Discover:Screen,* include sound in which the pictures, letters, words, and phrases talk.

Output Methods

AAC aids produce output that is either visual, auditory, or both. Visual output may be temporary, as with communication boards and liquid crystal displays (LCD), or may be permanent in the form of a printed copy (Tanchak & Sawyer, 1995). Most low-technology AAC devices that use visual output require the listener to be actively watching items being selected by the child. For example, when a child uses eye-pointing as a selection technique with an eye-gaze communication board, the listener needs to pay close attention to the target item.

Auditory output is available through high-technology devices, such as a computer or voice-output device, or through low-technology devices, such as a loop tape. Auditory output devices come with either *digitized speech* or *synthesized speech*. Digitized speech uses technology that records human speech. The sound is recorded digitally on a computer chip and requires large amounts of computer memory to retain a good quality of the recording. Most electronic AAC devices may be used to record any voice by directly speaking through an attached microphone. The spoken message is stored in the computer memory and, thus, sounds like the person who did the recording. *Macaw* and *Parrot* by Zygo as well as *AlphaTalker* by Prentke Romich use digitized speech.

Synthesized speech is computer-generated and uses a speech synthesizer. This type of speech uses text-to-speech translation, which means letters or words typed into the device can be spoken. The quality of the speech is related to the complexity and quality of the software that operates the system and the particular speech synthesizer used. Some speech synthesizers offer a range of child to adult male and female voices as well as the option of a customized, personal voice. Examples of AAC devices using speech synthesizers are Mayer-Johnson's *Link* and Adamlab's *Mega Wolf*. Recently, some communication systems combine both digitized and synthesized speech, such as Prentke Romich's *DeltaTalker* and *DynaVox 2* by Sentient Systems Technology. Finally, AAC systems may combine both auditory and visual output. Some devices offer a visual display with voice output and a built-in printer.

Current research suggests that young children show no preferences for the type of speech used with AAC systems (Burkhart, 1993). Some children respond better to synthesized speech, while others respond better to digitized speech. There are advantages and disadvantages to each type of speech. Digitized speech can be quickly programmed by recording anyone's voice. This helps a child remain actively involved in special activities, such as singing or making social comments. Since digitized speech can be easily programmed, the device can be cycled through different activities during the day. The main disadvantage of digitized speech is that the child is not able to produce his or her own messages since the devices need to be re-corded by a speaking individual ahead of time. In contrast, synthe-sized speech provides consistent feedback to the child since the sound is always the same. This consistency may help children with auditory processing problems and hearing disabilities (Burkhart, 1993). Syn-thetic speech may be robotic sounding, which can be motivating for some children. However, some professionals express concerns about children identifying with or imitating robot speech (Butler, 1989). As suggested by Burkhart (1993), the best voice-output devices would incorporate aspects of both types of speech, with the majority of vo-cabulary stored as synthesized speech and a small amount left for digitized speech.

AAC Strategies

Providing young children with a means to communicate does not automatically enable them to be active communicators (Behrmann et al., 1989). Besides access to AAC systems, young children need strat-egies that will help increase their use of the system in a generative and interactive fashion (Goossens' et al., 1994). Young children must be provided with frequent examples of interactive use of the AAC system in natural settings. As discussed earlier, play-based activities may provide excellent opportunities to facilitate communication and language development.

For very young children, it is often difficult to identify an appro-priate AAC device. Young children develop at different rates, and their need for a specific AAC device may change with their develop-ing skills. In addition, a child may need more than one way to com-municate, depending upon the needs of the child and the activity. Another consideration involves the funding and time required to se-cure the device. The process of identifying appropriate AAC devices and accessing the appropriate funding source, coupled with ordering the device and awaiting its delivery, may require months. By the time the device arrives, the child's needs may have changed, while valu-able learning time has already been lost (Burkhart, 1993). Therefore, it is suggested that a variety of communication aids be used that are currently available or easily acquired (see Goossens' et al., 1994, for constructing low-technology devices). For example:

> Linda is a 3-year-old child with cerebral palsy. She has good head control and good eye-movement skills. During circle time, she uses an optical head pointer to select the symbol for "sunny" on her communication board when a calendar activity is presented to her. During free choice, Linda chooses her center activity by eye-pointing to an eye-point horseshoe frame.

In addition, a number of inexpensive communication devices allow children to speak short phrases or messages. These devices can be used with different children and across activities. Examples of simple voice-output devices include *BIGmack* by AbleNet and *CheapTalk 4* by Toys for Special Children.

A number of AAC training strategies have been outlined by Goossens' et al. (1994, pp. 10–16) that are helpful when working with young children.

- *AAC training should be conducted within the natural environment.* Communication training conducted within natural settings with the relevant communication partners promotes the generalization and interactive nature of the device. Activities should concentrate on establishing the natural communication skills for the setting in which the device will be used. This may involve training parents, family members, teachers, and other caregivers in ways to integrate AAC devices in activities and routines at home and at school.
- *Children should be provided with frequent examples of AAC use.* Children do not automatically become proficient users of AAC systems. To become proficient users, children must observe other individuals modeling interactive, generative use of their AAC systems. This requires parents, family members,

teachers, and other significant caregivers to use the child's system to communicate with the child. The communication content should be concentrated enough to communicate frequently and interactively throughout the target activity or routine.

- *Children should have access to multiple communication displays.* Young children are involved in numerous activities and routines across the day. Some activities require different AAC systems to address the communicative needs of the child. For example, some activities require choice-making displays, whereas others require activity-based displays. A variety of display formats and selection techniques will be needed for the range of activities and needs presented by a child. It is essential that vocabulary be motivating to the child. A child's present and future communication needs should be considered when developing communication displays.

- *AAC training should foster communicative interaction between peers.* By integrating AAC devices into daily activities, social interaction among young children is encouraged. In a classroom setting, various children's communication systems should be created with some shared message content to allow children to interact with each other. In addition, children benefit from observing peers communicate, using the same message content to which the AAC user also has access. Activities should be planned so all the children in the classroom or all family members use the device in social, turn-taking interactions.

Finally, a substantial amount of early childhood software has been developed that can promote communication and language development. Software, such as *McGee* (Lawrence) and *Creature Antics* (Laureate), exists for interactive turn taking. Broderbund's *Living Books* and *Storytime Tales* by King-DeBaun promote emergent literacy skills. These typically enable young children to independently choose their story, turn pages, highlight, and have text read by hitting a switch.

Other software is available to build early vocabulary and labeling. Computer graphics and animation software encourages social and communication interaction for children with and without disabilities (Hutinger, 1996; Spiegel-McGill et al., 1989).

Assistive Technology and Mobility Skills

Locomotion and other motor skills allow children to master, control, and interact with their environments. For young children with physical disabilities, restricted mobility denies such opportunities for self-directed exploration. For these children, a variety of assistive devices are needed to make mobility possible. The development of new technology has contributed to the increasing use of powered mobility by children as young as 18 to 24 months (Butler, 1989).

Traditionally, professionals and parents have been reluctant to use powered mobility with young children due to several fears: (a) that children may lose or fail to develop the skills needed to walk due to powered chair use, (b) that children would injure themselves or injure peers who might get in their way while learning to drive powered mobility devices, and (c) that children might be less motivated to participate in therapy programs aimed at developing muscle strength and coordination for walking (Petty, 1994). However, research in the past decade has shown positive effects on young children who use powered mobility (Butler, Okamoto, & McKay, 1983; Butler, 1989; Paulson & Christofferson, 1984). Parents and professionals reported improved head control, trunk stability, and arm-hand function; increased motivation in other forms of movement; and more self-confidence in movement activities. Children also showed increases in communication, exploration, social interactions, and self-esteem, with no negative effects on motor development.

Based on this research, powered mobility is increasingly being made available to young children. The use of powered mobility may reduce the risk of further developmental and social delays by providing varied and appropriate experiences for young children in their homes, schools, and communities (Petty, 1994). With powered mobility and other assistive devices (motorized toy vehicles, walkers, scooter boards, standers), children can gain independence and a sense of control over themselves and their actions. Therefore, powered mobility should be made possible for children with disabilities as early as possible (Campbell et al., 1994).

Selecting the Mobility Device

A team approach, as described in Chapter 5, should be involved in the decision-making process when choosing a mobility device. The team involved in recommending and obtaining the necessary assistive mobility device should complete a functional needs assessment. Selection of a device should be appropriate not only in terms of the best anatomical alignment for the child but also in terms of the child's functional activities. Simple features that influence the usefulness of a mobility device may include its ability to fit under a table for meals or through the bathroom door in the child's home. A team composed of professionals and family members will have a wider range of perspectives for these details (Burkhart, 1993).

In order to assess the child's activities that require mobility, the team should begin by talking at length with the family, caregivers, classroom staff, and others who interact with the child on a daily basis. Members of the team should also spend time observing the child in all of the natural environments in which he or she participates. If children are able to communicate, either verbally or through AAC, it is important that they be given the opportunity to identify other places they want to go but cannot go without assistance (Gilson & Huss, 1995).

When assessing a child's need for an assistive mobility device, the child's strength, endurance, posture, sensation, energy level, and stamina must be evaluated before making a recommendation. Considerations for growth and future needs must also be taken into account. For example, young children quickly outgrow their walkers and standers. Other specific mobility device-related issues that need to be considered are listed in Table 2-3.

Table 2-3. *Specific mobility-device-related issues*

Issues	Questions to ask
Batteries	Where is battery and power system located on device? What types of batteries does device use? Are batteries rechargeable? What is the cost, and how easy is it, to recharge the batteries? How long will device operate after it is fully charged?
Braking	What type of braking system is used for stopping? Does braking system match child's physical and cognitive abilities?
Control methods	What control devices are available to maneuver device? Is more than one control option available for device? Can control methods be upgraded to accommodate physical and cognitive needs of child? Are control methods based on individual needs?
Displays	Are displays easy to see and read? Are displays easily programmable or changeable?
Environments	Does child have an accessible environment in which to use device? Do child's primary environments physically support powered mobility? Will use of device in child's primary environments create stress or other potential concerns for family?
Funding options	Can funding source secure device promptly? Is there a period of time for trial use of device before purchasing?
Maintenance and repair	Are loaner devices available during repair intervals? Are family/child willing to provide appropriate maintenance of device?
Noise	Does device make much noise?
Positioning options	Are there a variety of positioning options that meet child's needs? Can positioning options change as the child grows?
Seating system and compatibility	What seating systems are available that meet child's needs? Is the seating position optimal for child's physical development?
Size selection	Is device child-sized and user-friendly? Is seat height appropriate for child?
Stability	Is device stable when making turns, starting, and stopping?
Training	Will family and child be provided with the training necessary to operate device effectively?
Transportation	How will device be transported between settings? Is tie-down system adequate to secure device during transporting? Does device call undue attention to child/family during transporting?
Turning space	Does device need much space to make turns?

Other Considerations

Once the selection of the mobility device has been determined, other child needs must be considered. AAC systems may be integrated with a power mobility device. For example, an electronic AAC device could be mounted to a child's lap tray on the powered wheelchair. Making sure that the various systems are compatible and the AAC system is easily operable through the power of the mobility device is critical. In encouraging exploration and independence in young children, various mobility devices may be needed to meet all the child's therapeutic and functional needs. For example, a child may require one type of mobility device that provides postural support and another type that assists in independent mobility. Various battery-operated toy vehicles (e.g., Barbie's car or jeep) provide alternative options to more costly powered mobility devices, and the battery-operated toy vehicles may be more motivating for young children to learn to operate. These toy vehicles can be adapted for switch use and positioning. Specialized walkers, standers, push carts, and tricycles may be effective mobility aids for some children.

Equally important is having a training plan for the child and any others who will assist in the use and care of the mobility device. Toddlers and young children need to spend time operating the powered mobility device to learn about control of their own mobility (Campbell et al., 1994). This may take place in more open environments (e.g., gym, playground, or hallway) to learn to activate, stop, and steer and maneuver the device. For young children, it may be more effective to provide numerous short opportunities with the powered mobility device throughout the day instead of one longer session.

Future Directions

Today the value of assistive technology is increasingly recognized, and there are direct efforts by many individuals and service systems to adapt new technologies to meet the educational needs of young children with disabilities. Technology innovations are being developed at an extremely rapid rate. Developments in one area spawn applications in others, and as the impact of technological advances rapidly reaches the masses, it affects the lives of all people. Since these developments are often used for specific applications, there is a concerted effort on the part of the federal government and professionals in the disabilities field to investigate ways to reconfigure new technologies for the benefit of persons with disabilities. For example, NASA has a major technology transfer mandate. Using interviews and focus groups, they identify technology needs in the special education field and explore the feasibility of adapting current NASA technologies for a particular application. One such priority was the development of simple monitoring and life-support systems for medically fragile technology-dependent children in educational and community settings (Center for Special Education Technology, 1991). Due to the possibility and inherent consequences of human error, many transfer efforts are focused toward developing technologies to perform tasks that would be better executed by machine. "Smart technologies" developed for military and other scientific applications can provide consistent instruction matched to the learner's needs. Through such technology-transfer efforts, the power of computers and other technologies is becoming more accessible to individuals with disabilities.

The high computational power of today's computer chip is available at very low costs to all application fields. One application of the computer chip having implications for special education is in systems that store and simultaneously display information in multiple modalities, such as sound, graphics, and motion video. Coupled with the speed at which today's computers can process decision-making rules, interactive instructional systems are now a reality. Smart "virtual environments" in which young children can explore new worlds could soon be a reality. With today's adaptive access technologies and with those that will be developed in the near future, infants and toddlers with disabilities will be able to independently explore their worlds in safe and stimulating environments.

As research knowledge in the field of assistive technology increases, special educators will be in a better position to relate play, cognition, language, and other areas of early childhood development to assistive technology devices created by developers. Input provided by early childhood special educators provides developers with the necessary information to visualize how emerging technologies can be adapted to meet specific needs of young children with disabilities and their families. Such collaboration between educators and vendors will yield more developmentally appropriate programs and devices for young children with disabilities. Improved knowledge and understanding encourages developers to take the risk of creating applications for this underserved market.

CHAPTER THREE

Learning and Growing With Assistive Technology

Alice Wershing & Lois Symington

East Tennessee Technology Access Center

The field of assistive technology has blossomed and flourished over the past 10 years, offering expanded avenues for participation of young children with disabilities in home, school, and community environments. Failing to consider the potential role of assistive technology limits the many ways in which children with disabilities can participate in appropriate early childhood experiences. The following scenario illustrates how assistive technology can be used in an early childhood setting:

> Ten young children are gathered in a big room and are playing with a variety of objects. Two are taking turns operating a toy monkey that moves its tail and chatters. Two are experimenting with positioning a toy lion, zebra, and tiger under a chair that is decorated to look like a jungle. An-

Acknowledgments: Special thanks to Sammy Carver for creating the piñata, menorah, and other materials for use in the Holiday Theme; to Martha Iroff for her suggestions for latkes; and to Maria, Clara, Morgan, Michaeline, Andrew, Mike, Molly, Katheryn, Carolyn, Jessica, Alisha, and Ryan and their families for participating in the Kids' Time activities.

other is examining a stuffed elephant to see how it works. A two-year old is vigorously riding a rocking horse. While an adult sets up a computer and the opening screen of the software sings across the room, several children move towards the computer. One young child who uses a wheelchair is moved by her grandmother so she can join the group. Another young child moves beside her and asks to sit with her.

Although this sounds like a typical play group of young children, there are a few differences. This group includes children with and without disabilities. Additionally, all the toys have been adapted so that children with a variety of access methods can all play with them. Activities are designed to implement a theme—animals of the jungle —which has been selected on the basis of children's interests and experiences and which supports and encourages emergent literacy. Children can explore a variety of activities that have been designed to meet their various needs, ages, ability levels, and interests. Some enjoy hearing a book read to them, while others want to read the book by themselves. One wants to draw a picture using a mouse; another prefers to color, using a picture already drawn in *KidPix* (Broderbund) and made accessible through *ClickIt!* (IntelliTools). As with all young children, there are a multitude of noises as adults facilitate so that all can participate, enjoy, and learn. Reminders to take turns and to share abound amid the enthusiastic expressions of joy and excitement from the children who are waiting to use different kinds of computers and assistive technology, mostly for fun but also for learning.

This chapter discusses how computers, software, and assistive technology can be used as tools to enhance play and learning for young children with disabilities. Best practices in early childhood development and intervention will be discussed with specific ways children's play activities can be made accessible through the use of computers, software, and assistive technology. Readers will be guided through the steps of developing a thematic unit that incorporates assistive technology, and will receive guidelines to follow in considering modifications and access needs of young children. The software, voice output devices, and computer peripherals referred to in this chapter are listed in Appendices A–C (pp. 253-263).

Beliefs and Assumptions

Several beliefs and assumptions guide the practice of early childhood special education professionals. Best practices in education and early intervention of young children stress developmentally appropriate, experience-based activities that incorporate highly interesting content and elements of play, humor, and surprise. When these activities combine repetition, use of alliteration, and predictable stories, they are more likely to engage children and maintain their attention (Bredekamp, 1992). The following practices are consistent with current trends and best practices in the field of special education and early intervention:

1. Children with disabilities need access to the same experiences as children without disabilities to develop literacy concepts and a conceptual understanding of natural contexts. Children gain knowledge of natural contexts through experiences with people, objects, and events in their environments.

2. When children play, they explore, create, build, manipulate, learn, discover, imagine, imitate, pretend, interact, socialize, and communicate. They learn about natural contexts through play activities.

3. Play activities should be organized around themes based on the needs, interests, and capabilities of the children who are participating. Themes selected for play activities should be sensitive to children's experiences and cultures and be supported by the use of "best practice" curricular and commercial materials that are made available to all the children.

4. Participation in play and leisure activities promotes quality interactions between children with disabilities and their typi-

cal peers. Such interactions facilitate cognitive and language development.

5.   Assistive technology devices, including computers and software, enable children with disabilities to increase their active participation in a variety of play, leisure, academic, and therapy activities. Assistive technology devices also allow children with disabilities to experience and actively participate in age-appropriate activities with children who are nondisabled.

Assistive Technology and Young Children

Research focusing on preschoolers at play has shown that children engage in a wide variety of games, dramatic play, and linguistic play. Such activities have positive effects on personality and cognitive and language development (Vygotsky, 1962/1986). Most scholars note the transformational nature of play, since it combines game formats, exposes the child to contrasting sounds, images, movements, desires, and beliefs, and requires the child to switch in and out of contexts. In spontaneous play, children construct "microworlds" in which it is safe to explore unfamiliar or dangerous issues.

Children recreate the world in their own terms, selecting topics they think are important. One of their earliest activities is learning the concept of "fullness" or "cupness" by repeatedly filling and emptying a cup of water or sand. They take more pleasure out of playing with an empty box than with whatever was in the box. Much linguistic play is also transformational. When playing jump rope and in choosing rhymes, children explore the phonological, syntactic, and semantic rules of language well past the ages of the acquisition of basic sentence structures in a specific language. Children also transform facts they acquire about natural and cultural phenomena into play by making objects explode, become old, little, or obsolete.

Free play is often experimental or exploratory—children try out alternatives based on implicit principles of language, the social world, or other phenomena. Children experiment with the meanings of language (e.g., when they make up and repeat riddles). Similarly, they experiment with natural phenomena, such as gravity, when they try many different ways of rolling a ball. Some researchers have shown that through transformations of reality, language, and knowledge, children elaborate their emotional and cognitive understandings and construct their own models of how the world works. As children construct and control situations in the safety of play, they can release or overcome feelings related to confusion, doubt, or fear.

Assistive technology devices are tools that enable children with disabilities to explore natural environments. Software offers open-ended experiences and opportunities to design individual and unique experiences. Children with disabilities have an opportunity to play in simulated environments that might otherwise be difficult or impossible. For example, *IntelliPics* (IntelliTools) is a software program that can be used to provide access to books for a child who is unable to hold a book, turn pages, and independently read. Both text and graphics can be either scanned in or created and then accessed through a keyboard, mouse, *IntelliKeys* keyboard (IntelliTools), or switch access.

Switch-Adapted Toys and Alternative Input Devices

Children who cannot activate small switches on battery-operated toys often benefit from switch-adapted toys. When toys are adapted with switch interfaces, young children with disabilities may have the opportunity to develop concepts such as time (e.g., "make it go faster") and space and direction (e.g., "make it come to me"). Alternative input devices—e.g., adapted keyboards, such as the *IntelliKeys* keyboard (IntelliTools) or *Discover Board, Discover Switch*, and *Discover Screen* (Don Johnston)—integrate with software and allow adults to create custom overlays that provide unique opportunities for children to explore and learn concepts related to shapes, colors, numbers, object identification, event sequencing, and making nonsense words, phrases, and sentences. These tools also allow children to demonstrate competency and understanding with their peers in age-appropriate activities.

Augmentative and Alternative Communication (AAC) Devices

Since young children with disabilities need opportunities for autonomy and the development of emergent literacy skills, AAC devices may often be beneficial to accomplish these goals. Using simple AAC devices, such as the *AlphaTalker* (Prentke Romich), *Macaw* (Zygo), and *SuperHawk* (AdamLab), children can communicate needs ("I need to go to the potty") and preferences ("I want to read a book"), ask questions ("Where is Mommy?"), and participate in play. The *Super-Hawk*, an AAC device manufactured by the Wayne County Regional Education Services Association, can be programmed to provide nonverbal children with a "voice" that enables them to effectively participate in board games with typical peers. For example, when the child touches a space on the display panel or activates a switch connected to the SuperHawk, statements such as, "It's my turn," "I'll roll the dice," "I got a 3!" or "It's your turn now" might be spoken. Another new device from Ablenet, the *All-Turn-It*, provides access to games requiring the child to operate a spinner, roll dice, or make random selections.

Importance of Play

For children, play is an important context for the development of motor, cognitive, communication, and social skills. Although children with disabilities frequently have limited opportunities to explore their world through play, these experiences are just as important and beneficial to them as it is for children without disabilities. Through the use of assistive technology, children with disabilities have a set of tools to access parts of their world that are otherwise inaccessible. This enables them to act upon their environment, to cause events to happen, to exert some control over what happens in natural settings, and to make choices. In addition, assistive technology provides a scaffold for the development of social, academic, and language skills in ways that might otherwise be impossible.

Theories Contributing to the Role of Play in Child Development

Theorists who have contributed to the belief that young children learn through play include Vygotsky (1986) and Piaget (1962). An understanding of both theoretical perspectives provides adults with a conceptual basis for the use of assistive technology with young children who have disabilities.

Vygotsky's (1986) theories suggest that thinking and learning are social and dynamic. Parents, teachers, and peers act as mediators to help children move from their current level of functioning to a more advanced level. This is accomplished by (a) making suggestions, (b) providing hints or encouragement, (c) use of demonstrations, or (d) in some other way explaining the meaning of a task or activity. Children internalize the problem-solving strategies that are provided them socially by adult or peer mediators. Both thinking and learning are dynamic and occur in social settings with interactions between individuals.

A practical application of Vygotsky's theories may be observed when adults create parameters for children's play but allow children to set their own goals within those parameters. The social setting and the materials available will facilitate more cognitive change and language under these conditions than if adults controlled the event. Children actively engage and use available resources they encounter in natural settings. For example, a child encounters a large, empty box, and it becomes a magical toy during play. Cognitive change occurs when social relations and events become internalized and transformed into new knowledge by the child. Similar to Piaget's (1962) explanation of the importance of play activity, Vygotsky noted that a process of construction occurs during play and emphasized the origins of knowledge in the social interactions in which the child engages.

Piaget (1962) contributed to an explanation of how young children develop an understanding of objects, people, and relationships and how they code and store things in their memory without words. According to Piaget, object play is an important component of children's cognitive development. In their play with objects, children develop their understanding of natural contexts. This establishes the foundation for more complex thinking and language development.

Play may assume the form of simple explorations, imitations, searching for hidden objects (understanding object permanence), pretending, and experimentation. According to Piaget (1962), children learn best about their world through manipulation of real objects. Concepts such as time and distance are abstract, and children develop a more complete understanding of them when they are placed within the contexts of meaningful activities in which children can manipulate objects by seeing, feeling, hearing, or examining the results of their manipulations. Piaget seems to emphasize the fact that children are active learners and that they construct their own theories about the organization of natural environments.

In describing the characteristics of ideal play, Henniger (1994) noted that such play (a) is active, (b) is child-selected and -directed, (c) is process-oriented, (d) fosters imagination and creativity, (e) is low-risk, (f) reflects assimilative learning, and (g) is enjoyable. Yet for children with disabilities, especially those who have physical or sensory disabilities, play may not be active, child-selected, or child-directed, and it often is not focused on their imagination or creativity. For many children with disabilities, play may become a passive activity. Children may assume the roles of watching siblings, family members, or typical peers playing and not have any opportunity for involvement or independent actions in the observed play activities. Conversely, they may have opportunities to participate, but the level of participation may be controlled by others who make some or all the choices available for the child.

Adults frequently provide information to young children about natural settings rather than providing opportunities for children to experiment and learn firsthand about their world within these settings. For young children with disabilities, lack of opportunities for interactions within natural contexts can be particularly devastating. Children may fail to develop concepts related to time, motion, direction, and autonomy when adults in their environment (a) move children from place to place; (b) dictate when it is time to eat, sleep, or use the bathroom; and (c) place specific toys or objects within the grasp of children. Such dependence on others can result in learned helplessness (Seligman, 1975) and minimize the development of a positive self-esteem.

Assistive technology has opened a new world for these children, one in which they can learn about and act upon their world in ways similar to children without disabilities. Burkhart (1993) has noted that one of the most important assistive technology devices for young children with disabilities is wheeled mobility. Using a powered wheelchair or scooter, young children can develop important developmental concepts and gain greater control over their own lives.

Activity-Based Approach to Play

An activity-based approach to play includes a combination of adult-planned, child-initiated, and routine daily activities (Bricker & Cripe, 1992). Planned activities should be (a) developmentally appropriate, (b) exciting to explore, (c) motivating and interesting, and (d) focused on sustaining children's interest while they practice targeted skills. Child-initiated activities are introduced and maintained by children (Wershing & Symington, 1996). Routine activities occur on a predictable and regular basis, such as bathing, clean-up, arrival, and departure.

Goals identified in individual family service plans (IFSPs) and individual educational plans (IEPs) may be embedded in planned, child-initiated, and routine activities. Self-help and communication skills may be practiced within the context of activities and play. Choices on how the child can or will participate in ordinary activities, such as imitating gestures, recalling events, offering information, or paying attention to a story line, need to be considered.

In an activity-based approach, both children and adults are participants, and the need for artificial reinforcers is reduced. The child's attention is actively engaged as the adult and child respond to and add meaning to each other's initiations (Vygotsky, 1978). Feedback must be clear and consistent and must make sense to the child, which means the activity should take place within the context of a meaningful, relevant activity. The association between the event and the outcome is clear, resulting in effective learning. The adult plays a key role in monitoring learning opportunities by offering consistent and clear feedback, and the environment is tailored to enhance individual learning needs. Activities are meaningful and are related to or support goals identified in the IFSP or IEP. For the child with disabilities, this results in enhanced growth and development across natural settings, including the home, school and community. Learning occurs as each child participates and responds when activities and play are (a) related to meaningful themes, (b) structured around individual needs and experiences, and (c) facilitated by adults who add meaning and interpretation.

Use of assistive technology in activity-based play. Play activities might include shared activities such as taking turns (e.g., passing a switch between peers to activate a computer program), make-believe play (e.g., recreating real-life situations), and construction (e.g., building objects or scenes). It might be difficult for children to actually create a construction site, but children can experience it through commercial software programs such as the Road Construction portion of Richard Scarry's *How Things Work In BusyTown* (Computer Curriculum) and *Kids on Site* (Digital Pictures). Both programs allow children to direct either a cartoon character or a video clip of a bulldozer in creating a road. Children who have difficulty using a mouse to participate in computer-based play activities can use the *TouchWindow* (Edmark), *IntelliKeys* keyboard, or *Discover: Switch* as alternatives to a mouse or trackball to move items on the screen and create an animated sequence.

More independent activities might include painting or drawing, reading, playing music, or creating. *Blocks In Motion* (Don Johnston) is a software program that provides an environment for creating screen presentations of block-like objects having different colored shapes and animated features. The open-ended nature of this program allows children to create, experiment, and observe the results of their screen constructions. The following scenario illustrates how children can use assistive technology to indicate choices during playtime:

> In a large group setting, additional setups for AAC and choice-making using *Discover: Ke:nx* (Don Johnston) are used that provide some of the children with disabilities with a mechanism to indicate which blocks they want (e.g., "I want the red block") and its position, while peers place them on the screen [see Figure 3-1, below]. The *Say It Rocker Switch* from Enabling Devices is customized with a message that confirms the choice the child has made. The child simply touches one of the two switch positions, which says "That's the one I want" or "I want a different one."

Figure 3-1. *Communication overlays for construction activity*

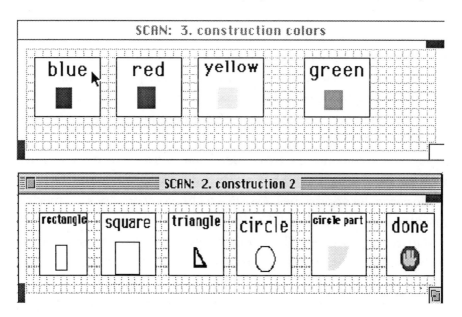

These overlays were designed using *Ke:nx Create* software, for a child to indicate choices during an activity using *Blocks in Motion* software. The first overlay can be used to allow a child to indicate color preference ("I want a blue one"), then branched to the second overlay to allow them to indicate shape preference ("I want a rectangle").

As noted in the preceding scenario, it is important to provide children who are using assistive technology with the opportunity to change or confirm choices made. This is especially critical when a physical disability may contribute to an undesired child selection if the object is restricted from reach.

When using software programs to create on-screen activities, young children with disabilities often must have a clear understanding of spatial relationships inherent in the programs. Adults should not simply assume that some children may not be able to use these programs. Assistive technology devices such as *Discover Ke:nx, Speaking Dynamically* (Mayer-Johnson), *BIGmack* (AbleNet), *Cheaptalk* (Enabling Devices), and other AAC devices or products can be used to enable children to participate according to their needs and abilities. If the software programs involve a series of steps to create a picture or activate animation, children can use AAC devices and software to indicate their preferences while another peer or adult completes the action. Such use of assistive technology enables all children to participate in completing a software activity while enjoying the process of cooperating with others.

Adult-planned and facilitated child-centered play is an initial step in overcoming the "learned helplessness" that may be evident when children begin school. A primary goal should be to give young children power within the natural controls of the environment or play group. In implementing activity-based play, assistive technology must be used in conjunction with creative instructional strategies and thematic curricular approaches. Assistive technology provides the mechanism through which all children can participate in classroom creative and learning processes. These tools allow children with disabilities to demonstrate their grasp of concepts and more fully participate in new learning experiences.

Importance of partial participation. A preferred alternative to passive or nonparticipation is partial participation and exploration in activities (Baumgart et al., 1982; Ferguson & Baumgart, 1991). For example, opportunities for friendship and creative expression might occur as a group of children with and without disabilities learn about holidays around the world. Similarly, during a candle-making activity, all children would benefit from rolling beeswax sheets into colorful candles since motor coordination is required. Even when a child can only partially participate (e.g., with a teacher providing hand-over-hand assistance, prompts, or cues), the young child with a disability is able to be fully present for a particular activity and perceived as an active participant rather than an observer. The following scenario presents a playtime experience in which active participation occurs through the use of assistive technology:

> A child with autism who is continuing to develop verbal language says "cheese pizza" spontaneously as "astronaut food" is divided among the group during a theme on space exploration. This same young child, using a single switch, *KidPix* software and customized *ClickIt!* files, waits anxiously for his turn. The child desires to draw along with *Harold and His Magic Purple Crayon.* He knows that the assistive technology can help him successfully participate along with his friends in the creative process of drawing the story on the screen.

In each of these examples, children with disabilities can more effectively participate with their typical peers and indicate preferences regarding choices of color, type of activity, or play partners.

Facilitating Language Development Through Play

Language development is influenced by both environmental and contextual factors (Burkhart, 1993). When language therapy is incorporated into play activities, it has to match the activity that is going on around the child and the child's response has to be appropriate within the context of the activity. Children also need to sequence words to communicate their needs, preferences, and thoughts to others. A software program such as *Speaking Dynamically* enables children to use a mouse or single switch to pair words and pictures to create speech.

In a traditional curricular approach, children might not be given an opportunity to participate in play-based and other learning activities with their typical peers. This may result in the development of splinter or isolated skills that are not part of more complex functional behaviors that children need in later years. Splinter skill development may be detrimental to the child's social and emotional development. To minimize the potential development of splinter skills, children need opportunities to practice important developmental skills by being immersed in the context of meaningful and functional activities.

Immersion is far more effective than providing drill and practice opportunities following direct instruction. For example, children who are nonverbal can participate by using an electronic AAC device that is programmed with language related to a particular play activity. This would allow interactions with others in which young children with disabilities hear appropriate language being modeled and use the programmed language on the AAC device. This is a more effective strategy than pulling children out of the natural setting for isolated therapy.

Games and play routines are excellent immersion activities for building interactive communication skills. Communication utterances that are encouraged in such interactions include: "It's your turn," "No, it's my turn," and "I won!" An excellent play activity in which children can be immersed is a birthday party. The young child with a disability can use a switch-activated hair dryer to blow out candles on a cake or use other assistive devices to assume more effective participatory roles in the activity. Immersion enables the child to understand that the participatory methods (use of the AAC device, signing, facial expressions, gestures, body movement, or pointing to pictures) being used for communication in such functional activities *are* language.

Adults should remain flexible and allow children freedom to make personal choices when immersed in play activities. While many instances might demand the need for children to demonstrate accuracy in the use of language rules, it is critical that children be afforded the opportunity to indicate individual preferences in natural contexts whenever possible.

Children who do not have oral language may not have developed the necessary schema for internal language to be well developed; thus, they may not be able to talk to themselves. Many of these children may exhibit what are perceived to be behavioral problems, when the child may actually be attempting to communicate by using primitive schemes. Consequently, AAC devices and software may need to be customized to provide the feedback children need for the development of both internal and oral language. If children are busy trying to communicate using physical behaviors, they may not have available the mental energy or attention required for cognitive or higher language learning.

The vocabulary children need to learn in immersion activities should match their environment and be age-appropriate. Even when children with disabilities demonstrate precocious abilities related to literacy (e.g., reading or mathematical ability), adults must be sensitive to the child's chronological age and not develop unreasonable expectations or exclude the children from age-appropriate activities.

Assistive Technology and Emergent Literacy Skills

Teachers and parents are facilitators of learning for the young child. Wells (1986) points out that literacy, like language, is acquired through a child's active involvement in daily encounters with other people and objects in meaningful and stimulating environments. Emergent literacy activities include (a) offering children opportunities to experience conceptual information, (b) helping children understand that they can use pictures and words to communicate, (c) helping children understand that pictures have meaning, (d) telling stories, (e) helping children understand that words have meaning and can be used to tell stories, and (f) helping children create their own stories using words and pictures. The precursor to becoming successful readers and writers is participation in literacy activities that are meaningful and functional from the child's point of view (Strickland, 1990).

Children's early play is a phase of literacy in which they begin to use words to name objects and request new ones. Assistive technology devices can facilitate the development of emergent literacy and conceptual development and provide a foundation for further learning and growth (Smedley et al., 1997). Young children who do not have disabilities acquire and explore emergent literacy concepts readily through daily experiences. Listening to stories read by family members, asking adults for information (e.g., "What does that say?"), and exploring the development of written expression through scribbling and other art activities are examples of typical emergent literacy opportunities for many typical children.

However, young children with disabilities are frequently unable to participate in such experiences, resulting in their exclusion from activities in natural settings. Children who are nonverbal may be unable to respond to adults when asked to name pictures or respond to questions about letters and words. It is often assumed that such children lack the cognitive abilities to participate with others and are "not ready" to engage in literacy activities.

Assistive technology devices can enable young children with disabilities to become active participants in literacy activities (e.g., turning pages in books or practicing forming letters with paint or other materials). As previously noted, computers and commercial software provide a means for young children with disabilities to actively and independently be included in and explore the same types of activities available to nondisabled peers. For example, using software such as *IntelliPics* allows a child to press a simple switch to display pictures of items and "speak" the label of the item. In many instances, animation accompanies the child's selection, offering more variety of stimuli presented to the child, which ultimately results in enhanced understanding of the item displayed. Individual thematic units can be customized to allow all children, including those with disabilities, to develop meaningful relationships with pictures, letter symbols, and words, while experiencing the simple pleasures of learning about and interacting with fun characters, such as Little Critter in *Just Grandma and Me* (Mayer, 1981) or Harold in *Harold's Trip to the Sky* (Leisk, 1957).

Assistive technology also provides young children with disabilities a means to demonstrate their conceptual knowledge to adults. Once children have learned to effectively use assistive devices, particularly computers and software, adults may have a "window" into the minds of young children with disabilities. This may be especially true for children who are unable to respond in ways comparable to their typical peers (e.g., speech and physical/written output). The following scenario illustrates how young children with disabilities effectively use assistive technology in a literacy environment:

> During a multicultural theme on the winter holidays, it is observed that each of the children participating in a play group has an accessible method of writing about the year in which they were born. The children take turns in creating a group story. Using an *IntelliPics* custom file, each child is able to select and print a picture for his or her birth year in the Chinese calendar [see Figure 3-2 on the next page]. The children also type a sentence about themselves and the animal they choose, using a custom *IntelliKeys* overlay for use with *IntelliTalk* (IntelliTools), a talking word processor [see Figure 3-3, p. 63]. Many choose an animal that does not correctly correspond to their actual year.

A recent study conducted by Howard, Greyrose, and Beckwith (1996) validates the claim that young children involved in computer-based activities demonstrate increased communication skills and active, animated involvement in computer activities. In this study (N = 45; age range = 18 months to 5 years), a 25% increase in positive affect was observed among children participating. Increases were noted in the areas of social play, social pretend play, communication, and affect. Those children who were engaged with computer activities exhibited more mixed and cooperative play outside the computer setting. Active waiting, defined as the ability to wait with interest and attention to a task while peers were taking turns or communicating, was prominent among children engaged in computer activities in this study. The results suggested that computer usage positively impacts language and cognitive development among young children and increases levels of cooperative and social play.

Figure 3-2. *Overlay for Chinese New Year activity*

IntelliPics is a multimedia tool that allows the insertion of graphics and content related to specific themes. Overlays are created to allow children to identify content-related vocabulary and to provide access to participating in group activities. The number of items on an overlay can be varied to meet individual needs (e.g., fewer items, larger pictures).

IntelliPics screens may be printed as each child makes a selection, using the custom overlay for the activity. Young children enjoy having a final product to take home. These can be used as prompts by family members, either through verbal speech or augmentative devices, to facilitate language at home related to the activity.

Figure 3-3. *Overlay for Chinese New Year writing activity*

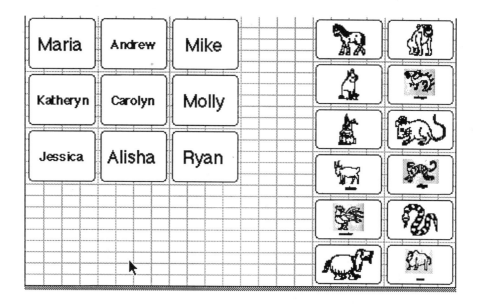

Custom overlays can be created with *Overlay Maker* to develop emerging literacy skills (e.g., name recognition) using pictures in combination with word labels.

Alisha is a dog. Andrew is a sheep. Morgan is a horse.
Clara is a dog. Maria is a snake. Ryan is a dog. Molly is a snake.
Jessica is a monkey.
Katheryn is a horse horse. Mike is a sheep.
Michaeline is a horse. Carolyn is a dragon.

Group story written with IntelliKeys and Custom overlay for Chinese New Year writing activity using *IntelliTalk,* a talking word processor. The use of the custom overlay allows each child to select their name and to hear their name spoken by the computer. Choice making is facilitated by the pictures offered and does not confine the child to making a "correct" choice. The child is free to select whatever animal they choose, which may not be their actual birth animal. The talking word processor highlights each word as it reads to the child, and group language is reinforced by hearing the entire group story.

Promoting Cognitive and Socialization Skills

Many studies from the 1980s noted the usefulness of computers in promoting cognitive skills and socialization in young children. Meyers and Beckwith (1988) found that children with Down syndrome demonstrated increased vocalization of real words and increased comprehension of words when interacting with the computer, as compared with their behaviors during noncomputer activities. In a similar study reported by O'Connor and Schery (1986), language usage was increased more among non-oral toddlers who had access to computer-assisted language therapy than among those in a traditional language therapy group. Shaperman, Howard, and Kehr (1989) found improvement in communication as well as on-task persistence and social interaction in a pilot study of the developmental effects of computer assistive technology with very young children who had a range of disabilities. Another study suggested that both children with and without disabilities demonstrated significantly increased socialization and turn-taking skills when engaged in free play centered around computer activities (Zippiroli, Bayer, & Mistrett, 1988). Most important, children without disabilities developed friendships with disabled children and demonstrated increased interaction with their friends around computer activities.

These studies seem to suggest that computers serve as social facilitators for children who have communication difficulties in social interactions. Children with disabilities demonstrate more socially directed behaviors when interacting with typically developing, socially competent peers while working together on the computer (Spiegel-McGill, Zippiroli, & Mistrett, 1989). Howard et al. (1996) reported that during computer usage, toddlers with disabilities showed more active waiting, less solitary play, and more simple play. These same young children also demonstrated more attention to communication when engaged with the computer.

Assistive Technology: Tools to Enhance Play and Learning

Assistive technology provides young children access to materials and activities according to individual abilities and needs. Many everyday activities would be inaccessible to young children with disabilities without some modification or without the use of assistive technology. Even at a few months of age, infants can learn to develop cause-and-effect relationships. Using specific input devices, such as a single switch, a switch interface, the *IntelliKeys* keyboard, the *TouchWindow*, or *Discover: Ke:nx*, young children with disabilities have access to exploring concepts that are learned by their peers without disabilities through play and exploration.

A child's ability to exert control over the environment and to complete tasks independently affects the development of self-esteem and social behavior (Mills, 1995). Without assistive technology, young children with disabilities may be excluded from opportunities to learn to direct an activity or to complete a project of their own. Using hardware and software chosen for specific activities, children can participate with their typical peers in such creative tasks as coloring, painting, and other activities that lead to the production of novel products, thoughts, and actions.

Voice output, sound, graphics, and animation have become standard in software for young children. Voice output provides feedback and modeling for children who are developing literacy and communication skills. Drawing, coloring, creating their own artwork, playing with shapes, constructing buildings, playing music, and other activities become accessible through computers, access devices, and software. Each developmental stage can be enhanced through technology, providing young children with disabilities with the power to reach their fullest potential.

The following scenario illustrates how modifications can be made by using assistive technology:

> A paper dreidel constructed from an activity book (Minelli,
> 1994) is attached to a switch-adapted Spin Art toy with

Handi-Tak from a local discount store. Children are divided into groups, and cards are made to match the symbols on the dreidel. The cards are distributed among the groups at random, and children take turns using the switch to spin the dreidel. If the group has a matching card, they receive a paper gold coin. Children are allowed to keep their gold coins at the end of the game.

Toy usage to facilitate play and learning. Toys offer a key component to a playful, motivating environment for young children. Toys become tools for communication and concept development in addition to facilitating opportunities for socialization with others. Creative play builds a foundation for the development of language skills and cognitive concepts. Social skills are solidified through cooperative play with peers.

For many children with disabilities, commercially available toys require modifications before they can be used by children. Many toys have small handles which may need to be enlarged or extensions added that allow independent play. Small toy pieces may need magnetic tape or Velcro added to them so they can be picked up when using magnetic wands or Velcro mitts. In some cases, the rules to games and materials may need to be modified so all children can participate. Many resources are available to assist adults in adapting toys for use with young children with disabilities (Burkhart, 1980; Burkhart, 1985; Levin & Enselein, 1990; Schwartz & Miller, 1988; Wershing, 1990).

Battery-operated toys. Battery-operated toys and methods for adapting toys provide a multitude of opportunities for switch activation beyond establishing cause-and-effect relationships. Many authorities have reported that the development of causality is facilitated by adapting battery-operated toys (Burkhart, 1980; Robinson, 1995; Wershing, 1990; Wright & Nomura, 1991) and through the use of switch-activated software. In addition, within group-learning situations, social interactions and turn-taking skills are developed when children use battery-operated toys effectively. These toys also (a) allow interactive and imaginative play to occur between siblings, family members, and friends and (b) facilitate development of critical concepts for language and cognitive development, particularly for children between the ages of birth and three years.

A Thematic Approach: Guidelines for Planning and Implementing Through Use of Assistive Technology

Thematic units (e.g., holidays, seasons, and community occupations) and activities are used across the curriculum for a variety of ages and grade levels (Croft & Hess, 1980; Flemming, Hamilton, & Hicks, 1977; McCord, 1995). A wide array of materials can be used to develop a thematic approach to instruction. When used in a classroom or child care setting, the thematic-unit approach integrates a particular theme across curricular or activity-center areas. The theme can also be extended across time.

The remainder of this section focuses on experiences reported by Wershing & Symington (1996), who have used assistive technology and thematic approaches within a community-based resource and demonstration center. These practitioners developed quarterly activities scheduled on Saturdays to accommodate children served at the East Tennessee Technology Access Center. Each Saturday session focused on a different theme, and the session length varied from two to four hours. While several sessions involved a small number of children, some included up to 10 children with and without disabilities, their siblings, family members, and parents (Wershing & Symington, 1996).

Themes used at the Center have been selected based on the interests of some of the children involved, available software tools, and the time of year. Some themes that have been used include winter, the jungle, things that grow, the ocean, the construction zone, and holidays around the world. An outline of the Holidays Around the World theme is presented in Table 3-1 on the next page.

Table 3-1. *Activity outline for Holidays Around the World theme*

Opening Activity

- Introduce the theme of holidays to children, who are sitting, standing, or being held in a circle. This activity can be scheduled for late November, prior to Chanukah and Christmas.
- Talk about other holidays that are celebrated in the wintertime in addition to holidays they may know about.

Adapted Dreidel Game

- Materials required: SpinArt toy adapted for switch use, a single switch (Buddy Button, Jelly Bean, Big Red, etc.), a paper dreidel, Handi-Tak to secure dreidel to SpinArt, accompanying cards to match dreidel symbols, and coins cut from gold paper
- To play the game: Group children. Give each group of children a set of cards and a cup to hold gold "coins." Pass the switch from group to group and let children spin the dreidel. When the dreidel stops, ask the children to show a matching card, and pass out gold coins. Play the game until all coins are distributed and all children have had an opportunity to spin.

Candle Making Activity

- Materials required: beeswax sheets, candlewick, scissors, and a Menorah (premade from clay, or borrowed).
- Discuss holidays where candles are included, such as Christmas, Kwanzaa, and Chanukah. In situations where the theme is extended over time, it may be possible to reinforce information shared about individual holidays.
- Give the children who are participating an opportunity to indicate their choice of color when making candles. Assistance may need to be provided to individual children in rolling the wax around the candlewicking. Let children take turns placing candles into the prepared Menorah, and provide enough materials so that each child can take at least one candle home.

Holiday Snack Fun

- Materials suggested: (a) colored frosting in tubes, with plain sugar cookies for decoration; (b) hashed brown potato patties with applesauce (Chanukah "latkes").

Adapted Piñata

- Materials required: premade piñata with a variety of candy (soft and hard), long dowel rod, wire and string to attach to piñata to the dowel rod, and soft material such as pipe casing to cover each of the dowel's ends for protection when used.

Table 3-1 *(continued)*.

- For a child who is using a wheelchair, position the dowel rod where it can be reached by the child in the chair. Assist children in holding the dowel rod and hitting the piñata. Provide turns for each child in the group until the piñata breaks. Prompting may be needed to insure that each young person receives candy and that no one is excluded when candy is gathered.

Chinese New Year Name Activity (as described in this chapter)

- Materials required: Macintosh computer, IntelliKeys keyboard, premade customized overlays made with *Overlay Maker*, IntelliPics software, *IntelliTalk* software, premade custom overlays using *Speaking Dynamically* software for switch access, printer, switch interface, and single switch. **NOTE:** While *Overlay Maker, IntelliTalk,* and the IntelliKeys keyboard are available for use on Windows platforms, *IntelliPics* is not yet available for Windows machines. IntelliTools, the developer of these products, anticipates that *IntelliPics* will become available for Windows and should be contacted for further information.

The 12 Days of Christmas Activity

- Materials required: Macintosh computer, IntelliKeys keyboard, *IntelliPics* software, *KidPix* software, *Overlay Maker* software, and a microphone.

- A customized *IntelliPics* file may be created with screens for each of the verses to the song, "The 12 Days of Christmas." Some of the children can participate in singing each verse for each screen and can be given a chance to play back their recordings.

Holidays Coloring Book Activity

- Materials required: Macintosh computer, IntelliKeys keyboard, *Holidays Coloring Book* software. **NOTE:** The *Holidays Coloring Book* includes predrawn files for use with the IntelliKeys keyboard or a single switch in order to provide access to coloring holiday pictures. This activity can also be done using scanned pictures, *KidPix* software, *ClickIt!,* and *Discover: Ke:nx.*

- Give each child an opportunity to choose several pictures—including a dreidel, present, and Santa—to color, using the coloring book.

Developing a Theme

In developing a theme, many issues must be considered. Each of these considerations is discussed in the following sections and is based on experiences reported by Wershing and Symington (1996).

Inclusion. Activities are developed based on the needs and abilities of the children involved. Providing activities that are accessible to all children participating is critical, even though many activities may be designed to include partial participation for children with disabilities by employing physical assistance from an adult or cooperative interaction with a peer. It may be necessary to provide a number of adapted access methods (e.g., switch access, voice output, or expanded keyboard) to insure that every young child can access software activities. For example, AAC devices and software programs have been used in a candle-making activity (see Table 3-1), providing children with a means to choose the color of the wax preferred, while being assisted by others to roll the candle. Whenever possible, having a wide range of activities and access methods available increases the likelihood that each child can participate in some way.

Material availability. Depending on the assistive technology and materials available within the local community, some themes may be more easily carried out than others. For example, a dinosaur egg hunt becomes a challenge to complete if the teacher plans to use plastic eggs and must buy them during a season other than spring. Budgets for supplemental materials often constrain what teachers and other adults are able to incorporate into a theme. However, many entertaining and ingenious activities may be developed at little cost if adults use creativity and teamwork.

Number of activities. The number of activities that can be incorporated into a theme depends on the time that can be committed to development and implementation. Given the limited attention spans of some children, it is preferable to have more activities than time allows to sustain their interest and attention. When working with young children of varied abilities, careful attention must be paid to behavioral indicators that children are tiring or need to transition to another activity within the theme. When the theme is extended over the course of a longer time period, such as several weeks, many activities may be completed at a later date. When a limited time is available to complete a theme, adults may have to decide which activities to exclude and save them for another time when the theme may be reintroduced.

Time constraints. A significant amount of time is needed to gather materials and prepare custom software files for use with children in play groups. Time must be allotted to (a) create accompanying materials, (b) modify software, (c) implement adaptive access to all software used, and (d) use assistive devices that include content relevant to the theme. The use of additional assistive technology (e.g., scanners to incorporate graphics for books, digital cameras to include actual photos, the addition of switch access through software and adaptive hardware) requires that time be made available prior to implementing these activities. The tools available and the amount of time needed to develop custom files and adapted activities must be taken into account when planning activities that meet the needs of a diverse group of young children.

A Sample Theme

Shown in Table 3-1 (pp. 68-69) are activities that we presented within the theme "Holidays Around the World." A number of resources were used in developing activities for this theme (Everix, 1991; Hearthsong Catalog, 1996; Minelli, 1994; Rozakis & Armstrong, 1993; Rutman, 1992; Waters & Slovenz-Low, 1990). This theme is provided as an example of a program in which children with disabilities may be included into thematic activities through the use of assistive technology tools. The following scenario illustrates how assistive technology is utilized in the thematic-unit approach:

Using the custom overlays depicted in Figures 3-2 and 3-3, each young child is given an opportunity to choose an animal according to his or her birth year. Prior to the activity, information provided by family members is used to make a list that indicates each child's birth year. The activity is introduced, using a photographic array of pictures on Chinese New Year activities (Waters & Slovenz-Low, 1990) and a chart that shows the animals corresponding to each year. The Chinese New Year Animal overlay is used with an *IntelliPics* file that states, "I was born in the Year of the [animal name]," as each child makes a selection. A child may need assistance in locating the corresponding animal; others may choose to select a different animal. After viewing the animal selected, each child's selection is printed. Finally, each child is prompted to use the Chinese New Year overlay with *IntelliTalk* so that he or she can print out a listing of all the names in the group and the animal that was selected, whether it corresponded correctly or not. The final listing is printed and copied for each child to take home.

Since some of the children participating may have difficulty accessing the *IntelliKeys*, an option for single switch access to the writing activity may be devised using *Speaking Dynamically* (see Figures 3-4 and 3-5). Each item is highlighted and voiced so that each child can select his or her name with a single switch and then move to a second screen to select their animal choice. The second screen also switches back to the first screen to build the story, using each child's choice in a separate sentence. A "read" button is included that allows either the entire story to be read or to read each individual sentence as it is added.

Conclusion

Federal law recognizes the significance of assistive technology in providing equal opportunities for children with disabilities to participate

Figure 3-4. *Writing activity using Speaking Dynamically*

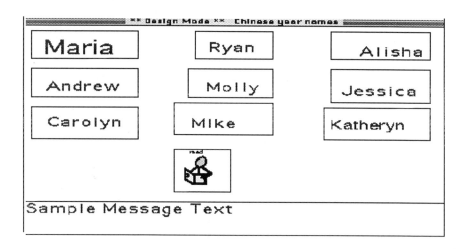

The screen was designed to allow individual children to select their names. Upon making a choice, the screen branches to the one shown below to complete the sentence. The "read" button allows text to be read aloud. This activity provides access to a variety of children, including those using a single switch. It also develops emerging literacy skills by providing auditory prompts for text on the screen and through reading the final sentence.

This screen automatically appears after selecting a name to allow the child to complete the sentence. The sentence appears in the message window and is read aloud.

Figure 3-5. *Writing activity using Speaking Dynamically*

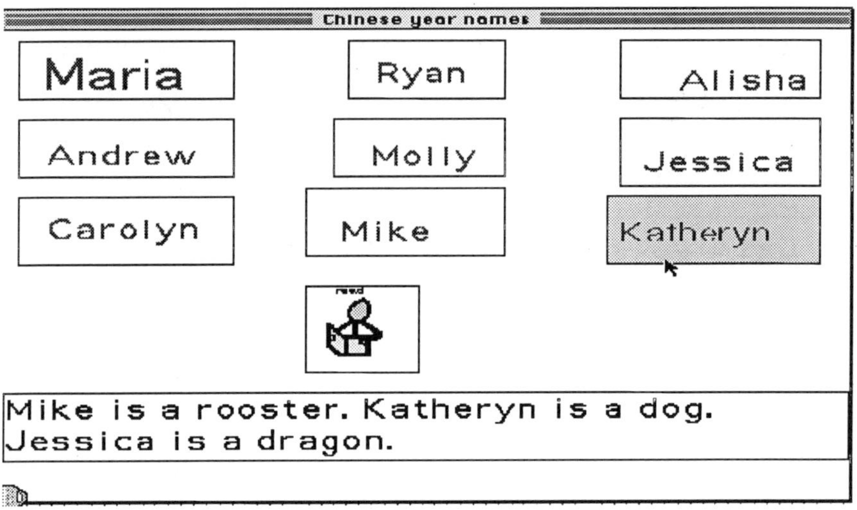

A sentence about each child is written while in the group and using the screens shown in Figure 3-4. The "read" button can be used to read the entire story when it is complete.

in play and learning activities. The Final Regulations of the Individuals with Disabilities Education Act of 1991 (IDEA) recognized the "critical importance of assistive technology in liberating many infants and toddlers with disabilities and their families from barriers encountered in all aspects of daily living, and in significantly enhancing learning and development." (pp. 12-13) The provision of assistive technology has resulted in less frequent reliance on labeling of children; increased opportunities for children to participate in integrated environments; increased confidence and ability levels for children; and heightened perceptions of child competence by family, peers, and service providers.

Inclusion of young children with disabilities may be facilitated by using a thematic-activity approach combined with the use of assistive technology. While assistive technology is not a panacea to ensure inclusion, it does provide teachers and family members with a mechanism for allowing children to participate in age-appropriate and developmentally appropriate activities that might not be accessible in any other way. Using creativity, open-mindedness, and a range of assistive technology devices, adults can create opportunities to allow all children to learn and grow, share and have fun, and move forward in exploring new horizons together.

CHAPTER FOUR

Software for Young Children

Patricia Hutinger & Joyce Johanson
Western Illinois University

When the right software is paired with a computer and enthusiastic children, the computer can sing or draw; tell stories or write stories; play individual games or operate a robot; and take its place beside books, blocks, toys, paint, and crayons in the lives of young children. Yet without software, the computer is mute. The more powerful the computer, the more interesting and the greater the variations and options the software can hold. Easy access to computers, adaptive peripherals, and appropriate software ensures abundant opportunities to do and learn, no matter what the child's abilities. Outcomes are sometimes surprising, and the results of the initial impact are lasting. The vignette below relates the story of Samuel. Computer activities, while not construed as a "cure" for Samuel's autistic behaviors, helped him participate in experiences and events that were interesting to him and furthered his interaction with other children and adults.

Authors' Note: We gratefully acknowledge the contributions of Macomb Projects' staff members Carol Bell, Letha Clark, Linda Robinson, and Carol Schneider. Macomb Projects has successfully implemented 17 externally-funded projects relating to young children with disabilities and technology between 1982 and 2000. For further information about these projects, contact Macomb Projects, College of Education and Human Services, 27 Horrabin Hall, Western Illinois University, Macomb, IL 61455, (309) 298-1634.

After two months in the preschool class, four-year-old Samuel and his teacher sat together at the computer watching Grandma give Little Critter a hug [characters in *Just Grandma and Me*]. "Hug," said Samuel. "Do you want to give me a hug?" asked his teacher. "No," replied Samuel, "hug Vinny." (Vinny is his personal aide.) Then he ran to Vinny and gave him a hug. When school began and until this critical incident, Samuel, who was diagnosed as autistic, was not social. He screamed loudly when anyone except his mother touched him. Yet, following this incident, he no longer rejected touch so vehemently. By the end of the school year, he had appointed himself as classroom greeter and met his classmates at the door each day. Video taken at the beginning of his second year in preschool shows him at the computer with a friend, who often reaches out to pat Samuel on the arm or fiddle with a lock of his hair.[1]

The software and activities discussed in this chapter, as well as examples of children's responses to it, are based on Macomb Projects' more than 15 years' experience developing model service delivery projects focusing on computer (and precomputer) applications for young children from less than a year of age to 8 (and sometimes older) with a wide range of disabilities. During that time, project personnel have worked with many children; trained hundreds of families and professionals; and developed curricular materials, software, and training materials. The discussions that follow are based on extensive, ongoing research and careful evaluation of the effects of various applications on children, families, and teachers.

The chapter includes a section on children and software, followed by a section intended for adults who plan to use software with children with disabilities. The children's section includes a discussion of

---

[1] Observations of Samuel are included in a classroom case study in the collaborative Early Childhood Comprehensive Technology System research project, funded by the U.S. Department of Education, Technology, Educational Media and Materials for Individuals with Disabilities Program, PR#HI80U50039.

benefits, adaptations, a look at earlier software, current software functions and applications, as well as preferences. The adult section includes a discussion of the adult's role, legal requirements, basic software considerations, and software evaluation. When the term *adult* is used, parents, caregivers, teachers, and other professionals are included. Examples of children's interaction with software are presented throughout the chapter. Information intended for different levels of computer users has also been interspersed with specific recommendations for software. Software referred to in this chapter is listed, alphabetically by publisher, in Appendix A. Readers are encouraged to skip over familiar information or use it to refresh their memories.

A Basic Definition

Software is an umbrella term for computer programs, the intricate combination of coding that directs a computer. Just as drivers don't have to understand a car's electrical system to turn on the headlights, computer users don't have to learn to "program" to use computers. Software programs may be found in different formats: (a) on bendable 5.25-inch magnetic floppy disks; (b) on the more rigid 3.5-inch magnetic disks housed in plastic cases; or (c) on CD-ROMs. CD-ROMs look like music CDs; in fact, with a compatible CD-ROM drive, newer computers can play music CDs. Since CD-ROMs store more coded data than floppy disks, software packaged in that format can include more sound, more color, more animation, more video, and more activities. Software to run some functions, including calculator, clock, and calendar, may (depending on the computer's manufacturer) reside in the logic board along with the software to run the operating system.

The Good News: Young Children Can Use Technology

The excitement children experience when playing with blocks, paints, and other toys translates to enthusiastic interactions with computer software, when it is coupled with a thoughtful selection of related environmental experiences. In 1980, Macomb Projects' staff were not sure that two- and three-year-olds could use a computer and software. Project personnel soon discovered that children could. In the beginning, some adventurous and trusting adults taught children to insert the floppy disk into the disk drive. Children did it! The rest, as they say, is history.

Young children *can* use and manipulate software. Children even younger than three years of age can use a mouse for input. Children can insert and remove CD-ROMs as well as disks from drives. They know how to start a software program, how to move through it, and how to end it—sometimes better than the adults. Many classrooms have a child who has become the "computer expert," and other children ask that child for help before going to an adult. Sometimes one child becomes an "expert" on one piece of software and another child is the "expert" for another.

The early childhood professional community now recognizes that children can learn to operate a computer safely and effectively when appropriate software is easily available. If clear, positive rules for software use are taught and followed, only occasional guidance from an adult or another child is needed.

Adaptations for Children with Disabilities

The same software used by children who do not have apparent disabilities is appropriate for young children with disabilities. The difference lies not in the content, approach, or function; instead, the real difference lies in the potential for adaptations. A list of features that can be built into software to facilitate useful adaptations is shown in Figure 4-1 on the next page. When software includes options to provide a variety of input methods—including switches—and can change response speed or sound volume, add prompts, determine how often prompts should be given, add scanning, or "crash-proof" a program, then children with a wide range of disabilities and developmental levels can use a program individually or in conjunction with other children and adults.

Figure 4-1. *Features that promote adaptations for use by children with disabilities*

Software containing multiple features that adults can customize to meet the individual needs or preferences of more than one child not only stretches the software budget, but also offers versatility. When evaluating software for such purposes, consider the following features:

1. The software can be accessed by alternate input devices
   - One or more switches
   - Alternate keyboards or touch tablets
     - IntelliKeys
     - Muppet Learning Keys
     - TouchWindow
     - PowerPad
2. The adult can set options for a child's individual preference or ability
   - Language (choices other than English)
   - Sound
     - On/Off
     - Volume control
   - Presentation options
     - Number of choices
     - Variety of skill levels
     - Scanning
       - On/Off
       - Set number of scans before prompting
       - Set number of choices for scanning array
       - Set time delay between scans
     - Auditory cues
       - On/Off
     - Prompts
       - On/Off
       - Set time before prompts begin
       - Set time between prompts
       - Choices for video and/or audio prompts

Currently, fewer adaptive peripherals are needed than were necessary in the 1980s, because more routines and options for customizing input and output are now built into both hardware and software. Examples of menus for customizing input and output are shown in the figures on pages 82-83. Figure 4-2 contains examples of adaptive input options in the software program *ArtSpace*,[1] while Figure 4-3 shows an example of software options adults can set to prevent unintended exits from the program. Extra options for auditory cues, a silencer, and a QuickTrip through the software, in this case the *ArtSpace* museum, are shown in Figure 4-4.

Lists of software for children with different disabilities may be comforting for adults, but such lists should be viewed with skepticism. Listing software in terms of the adaptive input it allows is more useful. Such a list is contained in Figure 4-5 (p. 84). If overlays are to be used with an input device, an adult should consider the availability of appropriate ready-made overlays and whether individualized overlays can be easily made. Determining the most effective input method (based on a child's most reliable movement) as well as child preferences and the purposes for software use should be undertaken during a team-based technology assessment such as Technology Team Assessment Process (TTAP).[2] Family members should be part of the team. Chapter 2 discusses team collaboration processes in detail.

Access Methods

Software that can be accessed via a *TouchWindow* has been quite successful, since children younger than 2 years and children with physical disabilities can easily use this input device. The *TouchWindow*

---

[1] *ArtSpace* (©1996) was developed by Macomb Projects through Expressive Arts Project for Young Children with Disabilities, a grant from the U.S. Department of Education, Technology, Educational Media, and Materials for Individuals with Disabilities Program, PR #H180D20019.

[2] TTAP is funded by the U.S. Department of Education, Early Education Program for Children with Disabilities, PR#HO24D40023. Assessment materials available from Macomb Projects include *Tap into TTAP* (training CD-ROM), *Technology Team Assessment Process Manual,* and *TECH-Access.*

Figure 4-2. *Example of useful adaptive input options*

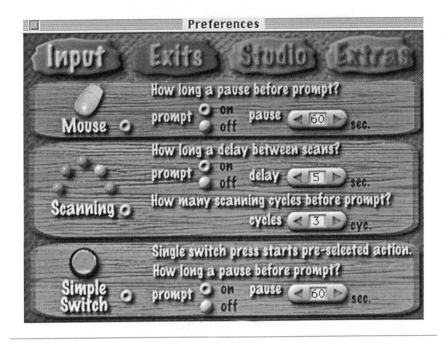

Figure 4-3. *Example of options to prevent unintended exits*

Figure 4-4. *Example of adaptations listed as "extras"*

Figures 4-2–4-4 used with permission: Macomb Projects, Expressive Arts Project for Young Children with Disabilities, *ArtSpace* ©1996.

Figure 5. *Examples of software for selected adaptive devices.*

Switch Software

101 Animations
aMAZEing Ways
Camelephant
Circletime Tales
Cross Scanner
Forgetful & Friends
Games 2 Play
Hit 'N Time
Millie's Math House
New Frog & Fly
One Switch Picasso
Press to Play Series
RadSounds
Sammy's Science House
Scan & Match #1 / #2
Scanning Picasso
Storytime Tales
Switch Intro
The Rodeo
Thinkin' Things
Toy Store
Workshop

Setups for KE:NX

Ke:nx Ready-Setups / Write:
   *Outloud**
Ke:nx Ready-Setups /
   *JOKUS**
Ke:nx Ready-Setups /
   *Storytime Tales**
Ke:nx Ready-Setups /
   *Circletime Tales**
*Millie's Math House Setups***

Easy Overlays* (=) and Easy
Scans* (+) for:
Arthur's Teacher Troubles +
Bailey's Book House =+
Berenstain Bears +
Dr. Seuss'ABCs +
Harry & Haunted House =+
Just Grandma & Me +

Kid Pix 2 =
McGee Series =+
Millie's Math House =+
Sammy's Science House =+
The Playroom =+
The Writing Center =+
Thinkin' Things Collection =+
Tortoise & Hare =+

Software for IntelliKeys

Buddy's Body
Click It!
IntelliPics
IntelliTalk for the Macintosh
Old MacDonald's Farm
Paper Dolls—Dress Me First
Seek and Find
This is the Way We Wash
   Our Face
Wheels on the Bus I / II / III
Zoo Time
Instant Overlays
   (IntelliTools):
Arthur's Birthday
Bailey's Book House
Harry & Haunted House
Just Grandma & Me
Millie's Math House
Sammy's Science House
Thinkin'Things

Software for the TouchWindow

Arthur's Teacher Troubles
The Backyard
Bailey's Book House
Blocks in Motion
Circletime Tales
Cosmic Osmo
Discis Series (A Long Hard
   Day on the Ranch,
   Cinderella, Heather Hits
   Her First Home Run,

Moving Gives Me A
Stomach Ache, Mud
Puddles, The Paper Bag
Princess, Scary Poems,
The Tale of Benjamin
Bunny, The Tale of Peter
Rabbit, Thomas'
Snowsuit)
EA*Kids Art Center
Explore-A-Story Series
   (Bald Headed Chicken,
   Princess and the Pea,
   Rosie the Counting
   Rabbit, Stone Soup,
   Three Little Pigs, What
   Makes a Dinosaur Sore?)
Kid Pix
Kid Pix Companion
Green Eggs and Ham
How Many Bugs in the Box
Imo and the King
McGee Series (McGee,
   McGee at the Fun Fair, &
   McGee Visits Katie's
   Farm)
Millie's Math House
Playroom
RadSounds
Storytime Tales
Storybook Weaver Deluxe
Just Grandma and Me
Little Monster at School
More Bugs in Boxes
Mr. Potato Head
Pippi Longstocking
Ruff's Bone
Sammy's Science House
Sheila Rae, the Brave
Silly Noisy House
Stellaluna
Thinkin' Things 2

* available from Don Johnston, Inc.   ** available from Macomb Projects
= Easy Overlays available   + Easy Scans available
Used with permission: Macomb Projects, Technology Team Assessment Process ©1997.

is pressure-sensitive, and even children with a very light touch are able to use it. Children don't need isolated finger movement; even a clenched fist will often accomplish the desired input goal. Children activate a program by pressing on the screen or moving their finger across the surface and then pressing on a hot spot (a spot programmed to begin an event). Hot spots can be large or small areas, depending on the program.

Software activated by a touch in a large area or even one touch anywhere on the screen is useful for children younger than 3 years of age, and particularly for those with little gross motor control. Programs such as *Baby ROM* (Bryon Press Multimedia) were developed to provide large activation areas on the screen. On the other hand, *McGee* (Lawrence Productions) requires a press in one of four large boxes at the bottom of the screen. If the child presses anywhere else on the screen, nothing happens. As children become accustomed to using the *TouchWindow*, they can begin to use such programs as *Just Grandma and Me* or other Living Books (Broderbund) software offering a variety of hot spots on each screen.

Access to software through use of a scanning method (a systematic series of hot spots) is essential for some children who have physical disabilities, whether they use a switch or another input method. A number of scanning options may be built into a software program; but whatever type is used should, at minimum, have the ability to control sound (when an auditory cue is needed) and the speed of the scan. Figure 4-2 (p. 82) shows an example of scanning options used in *ArtSpace*. Differing amounts of time between scans are options in the software Menu at the top of the screen.

When children begin to use scanning, the adult should use a program that contains simple graphics and sounds elicited by each switch press. The "Make It Sound" portion of *Switch Intro* is a good beginning program. A graphic image appears on the screen together with the corresponding sound of the object. The sound is heard for the duration of the switch press.

Other programs are available that reinforce causality and beginning switch skills. Increasing numbers of programs designed to reinforce switch skills are now available, such as *Switch Intro, Hit 'n Time, aMAZEing Ways,* and *Toystore* by Jokus. The *Make It Series* (Don Johnston), running on older machines, is useful to teach or reinforce switch skills. Two children each control their own switch and play cooperative games. More complicated programs, such as the *Train Game,*[3] can also be used by two children. The software runs the train after hardware modifications are made. One child presses a switch to make the train go for a specified distance and then must wait for the other child to press a switch to continue. By cooperating, children ensure that the train continues to run. If both children press the switch at the same time, the train stops. Children with severe physical disabilities have been observed playing this game with competence, enthusiasm, and laughter. They learned the rules more quickly than adults expected.

Teaching Switch Skills

Children do not know intuitively how to scan pictures or words, so this skill must be taught. If children will be using a switch as a communication tool and for other functions over time, a progression of switch skills should be taught. The child needs to learn how to indicate needs and wants by using a switch to scan across an array of choices. By beginning with simple, game-like software programs, children can master the skills needed to communicate, using a dedicated device such as the *Liberator.* Eventually children may be able to use switch input and "macro" commands to do word processing. Software that fosters the concept of causality (e.g., "when I hit my switch something happens") should be used initially. This is followed by software that requires a switch press at an appropriate time, rather

---

[3] *Train Game* was developed by James Keefe, John Boyd, and Steve Rosenberg for Project ACTT. Activating Children Through Technology, a tested and effective computer service delivery model for children with disabilities from 6 months to 8 years of age, was funded by the U.S. Department of Education, Early Education Programs for Children with Disabilities (EEPCD) from 1983 to 1996 and was the first technology project approved for funding by EEPCD.

than at random. Children then learn that specific switch pressing will result in the ability to communicate and obtain the desired consequences.

Software content for children with disabilities need not be different from that of software used in early childhood settings unless it is dedicated software that runs a communication device. Generally, computers assist children with disabilities to participate in inclusive settings and to do some of the same things other children do—draw pictures, play games, and communicate.

Criteria for selecting software specifically designed for children with special needs have been addressed for more than a decade. Recently, an article in the *Children's Software Revue* (1996) pointed out that programs intended for special education audiences often underestimate the individuality and variation of interests and abilities of children with special needs. While a particular child may need an uncluttered screen, many children with difficulties in learning can handle and need more control over the learning process. "If nothing else, the content should be highly engaging, and should take advantage of multimedia features (sounds and graphics), to present content in a variety of ways" (p. 19).

Software Paired with Computers Provides Benefits to Children

Undeniably, computers can function as tools for learning, communicating, equalizing opportunities, and creating positive changes in the learning environment of young children with disabilities (Sivin-Kachala & Bialo, 1996). Yet without software, computers do not and cannot live up to their promise and, therefore, face the danger of being abandoned by nonusers. Without interesting, developmentally appropriate software, novelty declines, and children soon lose interest. Participation may then be minimal, resulting in negative learning experiences ("I don't like this at all" or "I don't want to do this—no way").

Research results suggest that technology's impact in classrooms depends on the quality of the software, the attitude of the teachers, the physical and social arrangement, and the accessibility of the machine (Buckleitner, 1996; Campbell & Fein, 1986; Haugland, 1992; Haugland & Shade, 1990; Kristeller, 1996; Shade & Watson, 1990). Clements and Nastasi (1992) and Haugland (1992) found that open-ended software controlled by the child has different social and motivational effects and also creates different environments for learning than does drill-and-practice software.

All software is not of equal quality, and it varies with regard to design features, function, and content. Software designed and coded by knowledgeable developers who understand children or who have competent early childhood consultants has the potential to provide a unique medium for positive learning.

While children are busy learning about the world and the people in it, in all its variations, some software developers think that the main learning of children hinges on concepts, such as colors, shapes, counting, and the alphabet. These concepts do play a part in our world; yet they are not the most important learning topics for youngsters, nor are they as difficult to learn as some individuals suggest. Actually, most children learn about basic concepts, such as colors and shapes, in other less-expensive ways. Some currently available software often fails to make use of the extensive capabilities of computers. If software is no more than an electronic workbook, it is too expensive, regardless of the price.

Almost 10 years ago, simple drill-and-practice programs predominated in preschool classrooms (Becker, 1990). However, Haugland (1992) found that children using open-ended software made significant gains in intelligence, nonverbal skills, structural knowledge, long-term memory, complex manual dexterity, and self-esteem. At the same time, Haugland found that children using only drill-and-practice programs had significant losses in creativity. While several studies have found that drill-and-practice software increases preschool and primary-grade children's prereading or reading skills, the amount of practice was a critical element. A small number of sessions with simple readiness software is likely to have little or no effect (Clements, 1987; Clements & Nastasi, 1992).

In the decade of the 1980s, early childhood personnel complained that most software was uninteresting and not developmentally appropriate. Many early childhood professionals decided that since the software was "bad" (they probably meant developmentally inappropriate), then computers were also "bad" and "mechanistic." Therefore, technology should be kept away from young children and out of early childhood classrooms, because computers would "cheat" children of their childhood. Not until 1994 did the National Association for the Education of Young Children publish a useful guideline for using computers in early childhood classrooms, *Young Children: Active Learners in a Technological Age* (Wright & Shade, 1994). The publication provides a useful reference that should be part of any library of early childhood technology materials.

Integrating technology—including new, interactive computer software—into early childhood activities in the 1990s enjoys increasing attention among early childhood professionals (Becker, 1990; Buckleitner, 1996; Clements & Nastasi, 1992; Clements, Nastasi, & Swaminathan, 1993; Clements & Swaminathan, 1995; Haugland, 1992; Kristeller, 1996; Parette, 1996; Wright & Shade, 1994). Results of studies indicate (a) that preschoolers can work cooperatively with minimal instruction and supervision when they have adequate adult support; (b) that social interaction occurs frequently and positively; (c) that children cooperate, helping and teaching one another; (d) that children gain a sense of competence; and (e) that they can use the keyboard as input to the computer even though they do not know the alphabet, much less how to type (Brady & Hill, 1984; Campbell & Fein, 1986; Clements, 1987; Clements et al., 1993). One of the benefits of computers is that children can experiment with letters and words without being distracted by the fine motor aspects of handwriting (Clements, 1987).

Open-ended software, such as *Logo* (an interactive software program by Terrapin that is actually a computer language), can be used by young children and by graduate students in vastly different ways. *Logo* seems to produce higher-order thinking, partially due to the way children interact (Nastasi, Clements, & Battista, 1990; Watson,

Lange, & Brinkley, 1992; Yelland, 1992-1993, 1995a, 1995b, 1995c). As they use *Logo*, children frequently exchange information and re- solve conflicts by negotiating and talking through ideas. *Logo*, which is actively controlled by the child, has different social and motiva- tional effects and also creates different environments for learning than does drill-and-practice software. Teachers using a machine from the early 1980s, such as the Apple IIe, can still obtain a version of *Logo*.

Increases in children's problem-solving skills, their understand- ing of directions, and social-interaction skills (e.g., communication, following directions given by peers, turn taking) have been docu- mented as a result of curriculum activities using *ACTT Instant Logo,* a simplified version (Hutinger, 1987). Results of a study carried out by the ACTT staff (Hutinger, 1987; Hutinger & Ward, 1988) indicated that children with mild to moderate disabilities and developmental delays were able to use *ACTT Instant Logo* to solve a variety of prob- lems. Moreover, children retained those skills over a 6-month time span during the summer before *ACTT Instant Logo* was again used in the classroom.

Early Childhood Software Past and Present

The history of personal computers (in the 1980s they were called microcomputers) and software covers a period of approximately 20 years, but the history of their use in most early childhood classrooms is much briefer. If one examines the teaching strategies used by Froebel and Montessori, and by Native Americans and other cultures, it is clear that educational materials for young children have a long his- tory of representing smaller versions of adult objects. For example, child- sized furniture, miniature tepees, play cooking utensils, small shovels, trucks, bows and arrows, dolls, kachina, and other cultural trappings reflect accepted roles and traditions. However, computers in early childhood classrooms are not miniature adaptations of real- life objects. They are the same machines and are often just as power- ful as those used by children's parents in business and industry. Only the software and, sometimes, the input devices differ.

Then...

The idea of technology as an essential educational tool comparable to puzzles, paint, blocks, toys, and books in early childhood classrooms and homes is relatively new. When Macomb Projects personnel began developing software and activities for young children with disabilities in 1980, only a handful of people in the country were engaged in similar activities. A two-day seminar focusing on computer applications for young children with disabilities and attended by a small group of individuals was held in 1985 at Western Illinois University in Macomb. An article summarized the seminar's discussion and provided recommendations developed by the group (Hutinger & Gentry, 1986). Special attention was given to infusing computer technology with software being developed for use with children with disabilities. Some of the recommendations reflect the dated state of technology at that time, but some are still relevant.

Early software programs were simple. Programmers complained about the restrictions of machines with too little memory. Many software packages were not much more than electronic workbooks and provided little interaction. Some software today still retains this characteristic. Limited sound was available, and when sound was present, it was robotic and mechanical—yet understood more often by children than adults. Animation was awkward, images were poorly drawn, and fairly primitive line drawings prevailed. However, enough useful software was available for children to accomplish interesting activities.

Macomb Projects programmed *Master Blaster, Peek & Speak,* and *Switch 'N See*—software that allowed children to use a switch, a combination of switches, or a touch tablet to produce interesting results and to communicate. Project staff also produced some customized communication programs for individual children who were severely involved with cerebral palsy. Other groups and individuals were involved in the same endeavors, including UCLA-LAUDS,[4] which em-

---

[4] UCLA LAUDS, directed by Kit Kehr, is now known as the UCLA Intervention Program for Children with Disabilities.

barked on a major software development effort focused on children with physical disabilities. *Wheels on the Bus, If You're Happy and You Know It,* and *Switch-It-Change-It* were among many programs to emerge from the efforts of this project.

The first *Stickybear ABCs* and *Stickybear Numbers* (Optimum Resources) were hailed by proponents for technology and young children. The graphics were visually appealing, the color was exciting, the animation and sound were acceptable, and interesting things happened randomly. The screens were far more interesting than the simple line drawings that changed screen by screen as a key was pressed. Switch-press control required additional equipment, and often a customized adaptive software pre-boot program had to be loaded before the software itself to allow for switch input.

When *Stickybear Bop* (Optimum Resources) came along, with more options, together with *Animal Hotel* (Merit Software), *Rocky's Boots* (for children aged 5 years and older), and *Gertrude's Secrets* (also for older children; The Learrning Company), software began to provide more of the characteristics that made computers interesting to children. It also began to provide more than drill and practice (known in some circles as "drill and kill") with its academic, rote learning activities that are inappropriate for meaningful learning.

With the advent of *Logo* on personal computers, together with Macomb Projects' adapted version for young children, *ACTT Instant Logo,* personnel had software that would run robots throughout the classroom or along roads children painted on brown paper. Any number of goal-oriented activities could be created. For example, one teacher devised a simple activity where children used *Logo* to move a Turtle Tot robot to the carrot. Children worked together. One child operated the software; the others gave directions. Children who participated learned about directions, angles, and units of measurement.

Wrong answers often offered more interesting results than the right ones. A screen presentation of an animated man jumping up and down yelling was more interesting than a "Good Job" and a smiley face. This kind of interaction with the software still occurs. In such circumstances, the nature of the child's intent becomes a paramount issue. The child's intentions can assume a myriad of forms, and the answer depends on the child's thought processes.

And Now...

Interactive software based on good, children's literature and appropriate content is increasingly available. Realistic sound, faster animation, and more opportunities for interaction abound. Software runs faster than it did a decade ago. A storybook on the computer provides opportunities to "turn" a page, read the story (in English and other languages, including Japanese and Spanish), repeat highlighted words over and over as often as children wish to do so, and animate images. For example, 4-year-old Christopher spent hours with the English version of *Just Grandma and Me* (Broderbund); then he started using the Japanese version. He highlighted and repeated words, phrases, and the entire story; pronounced the words in Japanese; and listened intently. In a month he was finished and went on to explore *Thinkin' Things* (Edmark). Individuals or groups of children often use software such as *Harry and the Haunted House* or *Stellaluna* (Broderbund) with a copy of the actual book in hand as they progress through the story, repeat a page, or go back to a previous page. At the same time, their literacy skills are increasing.

Classifying Software and Computer Experiences

Software for young children's use can be organized according to a number of categories, including (a) function, (b) degree of interactivity, (c) content, (d) potential for peripheral use, (e) children's learning preferences, (f) developmental level addressed, and (g) an over-all qualitative judgment of design features. Any organizational system is, in a sense, rigid and may overlap into another; so Macomb Projects personnel encourage flexibility in applying any set of criteria. Software serves several functions or purposes regardless of its usage in a classroom or a home, the age of the children, or the extent to which it fits into the curriculum or the daily experiences of children. Learning outcomes, on the part of the child, should drive the decisions regarding appropriateness of the software in the learning environment. Narrowly framed software that focuses on limited content, function, and interactivity leads to narrow learning outcomes. However, software with a broad approach leads to a greater variety of learning outcomes for young children. Function must be determined on the basis of the desired outcomes—knowledge, skills and abilities, emotions, and attitudes.

Software Functions

While software packages perform a variety of functions, adults are responsible for deciding the purpose for using a program. Determining the purpose for software prior to use is a critical step in achieving positive outcomes. Adults must answer the question, "What do I want the software to do?" For example, if the objective is for young children to acquire concepts related to emergent literacy, then software such as *Green Eggs and Ham* (Broderbund) or *Storybook Weaver (MECC)* is more useful than *Mr. Potato Head* (Hasbro Interactive) or *Rosie the Counting Rabbit* (William K. Bradford). If the objective is to learn about other people and where they live, then *My First Amazing World Explorer* (DK Multimedia) or one of the *Magic Tales Collections* (Davidson & Associates) would be more appropriate.

An early functional classification of computers and software according to their purpose as tools, tutors, and tutees (Taylor, 1980) still has relevance to adults who are evaluating software. However, some argue that these terms reduce technology to known functions that ignore the potential variety of new uses of emerging and innovative technologies. While it is true that computers linked with telecommunications infrastructures allow complex simulations, data gathering, and information exchange unprecedented in the knowledge and experience of human cultures, Taylor's format provides a helpful structure for identifying, organizing, and evaluating software according to purpose. The tool function involves accomplishing a task such as word processing or drawing, while the tutor function refers to teaching related skills and content such as emergent literacy concepts to young children. The tutee function assumes that something is to be taught, such as *Logo*, and then a computer "learns" to perform tasks the individual "teaches." All three functions are related to interactivity levels. The basic questions remain: "What can children do with the software? What purposes does it serve in terms of children's use? How much interaction does the software provide?" In the following sections, the tool, tutor, and tutee functions of software are clarified.

Tool function. The purpose and tasks to be carried out determine what software children should use. For example, when children want to draw, *Kid Pix* (Broderbund) can be used. When children want to make music, *Tuneland* (7th Level) or *Lamb Chop Loves Music* (Phillips Media Software) provides the means to do so. When children want to write stories, *The Amazing Writing Machine* (Broderbund) or *Stanley's Sticker Stories* (Edmark) may be used. *KidDesk* (Edmark) provides appropriate desktop management, enabling children to select their own software or activity within the parameters of the software.

Tutor function. The teaching function of software applications predominates when content is of primary concern. Tutoring may assume the form of drill and practice if the teaching objective is limited to isolated skills, such as alphabet, numbers, colors, shapes. However, the tutorial function doesn't have to be so narrow. Field trips, such as museum trips in *ArtSpace,* the trips around the house or farm in the *McGee* series, and the wide variety of content and skills developed when children use the *Living Books* series, reflect a tutorial function. Similarly, the literacy programs, such as *WiggleWorks* (Scholastic), that are designed for primary children have a tutorial function. Software, like story books, can be used in numerous ways. Sometimes the software can be used to introduce a new curricular topic to the children or supplement a curricular theme (e.g., animals). Figure 4-6 on the next page presents examples of selected curricular themes and corresponding software.

Software can support concepts and develop skills (e.g., literacy);

Figure 4-6. *Examples of software titles that may be incorporated into selected curricular themes*

Software Uses	Products Containing Relevant Activities
1. To supplement a curricular theme	
Animals	*Camelephant, Let's Explore the Zoo, Putt Putt Saves the Zoo, Stellaluna*
Farm	*Big Job, Forever Growing Garden, Let's Explore the Farm, McGee Visits Katie's Farm*
Dinosaurs	*Dinosaur Days, Dinosaur Explorers, Dinosaur in the Garden, Dinosaur Kids, Talking First Dinosaur Reader, What Makes a Dinosaur Soar?*
People and Places	*ArtSpace, Richard Scarry's Busytown, How Things Work in Busytown, My First Amazing World Explorer*
Families	*Amanda's Stories, Arthur's Birthday, Berenstain Bears Get in a Fight, Just Me and My Mom/Dad, Just Grandma and Me*
2. To support concepts or develop skills	
Literacy	*A to Zap!, A Day at Play, Bailey's Book House, Circletime Tales, Dr. Seuss's ABC's, My First Incredible Amazing Dictionary, Stickybear's Reading Fun Park*
Math	*James Discovers Math, Millie's Math House, Nick Jr. -- Math Play, Thinkin' Things*
Science	*The Backyard, Ozzie's World, Sammy's Science House, Zurk's Learning Safari*
Creativity	*Amazing Writing Machine; ArtSpace; Blocks in Motion; Gryphon Bricks; Gus and the Cyberbugs Sing, Play, and Paint-A-Long; Kid Pix 2; Kid Works Deluxe; Lamb Chop Loves Music*
3. To help children understand other cultures	*The Magic Tales Interactive Storybooks Collections I and II (folk tales of Russian, Japanese, African, Irish, Italian, and Native American origin); Many Lands, Many Playgrounds*
4. To allow children to explore characters and situations in favorite books	*Arthur's Teacher Troubles, Green Eggs and Ham, Harry and the Haunted House, If You Give A Mouse A Cookie, Stellaluna*
5. To allow children to play favorite games	*Candy Land Adventure, Mr. Potato Head, Playschool Puzzles*

Used with permission: Early Childhood Emergent Literacy Technology Projects, Macomb Projects ©1997.

help children understand other cultures (*Imo and the King* [African] or *Liam Finds a Song* [Irish] by Davidson & Associates); or allow children to explore characters and situations in favorite books. Most software titles are likely to contain several different activities that can be used for varying purposes to meet different children's needs. For example, *Millie's Math House* (Edmark) contains matching and comparison activities and pattern/sequence activities, as well as creative activities and activities to develop critical-thinking skills.

If ongoing experiences in the classroom or at home influence the choice of software, then a theme of cooking, snacks, and nutrition might suggest the use of *Green Eggs and Ham* and *Stone Soup* (William K. Bradford). Sometimes the function of software is to influence children's activities. *ArtSpace* might lead to a classroom or home art gallery of children's work that includes images made with *Kid Pix*. Computer-generated art images can then be hung beside paintings, crayon drawings, and collages created by other children.

Characters, activities, themes, and concepts introduced in software can be expanded in off-computer activities that complement the information the software presents. Off-computer activities encourage knowledge and skill transfer and generalization to other areas. Teachers in Macomb Projects' demonstration and research-site classrooms have created many curriculum-integration ideas based on children's software. The possibilities for software-related activities are endless, requiring only a child's suggestion or an adult's imagination to integrate learning experiences for children. For instance, when children in one classroom used *Thinkin' Things* (Edmark) and became enamored of its Fripple Shop, the teacher suggested the class make its own Fripple Store. First, the children made Fripples in the art center out of lunch-sized paper sacks decorated with paint, yarn, glitter, and other materials. Then they set up their own Fripple Store in the dramatic play area where they took on roles of buyers and sellers, phone-message takers, and clerks. The teacher made up "Fripple Songs" by changing the words to familiar songs (e.g., "How Much is That Fripple in the Window?"), and children played games such as Guess Which Fripple ("I see a Fripple with black hair and blue and pink stripes").

Teachers take "snapshots" of computer screens and print them to make books, puzzles, and games for their classrooms. In addition, favorite characters from interactive story books have been printed; laminated; and used as finger puppets, play props, art activities, and classroom decorations. Similar screen prints have also been laminated and attached to a child's switch to provide clues for correct switch pressing or added to a nonverbal child's communication board to indicate choices.

One teacher used the pancake-making story in *Pippi Longstocking* (ahead media AB) to embark on a classroom pancake adventure. The dramatic play center became a pancake shop, complete with kitchen for "cooking" the pancakes children had made and decorated in the art center. The teacher created a *HyperStudio* (Roger Wagner Publishing) stack containing animated, written, and spoken directions for making pancakes. The children followed the directions and made pancake batter that the teacher cooked for snacktime. Later, the children made a graph showing their favorite choices of pancake toppings.

Tutee function. When the learner controls the software, he or she assumes a tutee function, and "teaches" a computer to do something. This kind of software is as open-ended as blocks and paint. Good preschool materials can be used in many different ways to accomplish a variety of outcomes. *Logo,* discussed earlier, meets these criteria, as does *HyperStudio,* a multimedia authoring program that can be integrated into early childhood experiences. *HyperStudio* provides many opportunities for young children with disabilities to make and use interactive, multimedia software. The subject of classroom-created software may focus on daily life activities using real-time video and digitized, still photographs. Children may create interactive software formats in authentic—and sometimes humorous and surprising—ways that do not rely on the "Saturday morning cartoons" mentality.

In one Head Start classroom, children and their teacher used *HyperStudio* first to develop a program about their classroom, showing who's who and using video images and voice. Children went on to develop a swinging "Five Little Mice Jumping on the Bed," which made use of a child drawing, child chants, and the opportunity to repeat any part of the poem. During production, children learned about the video camera, animating drawings, the sound pattern of their voices (speeded up, regular speed, or slowed down), and how they looked and sounded themselves. They planned segments (with adult help) and worked cooperatively with other children for a final product.

Another *HyperStudio* program developed at home by a computer-savvy grandmother and her 2- and 4-year-old grandsons involved the creative retelling of the children's favorite nursery rhyme, "Humpty Dumpty." The children's voices were recorded as they told the rhyme, and animation was added to the child-drawn Humpty Dumpty.

One rural, preschool special education class that participates in Macomb Projects took a field trip to the veterinarian's office. Since many of the children live on or near farms, veterinarians are part of their life experience. Video and photographs of the trip were made; and later a *HyperStudio* stack was developed, complete with children's recorded comments and sound effects, snippets of video footage from the trip, photos, and children's scanned drawings. The stack was loaded on the classroom computer's hard drive where children were free to access it to relive their visit to the vet's office. The stacks were printed on a color printer; and the pages were laminated, bound, and made into a book for the library center.

Function and Interactivity

Whether software serves as a tool, a tutor, or a tutee (Taylor, 1980), all three functions involve teaching and learning, are related to interactivity levels, and are closely related to educational purposes. Interactivity issues focus on how many things children can do and learn and how much interaction the software provides. Increasing software interactivity is related to advances in technology and to the intended function of the program. As used here, interactivity refers to the degree of interaction that occurs between the child user and the software program. The more interactive the program, the more the child is able to manipulate what happens when the program is used. Increased interactivity offers the opportunity for a greater number of option choices; a wider range of responses and outcomes; and greater control of design features, such as sound, graphics, text, and outcomes. The intended purpose of the software must be factored into selecting elements of interactivity. In a study of software design features that engage young children, Lahm (1996) reported that programs with higher interaction opportunities were preferred.

Figure 4-7 on the next page shows five levels of interactivity that guide selection of software included in the Interactive Technology Literacy Curriculum.[5] The intended outcomes relate to a range of emergent literacy concepts such as "a story has a beginning, a middle, and an ending," and "written letters and words are symbols that have meaning." A selection of current children's software classified according to those levels is also included in Figure 4-7.

Level 1 software, such as *The New Kid on the Block* (Broderbund), functions as tutorial software. It offers limited choices and follows a specific preselected path. It addresses a theme that is often part of children's daily experiences.

Level 4 software, such as *Stone Soup,* gives users many choices. Users can control the paths they wish to follow as they move through the story.

Level 5 software, such as *HyperStudio,* contains elements that are more interactive than Level 1 software, such as *Circletime Tales* (Don Johnston). Interactive options give children a greater number of options for control and a much broader set of outcomes. This level of interactivity contains elements of both tool and tutee functions.

Early childhood activities have a place for all five levels. However, given the presence of similar content addressing young children's developmental levels coupled with limited funds, it is preferable to

[5] The Interactive Technology Literacy Curriculum is a product of Macomb Projects' Early Childhood Emergent Literacy Technology Project, funded by the U.S. Department of Education's Technology, Educational Media, and Materials for Individuals with Disabilities Program, PR #H180G40078.

Figure 4-7. *Characteristics of five levels of interactivity*

Levels of Interactivity		Software Examples
Level 1	• Minimal choices are offered • Path is pre-determined • Choice response is fixed • Text (if any) is set and cannot be controlled or manipulated • Sound control is limited to on/off; up/down • Graphics are fixed and cannot be controlled or manipulated	*Amanda's Stories; Baby Bear's Bubble Bath; Chicka Chicka Boom Boom; Cinderella; Circletime Tales; JumpStart Toddlers; The New Kid on the Block; Peanut Butter and Jelly; Press to Play—Animals; The Rodeo; Storytime Tales; Switch Intro; The Tale of Peter Rabbit*
Level 2	• Multiple choices are offered • Path is divergent but predictable • Choice response is varied • Text (if any) is set and cannot be controlled or manipulated • Sound control is limited to on/off; up/down • Graphics are fixed and cannot be controlled or manipulated	*The Backyard; Bailey's Book House; Berenstain Bears in the Dark; Harry and the Haunted House; How Many Bugs in a Box; Just Grandma and Me; Just Me and My Dad; Little Monster At School; Magic Tales series; McGee series; Muppets on Stage; The Playroom; Stellaluna; Toystore*
Level 3	• Multiple choices are offered • Path is divergent and user is given moderate control • Choice response is varied • Text (if any) is set and cannot be controlled or manipulated • Sound control is limited to on/off; up/down • Graphics are fixed and cannot be controlled or manipulated	*A to Zap!; ArtSpace; Busytown; Green Eggs and Ham; Just Me and My Mom; Let's Explore the Airport; Let's Explore the Farm; Let's Explore the Zoo; My First Incredible Amazing Dictionary; Pippi Longstocking; Putt Putt Joins the Parade; Ruff's Bone; Workshop*
Level 4	• Multiple choices are offered • Path is divergent and user is given total control • Choice response is varied • Text (if any) can be controlled or manipulated • Sound control is limited • Graphics can be somewhat controlled or manipulated	*Big Job; Colorforms; Crayola Art Studio; EA*Kids Art Center; Explore-A-Classic series; Explore-A-Folktale series; Explore-A-Story series; Gryphon Bricks; Gus and the Cyberbuds; Kid Pix; Kid Works 2; KidWorld; Stone Soup; Storybook Theatre; Storybook Weaver; Thinkin' Things*
Level 5	User is given wide variety of choices, with total control over path, responses, text, sound and sound effects, graphics, & content	*Blocks in Motion* *HyperStudio* *Logo*

purchase the program with the highest level of interactivity since it can be used in the greatest number of ways for the widest range of purposes.

Software Addressing Multiple Intelligences

The range of children's learning outcomes and styles have been the focus of Gardner and his colleagues (1983, 1993). Their studies resulted in the formulations of generalizations related to multiple intelligences. *Frames of Mind* (Gardner, 1983) and *Multiple Intelligences* (Gardner, 1993) identified children's learning styles and abilities according to their identified intelligences, although educators and parents were aware that children learned at differing rates and had differing preferences.

Gardner's investigations were based on the assumptions that intelligence was multiple, that different intelligences demonstrated different characteristics, and that most roles and tasks require a blend or combination of intelligences. Gardner identified differences in the way children approach learning or preferences associated with seven intelligences: *spatial, logical/mathematical, bodily/kinesthetic, interpersonal, intrapersonal, linguistic,* and *musical.* In addition, he provided suggestions for reaching children with diverse learning styles.

Pracek and Atwood (1993) used Gardner's (1983, 1993) findings to classify software according to the intelligence to which it appealed. Macomb Projects' staff then extended their work to focus on software intended for use by young children. Figure 4-8 (pp. 103-104) contains suggestions for early childhood software that can be used to target children's varying intelligences and the preferred learning modes that accompany them. For example, a child whose spatial intelligence is dominant may prefer real blocks or *Busytown* (Computer Curriculum) to storybooks on computer screens, while a child excelling in logical/mathematical intelligence might prefer *Logo.* Gardner (1993) pointed out that instruction in the preschool years should focus on experiences for children to discover their own particular interests and abilities. He also noted that perhaps intervention at an early age might

Figure 4-8. *Multiple intelligences and related software*

Intelligences Identified by Gardner*	Characteristics of Relevant Software	Software Examples
SPATIAL INTELLIGENCE: • thinks in images and pictures • likes mazes and jigsaw puzzles • likes to draw and design things • likes to build models • likes films, slides, videos, diagrams, maps and charts	• contains draw and paint activities • reading software that uses visual cues or color coding • contains mazes or puzzles • uses maps, charts, diagrams	• *EA*Kids Art Center* • *aMAZEing Ways* • *ArtSpace* • *The Backyard* • *Kids on Site* • *Kid Pix Studio* • *Kid Works 2* • *Thinkin' Things* • *With Open Eyes*
LOGICAL/MATHEMATICAL INTELLIGENCE: • thinks conceptually • uses logical, clear reasoning • looks for abstract patterns and relationships • enjoys computing math problems in his/her head • likes brain teasers, logic puzzles, and strategy games • enjoys using the computer • likes experimenting and testing things • enjoys science kits • likes classifying & categorizing	• contains problem-solving activities • reading software that uses word patterns • contains simulations allowing children to experiment and observe results • contains strategy games	• *Blocks in Motion* • *Let's Explore the Farm* • *Logo* • *Millie's Math House* • *Mr. Potato Head* • *Muppets On Stage* • *Sammy's Science House* • *Silly Noisy House* • *Thinkin' Things*
BODILY/KINESTHETIC INTELLIGENCE: • processes knowledge through bodily sensations • communicates through gestures • moves or fidgets while sitting • learns by touching and manipulating • likes role playing, creative movement, and physical activity • demonstrates skills in crafts • enjoys fixing and building things	• contains keyboarding/word processing features • features instructional games in arcade-style format • science and math software that has accompanying manipulatives and probes • allows objects to be moved around the screen • uses animated graphics	• *Berenstain Bears Get in A Fight* • *Blocks in Motion* • *Dr. Seuss's ABC* • *EA*Kids Art Center* • *Just Grandma and Me* • *Kid Pix Studio* • *Pippi Longstocking* • *Sammy's Science House* • *Stanley's Sticker Stories*

* Gardner (1989, 1993).

Figure 4-8 *(continued)*.

Intelligences Identified by Gardner*	Characteristics of Relevant Software	Software Examples
INTERPERSONAL INTELLIGENCE • understands and cares about people • has many friends • enjoys socializing • learns more easily from cooperative learning experiences • enjoys group games • likes teaching other children • enjoys involvement in clubs and groups	• addresses social needs • allows group participation or decision-making • games that require two or more players • allows interaction with characters in a simulation or adventure format	• *Feelings* • *Games 2 Play* • *Green Eggs and Ham* • *Just Grandma and Me* • *McGee series* • *The Rodeo* • *Silly Noisy House* • *Thinkin' Things*
INTRAPERSONAL INTELLIGENCE: • enjoys working independently • likes to be alone • appears self-motivated • learns easily from independent study • enjoys individualized projects and games, self-paced learning • needs quiet space and time	• is self-paced • instructional games where the opponent is the computer • encourages self-awareness or builds self-improvement skills	• *Bailey's Book House* • *Feelings* • *Interaction Games* • *Millie's Math House* • *Just Grandma and Me* • *Kid Pix* • *Pippi Longstocking*
LINGUISTIC INTELLIGENCE: • thinks in words • learns by listening, reading, verbalizing • enjoys discussion • likes word games, books, records • remembers verses, lyrics, and trivia	• contains word processing features: stories, labels, word puzzles • contains speech	• *Explore-a-Story series* • *Bailey's Book House* • *Kid Works 2* • *The Playroom* • *Stellaluna* • *Storybook Theatre*
MUSICAL INTELLIGENCE: • thinks in tones • learns through rhythm and melody • enjoys playing musical instruments • remembers songs • notices nonverbal sounds in the environment	• combines stories with songs • contains music • allows children to create their own songs	• *Chicka Chicka Boom Boom* • *Lamb Chop Loves Music* • *How Many Bugs in a Box* • *Morton Subotnick's Making Music* • *Sound Toys* • *Stradiwackius* • *Thinkin' Things* • *Workshop*

Used with permission: Macomb Projects, Early Childhood Emergent Literacy Technology Project ©1997.

bring more children to an "at-promise" level rather than an "at-risk" level in intelligence.

In the process of selecting appropriate software, adults should consider the function of each of the activities and learning targets a software program offers and then decide which intelligence is addressed. Next, a chart might be created and used to ensure that software is available that appeals to individual learning styles and offers children opportunities to use and perhaps expand their less dominant intelligences.

Children's Interaction with Software: A Critical Element

While an adult who has learned to use a computer (and knows how to help young children use it) can select software, facilitate, encourage, and arrange the environment and events so that positive learning occurs, it remains the role of the child to do the learning and decide the fate of a software program's appeal. Ultimately children decide whether or not the software provides experiences worthy of their attention. When it does, children participate with excitement, exclaim with delight, interact with one another, dance a jig, repeat interesting events and invite other children to watch (or do), or perhaps say their first word. When it does not, they turn their heads, close their eyes, go to sleep, throw a disk across the classroom in disgust, or walk away and refuse to participate. Project personnel have observed all these behaviors in Macomb Projects' experience with computers, software, and young children who demonstrate a wide range of disabilities.

If *KidDesk* is used to manage the desktop on a classroom computer, children can control the choices they make while the applications and adult-produced documents stored on the hard disk are protected. The hard disk drive is protected from damage and files cannot be changed, moved, or deleted. Adults can personalize the desktops for individual children to indicate which files and programs each child can access. Desktops can be protected by passwords so adult files remain safe as long as children don't figure out what to do to get into the files by watching their parents or teachers set up desktops. Included in the *KidDesk* desktop features are a printable calendar, talking clock, working calculator, telephone, lamp, and gadget holder. E-mail and voice mail (where children can record a message) plus a note pad with different designs are included in the newest version. Each child's desktop access can be personalized with a scanned photograph of the child used instead of an icon.

When preschool children are given the opportunity to choose software from *KidDesk,* they become familiar with the software programs they prefer. *Harry and the Haunted House* is a perennial favorite in many early childhood classrooms. This software program starts with a baseball game in trouble: a long fly ball lands in a haunted house and must be found. Children are drawn to the words of the story and in some cases, pretend to "read" the story in time with the narration. The program lends itself to small-group work. Children return to the animations that have made them laugh and that provoked discussions in the past. Again and again they click on the spots that result in music. This sometimes results in the group jumping from their chairs and breaking into dance. Lahm (1996) suggested that the preschool children with disabilities in her study were compliant and would remain engaged with software they were given, whether it was interesting or not. However, Macomb Projects' staff have not found this to be the case in preschool classrooms where literacy research is being conducted. Perhaps classroom management and teacher's rules and expectations influence compliant behavior as much as or more than the characteristics of the software.

Computer Experiences Give Children Control

Using computers and software affords an opportunity where children can (and do) assume control of their experiences, deciding whether and when to repeat events, to go forward, to change the program; and they do so at their own speed and intent. Young children seldom experience this kind of control. Parents and teachers sometimes rush children through experiences designed for learning, such as a field trip to the zoo, seldom stopping more than a minute or two to give the children time to observe or ask questions. Time for contemplation and absorbing new visual or oral information is often limited, not so much by children's attention spans (which can be incredibly long when they are interested in doing something), but more by adults' need to hurry.

Given control of their own time and behavior on a computer with software they choose or enjoy, children spend as much or as little time as they please when timing is flexible. Children need uninterrupted blocks of time for learning. This is a basic tenet of Montessori classrooms, one that would benefit children if it was adopted in more homes and schools. Children are uncomfortable when they are interrupted and moved to another activity, just as adults are resentful when someone insists that they interrupt what they are doing.

Macomb Projects staff have frequently noted that teachers who are beginning to use technology with children limit children's time on the computer to five minutes each so that "everyone gets a turn," a basic belief in a teacher's view of what children need. However, this practice creates an unsatisfying experience for the child and sometimes leads to negative behaviors, especially when it is reintroduced after children in the classroom have enjoyed a period of flexible time. Setting time limits does not take into account individual needs. Few adults would think of limiting block time or easel painting to five minutes per child.

Adult impatience is an obstacle to children gaining a sense of control when they use computers. Macomb Projects' personnel have recorded many video segments highlighting adults' impatience. When adults tire of waiting for children to decide their next choice and step in to control the course of a computer program or to move to another program, the children lose a sense of autonomy.

While adults consider educational goals and the features of software, children express their likes or dislikes when they attend to particular programs for long periods of time and become thoroughly engaged. It is not surprising that children often use *Kid Pix*, since drawing, cutting, and pasting are frequent early childhood activities. As children use the software, they often repeat the "Oh, No" of the undo command, the silly sounds made by the different tools, and the motor of the moving van. Some children like *Logo,* while others prefer blocks or the housekeeping center. Some enjoy drawing with programs such as *Kid Pix,* but others never go near the computer when graphics programs hold forth. Instead, they wait for a program from the *Living Books* series.

As children become accustomed to using a computer and software, they also acquire worthwhile content about the world and learn socially acceptable behaviors such as turn taking and helping each other solve problems. For example, Zack, a 4-year-old in a rural preschool program, had a favorite software program, *Harry and the Haunted House.* Zack preferred playing with this software when he took his turn on the computer. Even when it wasn't his turn, he negotiated successfully with other children to get them to use it so he could watch.

Auditory feedback, whether it is instrumental, catchy tunes, speech, or nonsense sounds, seems to be a common feature in the software young children choose. The importance of auditory feedback is supported by Macomb Projects' work as well as Lahm's (1996) study of software features that engage children. Many children demonstrate a preference for music.

Children in Macomb Projects' research and model development sites (Hutinger, 1996; Hutinger & Bell, 1997) select software containing animation more frequently than they choose other types of software. Children repeatedly return to titles that include elements of animation paired with music and other sounds. This preference is supported by Lahm (1996). When the images, animation and sound refer to elements familiar to the child, the effects can be powerful. Recently a 4-year-old's response to an individualized *HyperStudio* stack showing members of her class and family surprised not only her therapist but her teacher and the principal as well.

Only once in the course of 15 years has a Macomb Projects' staff member observed a child throw a disk after removing it from an older machine. This happened in the fall just after the child entered a new preschool classroom after a family move. That classroom served as an emergent literacy research control site, a site that used technology but not the interactive curriculum being tested by the study.[6] The previous year, in another school, the child had participated in an emergent literacy research project using the latest in equipment and powerful software on CD-ROM. He liked *Stone Soup* and graphics software. Disgusted with the limited software available in the new classroom (programs without sound that required reading then finding a correct key to obtain a response) and the limited ability of the old 64K equipment, he actively demonstrated his displeasure. If more appropriate software had been available, his reaction might have been different.

Assessing children's preferences in software is an important element in determining the most effective technology applications for a particular child. Macomb Projects is currently completing *Something's Fishy*,[7] a software program designed for use in technology assessments to investigate the elements in software that are preferred by individual children. Dimensions of sound, color, graphics, animation, and video are varied to identify the elements to which children respond most favorably.

The Adult Role in Software Use

Even though children are the ultimate critics of software, adults (whether they are teachers, therapists, or parents) play an important part if benefits are to accrue to children. Adults must learn to use the technology themselves before they can incorporate it into work with children. This is a basic and necessary condition adults must fulfill. Stories abound about computers being abandoned in closets or left in

---

[6] This site became an emergent literacy technology curriculum site the following year and was not left without more appropriate resources.

[7] *Something's Fishy* is software on a CD-ROM that is part of Macomb Projects' Technology Assessment Software Package supported by the National Institute on Disabilities and Rehabilitation Research, #HI33G40141.

the original packing boxes because adults don't know what to do with them. After learning to operate the equipment and use elements of software, adults must (a) evaluate and secure hardware and software; (b) arrange the environment in inviting ways; (c) facilitate; and (d) play the demanding role of teacher in attempts to meet the needs of children, families, schools, and society.

Any discussion of software for homes and early childhood classrooms should address the importance of adult use of software. When adults are enthusiastic computer users, they are more likely to provide technology applications for children. Sometimes the authors of articles on early childhood software evaluations and computer use tend to overlook this basic fact of life in this age of communication. If parents and teachers are comfortable with word processing, spreadsheets, and databases as well as other software for adult "productivity" (a designation that includes spreadsheets, databases, word processing, communication protocols, e-mail, and Internet access to the World Wide Web), those adults are more likely to use computers and software with young children (Hutinger, Robinson, & Johanson, 1990). Software to assist professional staff write Individual Education Plans (IEPs) is available, while software such as the *Macomb 0-3 CORE* (Computer Recordkeeping Enhancer)[8] may be used in birth-to-3 programs to assist in determining appropriate sequences of activities for children in conjunction with families and to provide suggestions sheets to parents.

Software such as *PrintShop* (Broderbund) and *Card Shop Plus* (Mindscape) provide a format for greeting cards, banners, and other trappings of family and classroom activities that contribute to enthusiasm for technology and counter the computerphobia that remains with some adults, no matter what their age. Some software comes "bundled" with the computer or installed on the hard drive. Bundled software generally relates to activities for adults or children older than preschool age and is useful in establishing confidence in computer operation.

---

[8] *0-3 CORE* was developed as a product of Project ACTT.

Using Resources Wisely

Family and school decision-makers need to recognize that technology expenditures for hardware is only one part of the necessary resources. Sometimes schools and families spend a great deal of money on the hardware—the computer, monitor, and printer—then have little money left for software. Classrooms or homes that have a computer but little software that is suitable for young children are at as much a disadvantage as those who have powerful new software but lack the computers with the power to use it.

If budgets are limited and software must serve a variety of functions, then open-ended, interactive software that can be individualized and/or used by children with different skills and needs is preferable. This includes software such as *Logo, HyperStudio,* and good graphics programs, such as *KidPix.* The functions of these programs are similar to paint, crayons, and blocks because (a) each can be used differently by children at different developmental and skill levels; (b) they can be individualized in terms of difficulty, complexity, and content; and (c) they offer opportunities for a variety of learning outcomes across more than one content domain.

Software prices vary from catalog to catalog and company to company, sometimes by as much as $10. Prices advertised on the World Wide Web may be cheaper than other published prices. When resources are scarce, then consumers must do comparative shopping and use their financial resources for the most effective software purchases.

Shareware and Freeware

In addition to commercial software, shareware and freeware are available options to teachers who have limited funds for software purchases. Shareware is software that producers want consumers to copy and share with friends. Shareware is not free, however, and payment of some kind is expected for use of the program. Sometimes the producers simply want users to drop them a postcard and give them an opinion of the program. Most often money is expected. Some share-ware producers put their users on "the honor system," telling them how much they are expected to pay for the program if they like it and want to continue using it. Other producers build a specific number of "free uses" into the program. Once that limit is reached, if users want to keep the program, they must send payment to the producers, who will either send them a new unblocked copy of the program or will provide them with a password to circumvent the block. Prices for shareware range from $5 to $50 or more.

Freeware and public-domain software are, as the names imply, free to use, copy, and share with friends. Public-domain programs are not copyrighted and can be modified if users desire. Freeware is copyrighted. Like public-domain software, it can be copied and given away. However, it cannot be sold or modified. Some companies (see the list at the end of this chapter) distribute public-domain software for a minimal fee plus shipping and handling charges. The Internet can be a valuable resource for software. Adults may use available search engines and type in the descriptor "children's software." Com-mercial companies often provide demonstration copies of programs, hoping the preview will encourage the consumer to order the com-plete program. Shareware is available for downloading, as is freeware. A list of Uniform Resource Locators (URLs) for software-related sites is located in Appendix A (p. 253).

Legal Requirements: The Responsibility of Software Users

It is not always appropriate to share software. No one would think of copying a best-selling novel to share with other families or friends. If a person purchased a copy of the novel, enjoyed reading it, and wanted to share it, the person would loan their copy of the book to others or recommend that friends purchase it for themselves. However, the opposite practice is often commonplace where software programs are concerned. Perhaps this is because software, unlike a novel, is relatively easy, fast, and inexpensive to copy. Nevertheless, copying and distributing commercial software is illegal, whether the user's motivation is educational, altruistic, or profit seeking.

The Copyright Act of 1976, Public Law 94-553 (1996), contains language (§107 of Title 17) regarding fair use of copyrighted materials. Fair use allows copying without permission from or remuneration to the copyright owners because of minimal use of the materials. Teachers are among those listed in the law as having privileges of fair use. Guidelines for print materials allow for only relatively small portions of the work to be copied (e.g., 250 words of a poem; a complete article of less than 2,500 words; 10% of a prose work, up to 1,000 words).

Software is another matter. It isn't possible to copy just part of a program. A 1980 revision (§117) to the Copyright Act addressed fair use of copyrighted computer programs. Consumers have the right to make one back-up (archival) copy of a program. If the consumer has sold the software or given it away, legally he or she is required to destroy archival copies of programs or to include them as part of the transaction. Consumers may not use back-up copies to make replacement copies of a program that has been sold or given away. Multiple copies of a program to sell or give away may not be made, even if the intention is to distribute them only among teachers within the district that purchased the program.

Licensing and Consumer Rights

What rights do consumers have when they purchase a program? Users may or may not be able to install software as often as they expected. For example, one of this chapter's authors (not a novice computer user) purchased a $295 software tutorial writing program and was shocked to learn, on reading the documentation after the software arrived, that it could be installed only twice. The third time an installation was needed, the program had to be uninstalled from a computer where it was being used. A fourth installation was out of the question since the software was programmed so that it could not be used again.

The developers' intent was to add a rigid dimension to prohibit sharing or copying the software, thereby depriving the originators of their rightful income and creative property; however, such a practice deprives the consumer of value and property. Books don't disintegrate after the first three readings, nor do newspapers or World Wide Web sites. A consumer's hard drive, on the other hand, does crash, logic boards do go haywire, and accidents do happen. Back-ups must be available. But, as noted earlier, making copies of the program and distributing them to friends is not only unethical and unacceptable, it is illegal.

Licensing requirements and agreements differ, depending on the software. Consumers should be sure they know what the requirements are prior to a purchase. Sometimes software is licensed to a purchaser and can be used on many machines owned by the entity (for example, a school district). Such a license is more expensive than a single piece of software used by an individual user. Other software must be used on only one machine at a time; if multiple machines are to be used, the owner must purchase multiple copies of the software. Information about site-licensing agreements is contained in a company's catalog or from a customer service representative.

Useful Considerations

Users must consider software "housekeeping" or "management" information. Backing up software, returning faulty programs, and acquiring upgrades are part of the underlying requirements for effective and satisfactory computer use.

Back it up. Consumers should make a back-up version of the software in case something does go wrong. A 3.5-inch disk can be write-protected by sliding the small plastic tab on the back of the disk to uncover the square hole in the upper right-hand corner. A 5.25-inch disk can be write-protected by covering the notch on the side of the disk with a piece of tape. If a software program on floppy disks does not provide or allow back-ups, consumers might reconsider its purchase. Backing up software purchased on a CD-ROM is a different matter because so much data is stored on each silver disk. However, currently CD-ROMs are "read only" and information cannot be accidentally deleted, although the disk can be damaged.

While disks won't shrink, spilled water or soft drinks render them unusable. Because magnets remove electronic code and erase a program, keep all magnets (including telephones) away from computers and disks. Accidentally deleting files or initializing a disk may occur due to confusion or carelessness. Therefore, back-up copies must be made and the write-protection safety on disks should be used. Make a back-up copy prior to installing the software. Also, as you are working on the computer, files must be saved frequently. Making a back-up disk of any files constructed while using adult productivity software is a necessary precaution.

Return policies. The dealer's return policy may be to offer consumers a money-back guarantee or a replacement, but *not* if the entire program has accidentally been deleted. If a CD-ROM or disk has been scratched or damaged from a crayon or marker, most companies will replace it for a small fee. When a software warranty accompanies a purchase, wise consumers fill it out and mail it promptly. Buyers *do* have some responsibility to use disks wisely.

Consumers should buy software from dealers who are reputable, reliable, and knowledgeable. Return policies for software vary. Some companies have a policy that allows consumers to purchase and view the software for 30 days then return it for a full refund with only a few restrictions. The process is initiated with a phone call requesting a special Return Merchandise Authorization number. Then the reason(s) the consumer doesn't want the program must be put in writing, and a form must be filled out. If a problem arises with any software, the software "Help" service (also known as "technical support") should be contacted immediately to determine whether or not the fault lies in the software or the user. The "Help" service assists in determining whether the user is forgetting something or doing something wrong. If the service representative's suggestions don't solve the problem, the program should be returned immediately.

Upgrades. When upgrades are released, if a warranty card has been returned, users will be given the opportunity to purchase the new version for a small fee rather than paying the entire purchase price. Upgrades are intended to provide a more useful product with fewer "bugs" and more options than the previous version. If consumers register the software, some companies automatically notify them of upgrades. However, consumers should regularly read at least one computer magazine for current information regarding upgrades.

Recordkeeping. Recordkeeping was heralded by some in special education as being a necessary addition to software. Whether or not recordkeeping is needed depends on the function of the software. At the present time, bookmarks can be added to some interactive software so the user can easily find his or her place again. Some software (e.g., the literacy package *Wiggle Works,* intended for the primary grades) has the potential to keep track of the progression of an entire class through a series of activities and exercises. Identifying and keeping track of errors is useful when older children need to practice a discrete skill (i.e., adding or subtracting numbers, spelling words correctly), but has little place in current problem-solving software for young children. This is not to say that, with the appropriate theoretical framework and hours of work and discussion, software that keeps track of young children's problem-solving abilities is not possible. However, it is probably not possible at the present time in terms of expense and marketability. Adults and children can keep track of *Logo* moves and construction and have had that capability for years. Recordkeeping may involve no more than keeping a hardcopy or examples of children's work on disk, using a portfolio approach to evaluation.

Nuts and Bolts: Important Software Features

Aside from legal considerations, content, design, developmental appropriateness, and appeal, consumers have a right to expect that purchased software comes with some basic and essential technical features. A checklist of basic technical elements, beginning with compatibility components, is shown in Figure 4-9 on the next page. While consumers might assume that the features discussed are present in both child and adult software, that assumption is not accurate.

The Basic Question: Will It Run On Our Computer?

Compatibility is a critical consideration and requires that beginners and experienced users alike ask questions about software requirements when a purchase is imminent. For example, software embedded on a CD-ROM requires a CD-ROM drive in or attached to a computer. Figure 9 contains a checklist of compatibility essentials together with other basic considerations when selecting software.

In order for applications to operate effectively, the requirements of the equipment must be consistent with the requirements of the software. The documentation details requirements. The newest software and computers have more power and, therefore, can perform more functions than older models. However, software appropriate for children and for the equipment is still available for a 64K or a 128K machine. As early as 1980, Macomb Projects' staff were doing interesting things with 48K machines, software, and young children. When staff discovered that a baby could use a suck (sip 'n puff) switch to turn computer-controlled events on and off,[9] applications were developed, including cause and effect software such as *Switch 'N See* for children with disabilities under the age of three or four years.

The current interest in getting tax deductions for charitable donation of computers results in older computer models becoming available to schools in many parts of the country. The National Cristina Foundation was a forerunner in this effort; then other groups, many resulting from state assistive technology projects, followed suit. Most groups refurbish the computers to make sure they are in good working condition before they are given to schools. If it still works and *if*

---

[9]Thanks to Warren Brown, who at that time was the computer guru with FDLRS (Florida Diagnostic and Learning Resources System) in Sarasota, Florida.

Figure 4-9. *Basic software features*

1. **Compatibility.** Check the software's requirements (usually clearly printed on the software box or given in the catalog description) against your computer's system. Consider the following:

- RAM (Random Access Memory)
- ROM (Read Only Memory) and/or hard drive space
- Operating system requirements
- Monitor size
- Color and graphics capabilities
- CD-ROM drive requirements

2. **Program features.**

- Reading should not be necessary for children to operate the program independently.
- The program should not freeze or crash if an incorrect key is pressed.
- An "undo" feature should be available for correcting errors in graphics or storywriting software.
- Children should be able to bypass the introduction or title screen.
- Animated and video routines should be interruptible.
- Children should be able to "exit" or "go back" at any time in the program.
- Printing options should be available for all writing and graphic programs.
- A save option should be available in all writing and graphic programs.

3. **Company support.**

- The program should come with understandable documentation and include troubleshooting tips.
- The software company should provide a customer service help line.
- The warranty, guarantee, and return policy should be clearly stated.

Used with permission: Macomb Projects, Project ACTT ©1996.

appropriate software is available, the opportunity to acquire a classroom computer should not be ignored because it is old. Once parents and administrators see the advantages computers and software offer children with disabilities, efforts are usually made to update the equipment. Many of the companies listed in Appendix A, including Commercial Software Resources and Public Domain Software Resources, still sell software for older computers.

Basic Features

Figure 4-9 lists basic design features that users can reasonably expect from any software program. Software should be "crash-proof": an accidental keystroke, combination of keystrokes, or movement should not shut down the program or freeze the computer. Shareware and public domain software should meet the same standard. Sometimes software still has bugs the developer has not yet found or removed. A program should have an easy way to "escape" at any time as well as a way to interrupt an animated or video routine. Children should find it easy to go back to an earlier screen or forward to the next screen.

If software on CD-ROMs does not have to be installed on the hard drive in order to operate, it will run independently of the computer's storage capacity. When applications include options for creating individual files (i.e., writing stories, producing graphics), then the software must be installed on the hard drive. This factor is not critical when the hard drive has gigabytes[10] of read-only memory (ROM). If a hard drive has limited ROM and if CD-ROMs must be installed on the hard drive in order to function, the software takes up space that may be needed to run other software. The capability of the machine must be considered.

Documentation should be clearly written, concise, and provide examples from the program screens. Programs for young children should be intuitive in terms of operation or have sound to guide the child rather than depending on the ability to read words.

Software should do what its advertising claims purport it will do in all sections of the program. All the parts of a program should run, and nothing outside a beta (or test) version should be "under construction." Sometimes software is advertised and promised well before the date it is completed. Software featured in magazines may not be immediately available. The actual ship date may be as long as six to eight months after the first-promised ship date.

---

[10] A gigabyte is one billion bytes of memory. A CD-ROM holds 0.65 gigabytes of data.

Software Design Features

Design covers a wide range of elements, including those discussed in the sections on adaptations, interactivity, and basic features. The characteristics of appropriate design addressed in this section are based on Macomb Projects' research findings and model development activities (Hutinger, 1996; Hutinger & Bell, 1997) and on criteria suggested by others (Ainsa, Murphy, Thouvenelle, & Wright, 1994; Bowman & Beyer, 1994; Buckleitner, 1996; Kafai & Soloway, 1994; Lahm, 1996; Pierce, 1994). Design concerns relate to the nature of software content and reflect the developmental characteristics of children. Design features are not always apparent to the user. They are transparent, residing within the coding, and contribute to ease of use. Appropriate design features can be found across a range of software.

Software content. Software design, good early childhood practices, and good children's literature share many of the same characteristics. Programs should be designed around strong content that is interesting, engaging, and addresses a range of topics, including children's real life experiences and imaginative situations. Content and activities should go beyond the Saturday morning cartoon mentality and address cognitive abilities that require decision-making and judgments and that invite further exploration and actions that extend further than rote memory activities. Well-designed software provides time to pause and reflect rather than presenting children with a rush of flashing pictures and an overload of sensory stimulation. Software should be enjoyable and sustain children's interest, encouraging children to laugh, to use their imagination, and to explore.

Programs should contain more than one activity. Moreover, gender, cultural, and racial stereotypes should not be employed. Content should reflect children as socially competent beings who have different characteristics, demonstrate positive social values (i.e., people can get along with one another), and portray the world as an interesting and exciting place.

Literacy and developmental concerns. Emergent literacy is an important part of young children's experiences that can be achieved and enhanced via computer use (Erickson & Koppenhaver, 1995; Hutinger & Bell, 1997; STARNet, 1996). Software that addresses literacy concepts includes storybooks, writing, and graphic programs. In the case of the latter, printing and "save" options should be available for all writing and graphic programs. An "undo" feature should be available for correcting errors in graphics or storywriting software.

Storybook software should not always have to begin at the beginning. Children should be able to start at the page where they previously stopped. If there is text, the user should be able to select different options. For example, children should be able to turn the highlighting feature off and on text when it is read. Features that permit children or adults to select different languages and different ways to move through the text enhance the potential of the software.

Design Addresses Characteristics of Young Children

Software should be designed so young children can control the pace and path of the software and use the program independently. Good software appeals to children's multisensory learning styles and takes advantage of the capacities offered by powerful computers. Children should be able to determine the order in which they want to use activities, and activities should be easy to access or change. Novelty and surprise should be built into the design, and content should change with each use of the software. Play and imagination should be encouraged.

Good software has a high degree of interactivity, requiring active participation rather than passive sitting and watching. It requires frequent reactions, decisions, and/or creative input (Buckleitner, 1996), and "using" rather than doing (Lahm, 1996).

Child control. Children are in control when software is developmentally appropriate. Icons should be easy for children to understand. Access and options should be designed to allow children to explore and discover. Reading should not be necessary for children to operate the program independently. Images or speech should guide the path through the software.

Individual differences. Good software design often allows for the software to be personalized for preference or ability. Perhaps it can be personalized with sound, voice, or the child's name. It can be used by children of differing abilities and developmental levels. Responses should be short; long narratives do not appeal to young children.

Levels of difficulty or new challenges should be varied either by the number of choices offered or variations in the activity. Different levels should be available for selection by child or adult. Levels may change automatically as the child's skill increases. Software design may provide layers of complexity and greater fluidity in organizing and presenting ideas (Kafai & Soloway, 1994).

Design Elements

Software should be easy to use. Programs should load quickly so children don't have to wait for long periods of time for a response to their input. Feedback should be instantaneous. On-screen help may be available or it can be turned off. Software may include options so children can save, reuse, and change their products. It should be easy to pause within a program, and children should be able to bypass the title screen and interrupt animated or video routines. Children should be able to "escape" and go back to a previous screen at any time. Sometimes bookmarks are used to mark a place. In some software, adults can review what children have done.

Sound. With the right equipment, software can allow voices, music, and other sounds to be recorded. The program itself should contain interesting and appropriate sounds and music related to the learning activity. If speech is used, it should be clear and understandable and include children's voices in addition to adult voices. Sound can be turned off or on and adjusted for volume within the software without having to access hardware volume control.

Graphics. Engaging, well-drawn images of the same quality as found in good children's literature should be evidenced. Graphics are a form of art and can be evaluated as such. Pictures should be clear. Images, in both drawn and photographic format, should include those of children and adults, not just animals. Examples of children's work both visually and in other elements, such as voice and story, should sometimes be used.

Good software has well-designed, coherent, simple screens with appealing color, free of distracting decorative elements unrelated to the theme or content. Graphics designers involved in developing good software typically do not use every available gimmick in the graphics arsenal (e.g., marble textures to a full rainbow array of distracting colors). Instead, elements are selected that are pleasing to the eye. The term "simple" used here does not encompass the context of cognitive elements. Children with disabilities can often handle the same software complexities as "typical" children. Rather, the term addresses universal elements of design related to line, color, value, and composition.

Animation and video. Given the power of new equipment and software, programs can be expected to contain smooth and immediate, not slow and jerky, animation routines. When children access objects and characters that are animated, the response is immediate. Video, if it is used, is clear, not jerky, and appropriate to the topic.

Errors. The software program's response to mistakes (incorrect keys or incorrect choices) should contain appropriate messages. Responses to mistakes (incorrect keys pressed or incorrect choices made) should not be negative or criticizing. The child should be given the opportunity to make another choice before a correct answer is given. Children can correct an error at any point in time. Moreover, the program does not automatically return a child to an earlier level or screen if a mistake of any kind is made. At some point, if correct answers are required, the answer should be given.

Software Evaluation

Software that contains a variety of components designed to meet children's changing developmental needs is essential if technology is to enhance early childhood experiences. Selecting such software and finding creative ways to use it to support or initiate curriculum-based or daily activities and children's interests is an important responsibility for early childhood special education teachers, staff, and families. Throughout the chapter, criteria that can be used to evaluate software has been suggested. Many evaluation forms exist that may or may not be useful in a specific situation. Using elements suggested here, an individualized evaluation form can be constructed that will meet specific needs.

Software selected for a particular setting must relate to the goals for using that particular program. The objectives for using software are more important than the goals suggested in the software packaging. The two must mesh if the software is to be used successfully. First, parents or teachers must know what they expect the software to do, and they should answer questions such as those that follow. What is its function? Both IEPs and IFSPs provide direction for making software selections for a particular child or groups of children. Is the program, or parts of it, appropriate for a broad age range, including children younger than three? Can it be used differently by children of differing ages and abilities? Is the purpose to secure software that supports emergent literacy, or games that promote social interaction? Is the software intended to introduce children to a variety of cultures and people? What are the curricular goals? Parents and teachers should keep children's needs in mind when reading descriptions and reviews of various software and evaluating programs and then purchase software that will address those needs. The need should determine the tool rather than the tool determining the need.

When reviewing and evaluating software for inclusion in a software library, adults should consider its possibilities for extending the curriculum. Ways to extend the content of the software beyond the computer center should be explored in order to provide a creative learning environment for children and, at the same time, get the most from software purchases. Some software contains a separate section within the program, addressing further useful activities and information for adults. Other software has accompanying written curricular materials.

In order to optimize the financial investment in software, an early childhood special education professional should be a member of the selection team when purchasing decisions are made. Time spent previewing software is well spent. However, the feature that adults dislike may turn out to be popular with children, or vice versa. Adults should be aware of the danger of becoming so enamored of one intriguing feature (e.g., the confusing video on a recently released construction site program or the popularity of a well-known singer on a program featuring a children's song) that they don't view the software from the child's perspective. Adults can preview and evaluate software, but until they have used it with children, adults may be mistaken about the appeal of a feature.

A wide range of software is currently available, and it contains a variety of positive and negative elements. Software reviews and databases, such as the *Guide to Software Recommendations*,[11] are helpful resources for parents and teachers who are looking for software that will meet the needs of a child. These resources will help adults narrow down the choices for software purchases but should not replace a thorough evaluation of the software after a purchase has been made.

---

[11] *Guide to Software Recommendations* is a product of Macomb Projects' Technology Assessment Software Package. The database can be used to match software with a child's input abilities and preferences for sound, color, motion, and images.

Summary

The adult role in selecting software is similar to choosing any effective learning tool for young children with disabilities, whether books, toys, blocks, paint, or other materials and equipment. Highly interactive software accompanies more powerful hardware, replacing earlier programs that reflected narrow learning outcomes. Computers and accompanying software provide children with the means to use and control tools that produce exciting learning outcomes that cannot be attained in any other way. However, technology will not replace customary early childhood materials, nor will it interfere with social interaction. Pages can be turned and pictures can be viewed in a good storybook, but if a child cannot read, she or he needs another individual to read the narrative. Storybook software on a computer can be set to read the story, pictures can be animated—the young child is in control and competent. Software adaptations for children with varying disabilities are available and provide benefits across many areas of development. Software functions (i.e., tool, tutor, and tutee) provide a framework for evaluating programs, elements of interactivity, and individual differences in preferences. The references and resources in the Appendices are included to provide further information related to both recent and older software.

CHAPTER FIVE

Assistive Technology Decision-Making Strategies

Sharon Lesar Judge
The University of Tennessee, Knoxville

Howard P. Parette, Jr.
Southeast Missouri State University

While descriptions of assistive technology assessment processes have been provided in the professional literature, they have generally been directed toward school-age children and adults, with relatively little attention being given to young children and their families (Bowe, 1995; Bradley, Parette, & VanBiervliet, 1995). This chapter presents extensive reviews of the existing literature pertaining to assistive technology decision-making and early intervention "best practices," with implications being drawn for the field of early childhood special education. Issues that will be addressed include team collaboration considerations; parent-professional partnership building; and child, family, technology, and service system domains that should be considered during assistive technology assessment processes.

Team Collaboration

Assistive technology for young children with disabilities cannot be appropriately provided without team participation. Descriptions of teams in the professional literature emphasize the involvement of related service personnel and early childhood special education professionals collaborating with the child *and* family members. Assistive technology teams are necessary since no one individual or discipline will have all the information available regarding the range of assistive devices that might be helpful for a child (Smith, Benge, & Hall, 1994).

Different models of teaming have been identified in the early intervention literature. The *transdisciplinary team model* (Lesar, Lowe, & Bartholomew, 1994) has proven to be an effective way to develop and organize the delivery of assistive technology services for children and families who require the involvement of professionals from a variety of disciplines and agencies. This approach differs from other team models in that it attempts to overcome the confines of individual disciplines in order to form a team that crosses and recrosses disciplinary boundaries and thereby maximizes communication, interaction, and cooperation among team members (Bruder & Bologna, 1993; McGonigel & Garland, 1988; Woodruff & McGonigel, 1988). The transdisciplinary team pools and integrates the expertise of team members so that more efficient and comprehensive assistive technology assessment and intervention plans and services can be provided. Typically, decisions regarding assessment and intervention are made by team consensus. Family participation on the team is crucial. Potential team members that might be involved in decision making about assistive devices for young children with disabilities and their families are presented in Figure 5-1 on the next page.

Parent-Professional Partnership Building

Current practices in family-centered early intervention highlight the importance of parent and professional partnerships. Operationally, a parent-professional partnership is defined as an association between a family and one or more professionals that functions collaboratively, using agreed-upon roles in pursuit of a common interest (Dunst & Paget, 1991). Through parent-professional partnerships, opportunities are created for partners to become empowered to make informed

Figure 5-1. *Potential assistive technology team members*

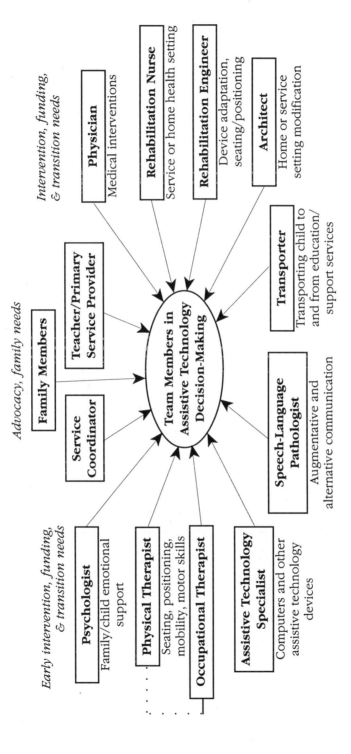

Source: Parette, H. P. (in press). Assistive technology effective practices for students with mental retardation and developmental disabilities. In A. Hilton & R. Ringlaben (Eds.), *Effective and promising practices in developmental disabilities*. Austin, TX: PRO-ED. Adapted with permission.

decisions about the best course of action to achieve a common goal or interest.

A family-centered approach to assistive technology considers partnership building as a mechanism for empowering families to be involved in all aspects of assistive technology assessment and service delivery. This approach to the implementation of assistive technology contrasts sharply with the traditional role relationships between professionals and families. Family involvement during assistive technology assessment and implementation has often been limited to that of information provider and trainer rather than decision-maker (Parette & Angelo, 1996). Use of partnerships encourages shared responsibility and collaboration between the family and professional rather than client-professional relationships focused solely on the child.

Partnerships are characterized by certain features that make them different from other types of cooperative endeavors. *First,* the decision-making process in all aspects of assistive technology assessment and intervention must consider the changing needs of the family and allow for such flexibility. A major duty and responsibility of the professional is to provide all necessary information to assist the family in evaluating different options so that the parents can make informed decisions regarding the selection and use of the assistive technology device. The final decision, however, about what devices appropriately match the needs of the child, what goals and interests should be pursued, and what courses of action will be taken to attain them, must rest solely with the family. Otherwise, lack of consensus may occur, resulting in limited device use by the child and family or abandonment of assistive devices. Even if the professional disagrees with the family's decision, parents still need the professional's advice, encouragement, and support after the decision has been made.

Second, partnerships developed between the family and professionals evolve from mutual trust, honesty, respect, open communication, and respect for cultural diversity. Honesty, trust, and commitment are the backbone of any effective helping relationship and are absolutely necessary for a partnership to be effective (Dunst & Paget, 1991). Professionals who enter into collaborative arrangements with families must give complete loyalty to the partnership; provide families with relevant, accurate, and up-to-date information; and use effective communication skills so that trusting partnerships can be developed and enhanced. The professional must be able to instill confidence in the family and understand the responsibility of providing the necessary information so the family can make informed decisions regarding appropriate assistive technology services for their child. This is a very important step in creating an equal partnership and putting the parents on equal ground with the professional, assuming that the family desires equality in the relationship (see Chapter 7 for a discussion of cultural influences).

Third, partners recognize the benefits of a collaborative arrangement and openly agree to pool their respective resources (knowledge, skills, etc.) and to work toward a mutually agreed-upon goal or interest. Both the parent and professional must discuss the assistive technology "joint venture" and then proceed to define the mutually agreed-upon roles that will be used in the development of the partnership. This process is driven by family-identified needs, resources, routines, and values. The family is provided opportunities to evaluate the progress made at various times during the process and to renegotiate the mutually agreed-upon roles as well as the goals.

Partnerships in early intervention benefit everyone involved, including the child. Building partnerships with parents and involving them purposefully and meaningfully at all levels within the assistive technology process promotes the incorporation of the parents' views on choosing devices and implementing and supporting their use. Presented in Figure 5-2 are issues to consider when developing and cultivating parent-professional partnerships.

Assistive Technology Decision-Making Domains

When making decisions about assistive technology devices and services, four interrelated domains should be the focus of professional and family assessment efforts: *child characteristics, family issues, technology features,* and *service system issues* (Parette, in press; Parette &

Figure 5-2 *Assistive technology partnership-building questions*

- Are parents asked about the level of involvement they desire at all stages of the assistive technology assessment process?
- Are family members asked about their preferred methods of involvement and communication?
- Does the decision-making process consider the changing needs of the family and allow for such flexibility in the plan?
- Are partnerships developed between the family and professionals that evolve from mutual trust, honesty, respect, and open communication?
- Are there opportunities for the family to evaluate the progress made at various times during the process (evaluation of the entire process as well as individual goals)?
- Does the family have the final decision regarding whether to accept or reject the advice?
- Has professional help been offered that matches the family's appraisal of their needs?
- Are professionals positive and proactive in all aspects of interactions with the family?
- Does the process clearly show that family-identified needs, resources, routines, and values drive the process with the collaborative support of professionals?
- Are families asked about their preferences concerning times and locations for interactions and assistive technology services?

Angelo, 1996; Parette & Brotherson, 1996; Parette, Hourcade, & VanBiervliet, 1993). When professionals are identifying appropriate assistive devices for any young child with a disability, an examination of the linkages among the four domains is necessary. Each of these domains will be addressed in the following sections to insure that decision-making strategies promote child and family competencies in assistive technology.

Child Factors

Since the historical focus of assistive technology service delivery has been the user or individual who is the recipient of devices and services, child factors are crucial in assessment processes. Early childhood special education personnel involved in assistive technology assessment processes must examine specific child-related factors to identify *appropriate technology* that can be appropriately used by the young child with disabilities and the family.

Appropriateness has been defined in various ways. From a more traditional perspective, assistive technology devices are appropriate when they meet three criteria: (a) they are related to specific and clearly defined goals that are meaningful to the child and family; (b) they are compatible with practical constraints, such as the available resources or amount of training required for the child and others to use the technology; and (c) they should result in the child and family achieving desirable and sufficient outcomes (Office of Technology Assessment, 1982; Parette, in press). Since the provision of assistive technology devices and services are linked to the development of the Individual Family Service Plan (IFSP) and Individual Education Plan (IEP), devices and services should be viewed from the perspective of child strengths and needs in *naturalistic settings.*

The IFSP/IEP must include a statement of the child's present levels of development in physical, cognitive, communication, social and emotional, and adaptive development. This provides a tentative starting point for examination of child characteristics by providing the team with important information relating to the child's functioning in various domains. Several discussions of these factors have been addressed in assistive technology curricula developed for family members (Parette & VanBiervliet, 1990a, 1990b). An understanding of *gross- and fine-motor abilities* will help the team to best select devices that can be held, manipulated, or transported by the child in naturalistic settings. *Cognitive skills* become important considerations given that certain devices require higher levels of cognitive ability to use efficiently. An understanding of the child's *communication skills* is necessary to identify the language that will be associated with the use of appropriate augmentative and alternative communication (AAC) devices. This also becomes an issue when children must use assistive technology devices cooperatively with others. Knowledge of the child's *social and emotional skills* enables the team to effectively consider assistive technology devices that (a) may require focused concentration by the child, (b) will be used in play settings with other children (e.g., requiring turn taking), or (c) are responsive to the child's emotional states (e.g., a child who is emotionally labile and inclined to throw, tear, or bang materials). Finally, recognition of the child's *adaptive skills* will provide the team with an understanding of the degree of self-sufficiency or independence with which the child can be expected to use an assistive technology device in naturalistic settings. While the child's level of development provides an initial starting point for assistive technology decision-making, other specific device-related issues may also be considered (see Figure 5-3 below).

Consideration of *age* is important since certain assistive devices have been designed specifically for use with young children. *Gender* may be an important issue; for example, an electronic augmentative and alternative communication (AAC) device featuring a female voice would be inappropriate for a male child. Furthermore, certain colors or materials may be viewed by the family as being appropriate to a specific gender (e.g., preferring pink or even green for a daughter's

Figure 5-3. *Important child characteristics that influence the selection of appropriate assistive technology devices*

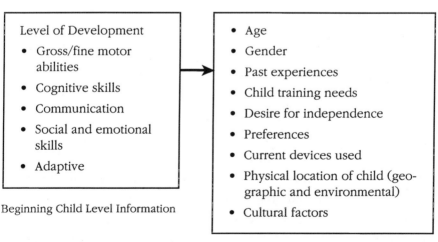

Level of Development
- Gross/fine motor abilities
- Cognitive skills
- Communication
- Social and emotional skills
- Adaptive

Beginning Child Level Information

- Age
- Gender
- Past experiences
- Child training needs
- Desire for independence
- Preferences
- Current devices used
- Physical location of child (geographic and environmental)
- Cultural factors

Specific Assistive Device–Related Issues

equipment, rather than blue). Such preferences often have a cultural component (an issue discussed more fully in Chapter 7).

The child's *past experiences* in using assistive technology devices are of particular importance since this information provides insights regarding both successful and unsuccessful interactions that can guide decision-making. *Training needs* associated with any assistive technology device will have an impact not only on the child but also on service system personnel and family members, since all persons in the child's naturalistic settings may need to learn to use the device (Behrmann, 1995; Carey & Sale, 1994). The child's *desire for independence,* or the family's desire for child independence, may be an issue for some families—particularly depending on their cultural context—and influence decisions regarding the most appropriate device for the priorities, concerns, and resources of the family. *Child preferences* for devices may be an issue for toddlers who are beginning to make choices and show early preferences for devices constructed of specific materials or with features that are novel and of interest to the child. While family members often report little consideration being given to the child's preferences during decision making (Hutinger, 1994; Parette & VanBiervliet, 1995), professionals have reported that user preferences *are* considered (Van Dyck, Allaire, & Gressard, 1990), though the influence of assistive technology on young children's opinions varies markedly depending on the child's developmental age and status (Allaire, Gressard, Blackman, & Hostler, 1991).

Current devices used also provide team members with information necessary for decision-making, enabling team members to examine the efficiency with which a child can use a particular device and allowing them to evaluate the child's potential to use more sophisticated devices that might potentially be considered. *Physical location of the child* refers to the naturalistic setting in which the assistive technology may be used. Devices that will be used across several naturalistic settings will need to be transported. Wheelchairs and other mobility devices may require environmental modifications to enable efficient operation. Cultural issues specific to the child and family also need to be considered.

Family Factors

Until recently, assistive technology decision-making practices have reflected more traditional and less family-centered approaches. P.L. 101-476, the *Individuals with Disabilities Education Act of 1990*, reflects a clear intent for related service personnel to facilitate greater family involvement in assistive technology assessment processes because family members are recognized as primary decision-makers and sources of assessment information, particularly for young children with disabilities.

When parents and primary caregivers collaborate with professionals, there is a recognition that (a) the family is the constant in the child's life, while services and professionals within the system are always in a state of flux (Parette, 1995); and (b) assistive technology device recommendations must be flexible, accessible, and responsive to family needs (Bradley et al., 1995; Parette & Brotherson, 1996). When family members are involved in decision-making regarding assistive devices, they are more likely to perceive ownership of the interventions recommended (Beukelman & Mirenda, 1992; Parette & Angelo, 1996). Such participation has also been reported to result in both family satisfaction for devices prescribed and more favorable regard for professionals (Crais, 1991).

When family members are not involved in assistive technology decision-making, important family issues may not be addressed, resulting in the prescription of inappropriate devices. This, in turn, can result in noncompliance or abandonment of recommended intervention strategies using the device. Device abandonment has far-reaching implications, including (a) an exacerbation of the effects of disability on the infant or toddler who could potentially benefit from their usage (Brody & Ruff, 1986), (b) excess personal and financial costs (Luborsky, 1993; Parette, 1996), and (c) inefficient use of finite service system resources (Bradley et al., 1995; Parette, Brotherson, Hourcade, & Bradley, 1996)—in short, considerable waste.

Family expectations of assistive technology. Parent concerns are likely to focus on characteristics of the service system environment and inadequacies of equipment rather than inadequacies of children and activities. Several researchers (Culp, Ambrosi, Berniger, & Mitchell, 1986; Naisbitt, 1984) have noted the tendency of some people to believe (or hope) that technology is a panacea, thus abdicating personal responsibility for appropriate use of devices. During assistive technology assessment, such parental attitudes cannot be ignored since they may contribute to disappointment and anger when the technology fails to live up to their expectations. Consequently, it is critical that professionals working with family members *clearly understand* the expectations that families have for assistive technology devices and provide meaningful information to families regarding device features and capabilities as well as anticipated involvement of families and intervention personnel to ensure success of the device.

Angelo (1997) commented that parental anticipation of benefits expected from assistive technology may be diminished when families must modulate their routines and schedules with the demands required for device usage. Families also have expectations regarding quality of life and attainment of personal values and goals, though such expectations are typically not considered in assistive technology decision-making. If family members are placed in the position of having to choose between increased stress (due to assistive technology usage demands) and a more reasonable family routine (and enhanced quality of life), families often choose not to use the assistive technology device (Parette, 1996; Parette, Brotherson, Hoge, et al., 1996). This will be discussed in greater detail in Chapter 6.

Professional and parent perceptions of technology usage also differ markedly. Parents of younger children have been reported to use technology for social and emotional purposes, while parents of older students typically use technology for cognitive purposes. For example, Swartz (1994) found that home usage of technology was strongly influenced by parent and sibling assistance as well as the demands placed on the child by the service system to use the technology. Swartz further reported that more family-sensitive models of collaboration should be developed that are responsive to a wide range of family needs, strengths, and abilities. This supports findings that technology needs change across the life cycle (Luborsky, 1993; Male, 1994)

Changes in family interaction patterns and stress. If appropriate assistive technology devices are to be identified and IFSP/IEP implementation is to be effective, family values, routines, and resources should be considered by team members. When assistive devices are introduced in the home and other naturalistic settings, unexpected outcomes may sometimes result. In a study involving family use of computers in home settings, Margalit (1990) found that the introduction of computers affected the interactional styles of families. Some families reported substantial modifications as a result of technology impact, while some families reported none. This study suggests that technology introduction and usage cannot be expected to create significant results unless the *contextual features* in which the technology is integrated are dynamic and open to change. Parents sometimes use technology with an emphasis on products, rather than process, resulting in "mindless" involvement with the assistive device. The optimal learning environment is one in which "mindful" involvement is demonstrated by family members and learning processes are emphasized; parents and children together learn new tasks, find enjoyment in overcoming obstacles, and use effective problem-solving strategies (Brotherson, Cook, & Parette, 1996; Margalit, 1990).

Kaplan (1996) notes that technology is merely a tool, and compromises may need to be made during decision-making. What children and families receive may not be what is best, as perceived from a technical point of view by professionals, but rather what the child and family believe they can accept. Studies have shown that higher levels of stress may occur if (a) increased caregiving demands are placed on families (Angelo, 1997; McNaughton, 1990; Parette, Brotherson, Hourcade et al., 1996), (b) great amounts of time are required for family members to provide team-identified interventions (Brotherson & Goldstein, 1992), and (c) the specific assistive devices provided require family time and resource commitments (Allaire et al.,

1991; Angelo, 1997; McNaughton, 1990). Sensitivity to the changes that might potentially occur in families reflects respect for the family and may encourage greater family participation in the child's early intervention program. (For recommendations, see Parette, in press; Parette & Angelo, 1996b; Parette & Brotherson, 1996; Parette, Brotherson, Hourcade et al., 1996.)

The social environment. Brotherson et al. (1996) reported on the importance of the home and social environments when attempting to make appropriate decisions about assistive technologies. Family expectations regarding how the home environment is to be used may inhibit use of assistive technology. Johnson (1987) noted that the home environment of children is one of the most restrictive that they encounter and recommended that homes include (a) play areas in the main living areas of the home and in the kitchen, (b) improved access to the household based on the sizing and positioning of various fixtures, and (c) consideration of both privacy and active-play needs within the home. The social environment is of particular importance, and each technological solution considered for a child should examine how it makes the child look, sound, and behave differently from others.

Assistive Technology Device Factors

Specific features of assistive devices are typically examined after an understanding of the child's characteristics and family issues have been determined (Inge & Shepherd, 1995; Parette, in press; see Figure 5-4 on the next page). As there may be numerous aspects of devices crucial to making an appropriate selection for the young child with a disability, such an examination should be more than cursory in nature. The *range of available devices* that are potentially appropriate should be examined. A review of products advertised in various catalogs can provide the team with potential devices that might be appropriate for the child. Vendors may also be contacted and requested to provide demonstrations and hands-on opportunities for children

---

Figure 5-4. *Important device features that influence the selection of appropriate assistive technology devices*

- Range of devices available
- Potential to increase child's performance levels
- Costs (hidden as well as advertised)
- Ease of use
- Comfort
- Dependability
- Transportability

- Longevity and durability
- Adaptability
- Compatibility
- Hands-on opportunities to try out the device
- Longevity and durability
- Safety features
- Repair considerations

---

and families to use devices that are being considered by the team. Many states have demonstration centers that afford families hands-on experiences with a range of assistive technology devices.

Numerous state and national databases are also available to assist team members in examining the range of assistive technology devices available (Parette, 1995). ABLEDATA is a U.S. Department of Education–sponsored database containing a detailed description and manufacturer information on approximately 19,000 products from over 3,000 manufacturers. ABLEDATA is one of the first public-domain databases to be distributed widely through a low-cost CD-ROM, entitled *Cooperative Database Distribution Network for Assistive Technology* (CO-NET). It is internationally distributed by the Trace Center at the University of Wisconsin. Two user-friendly computer programs, DOS-ABLEDATA (VanBiervliet & Cox, 1991) and Hyper-ABLEDATA (Smith, Vanderheiden, Berliss, & Angelo, 1989), have been created to make it easy to access the ABLEDATA database on both IBM and Macintosh platforms. The programs have also been uploaded onto electronic bulletin boards for access by modem. CO-NET also contains 11 easy-to-use national directories of disability-related services that cover certain states plus regional and nationwide data sources (CO-NET, 1991; Vanderheiden, 1990). The new version of the CO-NET CD-ROM contains a complete, 41,000-entry REHABDATA database along with three additional databases.

The assistive device's *potential to increase performance levels* must also be carefully examined. Once a child's performance levels are known by the team, a plan may be developed that addresses the family's priorities, concerns, and resources. Many assistive technology devices are designed to perform specific functions in naturalistic settings, while other devices may have multiple uses across tasks and settings (Parette, in press). Some devices will be accompanied by product manuals that provide documentation regarding device functions and limitations. If such documentation is not available, team members may need to directly examine devices being considered by requesting product demonstrations by vendors or obtaining information from families who have used the devices being considered.

The *cost* of assistive technology is often identified as a primary barrier to acquiring technology for children with disabilities. Of particular importance to the team is the cost of the device, including costs associated with assembling, special batteries, parts, maintenance requirements, and additional assistive devices that are required to operate the device being considered. When hidden expenses are initially explored, they may be written into the child's IFSP/IEP as an assistive technology service, with specified providers being identified to pay for the necessary services.

Ease of use, or simplicity of operation of an assistive technology device, is an important consideration for young children with disabilities as well as family members. When complex devices are prescribed that require inordinate training-time commitments by service providers, family members, and children, reluctance to make such time investments may be exhibited. If the cognitive or motoric demands of the device exceed the child's performance levels, the child and family may be resistant to using the device, resulting in technology abandonment.

Comfort of assistive devices has also been identified as a potential factor for consideration during decision making. Careful thought must be given to the physical demands placed on the child to operate or use any assistive technology device and the level of comfort experienced during use in naturalistic settings. Some devices may be used with great ease and comfort, while others can only be used for short periods before the child will become tired or uncomfortable.

Dependability of the device includes the extent to which (a) device performance matches manufacturer claims and (b) the device meets the needs of the child. Team members must examine the ability of assistive technology devices to provide performance or evaluation data necessary for the documentation of the child's progress toward meeting goals that reflect the family's priorities, concerns, and needs. When information regarding device dependability is not available, team members may contact persons with disabilities who have used the device to obtain their perspectives of its dependability.

Transportability of the device across and within naturalistic settings may also be an important factor for team members to consider. Sometimes bulky or heavy devices may be chosen for young children who may not have the strength to carry them around in the environment. This places responsibility on adults working with the child to ensure the availability of the assistive technology device for targeted tasks identified in the IFSP/IEP. Smaller devices may be cumbersome for some young children to transport, requiring a special case, satchel, or bag—or a designated adult—to assist in transportation across environmental settings.

The *longevity* and *durability* of devices become an important consideration given that some assistive devices must be handled carefully and cannot be subjected to even moderate abuse (e.g., drooling, spills, being dropped) while other devices are specifically designed to resist very rugged use by young children with disabilities. Product manuals should be examined for information regarding longevity and durability; if unavailable, direct contact with the manufacturer may be helpful.

Since many technologies will be used for a long period of time, *adaptability* to meet a child's changing needs over time must be carefully considered. Devices that may be used across many naturalistic settings may be preferable (and more cost-effective) to those which perform only one function. However, some devices are designed to perform a specific function and cannot be adapted. Before an assistive technology device is purchased, team members should identify potential modifications needed for the device over time. Such needed modifications should then be weighed against available fiscal and human resources in the service system (e.g., school personnel, community volunteers) necessary to make the needed modifications.

Compatibility with other devices, or the extent to which a device being considered can be used with other assistive technology, may become an important consideration for some young children with disabilities. Team members should give thought to both the child's *present* and *future* needs when examining the ability of the technology to be used with other devices.

Hands-on opportunities to try out and use the device have repeatedly been identified as a prerequisite to assistive technology decision making by both family members and persons with disabilities (Hayward & Elliott, 1992; Hutinger, 1994). Team members should attempt to insure that the child has an opportunity to use an assistive technology device before purchase.

Safety features should be a consideration during team decision-making, since not all assistive technology devices may be safe for use with all young children with disabilities. Small devices that could be easily swallowed might not be appropriate for young children having a tendency to mouth objects. Other devices might have sharp edges that could injure young children during a fall or handling, while others might cause electric shock if placed in water.

Since some assistive devices require lengthy or frequent repair intervals, and because of the potential effects of this down-time on the child's progress, *repair considerations* should be considered by team members during decision-making processes. Team members should request information from vendors about product testing, reliability, and repair records for devices. Persons in the community who use the devices being considered should be contacted to obtain a user perspective regarding repair issues. Team members should also ask vendors whether the child and family will have a backup or "loaner" device provided by the manufacturer while the device is being repaired and whether a warranty is available. If a warranty is not available, team members may identify (a) local shops or companies that can provide parts or repair damaged devices or (b) students, parents, and school personnel who might have the tools and skills to repair assistive technology devices.

Service System Factors

The fourth area of concern that has traditionally been addressed by the IFSP/IEP team includes factors directly related to the service system's ability to provide needed assistive technology devices and services (see Figure 5 below).

Financing of assistive technology devices is sometimes perceived by professionals as the most critical service system issue (Church & Glennen, 1992; Klein, Walker, & Foster, 1994/95; Wallace, 1995). Assistive technology services identified in P.L. 102-119 include evaluations, purchasing, leasing, maintenance, repair, training, and other services (34 CFR §303.12). However, the reality of potentially limited funding of the Part H system (Gallagher, Harbin, Eckland, & Clifford, 1994) presents a major challenge to team members, and underscores the effective practice of *identifying appropriate technologies* for young children with disabilities. State, federal, and private sources other than Part H funds (e.g., Medicaid, Social Security Administration, CHAMPUS, private insurance) typically must be accessed. Inexpensive assistive

---

Figure 5-5. *Important service system characteristics that influence the selection of appropriate assistive technology devices*

- Cost
- Protection from theft and damage
- System's ability to modify, customize, or make inexpensive devices

- Early intervention personnel training needs
- Transportation
- Transition needs

---

devices or those that can be modified, customized, or made by the service system personnel at minimal cost may be appropriate for some young children with disabilities. Team members may consider *leasing* as an alternative to purchasing expensive devices, thus minimizing hidden expenses. Another effective practice solution is to use community resources as an alternative funding source when severe fiscal resource limitations are present.

When devices are prescribed for young children with disabilities, *protection from theft and damage* may become an issue. This is particularly true when young children will be using devices across a range of naturalistic settings. While a particular facility where early intervention services are provided may have coverage for theft or damage while a device is on-site, liability issues may need to be examined if the device leaves the facility.

Integrally linked to the financing of assistive devices are *early intervention personnel training needs* (Behrmann, 1995; Carey & Sale, 1994). Effective team members should not ignore the necessity of training personnel in the appropriate use of assistive technology devices. While many assistive devices can easily be used without training, more sophisticated devices (e.g., keyboard emulators, nondedicated speech devices, environmental control systems) may require considerable personnel training commitments. Thought should also be given to the attitudes held by professionals who require training in the use of assistive devices. Some professionals *do not want to learn* to use technology, just as some children show no interest in using specific applications (Hutinger, 1994). Professionals' opinion of how successful they think the outcome will be determines whether or not they make the device accessible to the child (Hutinger, 1994; Parette, 1996). Moratinos (1995) found that teacher perceptions of students' abilities to learn to communicate were the strongest predictors of their intentions to provide and use AAC systems in classroom settings. These perceptions, however, were also found to be strongly affected by their own skills and responsibilities to provide AAC training in the classroom.

While technology benefits for young children with disabilities and their families may occur after their delivery, the resources of the service delivery system; belief in technology benefits; technology competence of professionals who work with the child and family; the child; and the interest, resources, and persistence of families all appear to be related to positive outcomes (Hutinger, 1994).

Transportation may become an issue for some children, particularly when medical technologies (e.g., apnea monitors, respirators) or powered mobility devices must be transported across naturalistic or other service settings. Team members should give careful consideration to the coordination of services necessary to insure that assistive devices prescribed for young children with disabilities may be safely and efficiently transported within and across service systems.

Transition needs of individual children and families must be addressed as part of the IFSP/IEP (P.L. 102-119, 34 CFR §303.344). Infants and toddlers with disabilities may require varying types of assistive technology devices across environmental settings. Device needs may also change as the child transitions into various components of the service system (e.g., hospital to home, home to center-based program, center-based program to preschool). In all instances, team members will need to consider assistive technology devices and services for the child and family that will insure smooth transitions.

Conclusion

With the increasing emphasis on family-centered early intervention, family involvement must be of paramount importance when planning for implementation of assistive technology services. The use of parent-professional partnerships can dramatically impact how families perceive assistive technology as a means for meeting their child's needs. Because of this, we believe that early intervention programs that provide assistive technology services for young children and their families need to incorporate parent-professional partnerships as the cornerstone of their services. While the selection of the assistive technology device is important, the accommodation of the device within the family system and the child's routines and activities is more critical to the overall process. An assistive technology decision-making process that takes into account the linkages between the four domains of child, family, device, and service system factors discussed in this chapter should result in the selection of assistive technology devices or systems that promote a child's overall development and have a positive impact on the whole family.

CHAPTER SIX

The Impact of Assistive Technology Devices and Services on Children and Families

Howard P. Parette
Southeast Missouri State University

Dianne H. Angelo
Bloomsburg University of Pennsylvania

The practice of providing assistive technology devices and services hinges on anticipated benefits for the recipients—both the child and the family. Improvements in specific functional capabilities for the child, such as communication with others, increased mobility in natural settings, and greater control over the environment, are frequently identified by family members as primary goals for young children with disabilities during the development of service plans (Behrmann, Jones, & Wilds, 1989; Parette & Angelo, 1996; Parette & VanBiervliet, 1991). Others have noted that assistive technology may contribute to the

This chapter is supported in part by Grant No. H029K50072 from the U.S. Department of Education. Opinions expressed herein are those of the authors alone and should not be interpreted to have agency endorsement.

integration of children with disabilities into community settings and increase their levels of independence (Church & Glennen, 1992; Mann & Lane, 1995).

Assistive technology has the potential to bring about significant changes in the life of a child with disabilities in the home, school, and community. It also has the power to affect the family, both positively and negatively, in ways that can influence intervention outcomes. Recently, it has become more obvious that the impact of assistive technology devices and services on the child should be considered from the perspective of the family (Parette & Angelo, 1996). Recognition of family issues in assistive technology is increasingly reflected in our assessment and intervention practices and is critical to bringing about successful educational and social outcomes for children with disabilities (Angelo, Jones, & Kokoska, 1995; Angelo, Kokoska, & Jones, 1996). Involvement of families increases the likelihood of success and promotes consumer satisfaction with assistive technology devices and services (Angelo, 1996).

P.L. 101-476, the *Individuals with Disabilities Education Act of 1990* (IDEA), and its recent reauthorization (P.L. 105-17) reveal a clear intent for related service personnel to facilitate greater family involvement in assistive technology assessment processes. It suggests more active family involvement, particularly in the areas of decision-making and problem-solving. The interpretation of the underlying family-centered intent of the legislation requires new practices, attitudes, and skills for working with families that differ from those used in the past. The growing interest in extending the family-centered focus of the Individual Family Service Plan (IFSP) to 3- through 5-year-old eligible children (Council for Exceptional Children, 1994; Rose & Smith, 1994) suggests that family involvement in assistive technology decision-making should be encouraged and supported throughout the preschool years.

Although numerous professional writings have described guidelines for selecting assistive technology devices for children with disabilities (e.g., Inge & Shepherd, 1995; Mann & Lane, 1995; Parette, Hourcade, & VanBiervliet, 1993), these guidelines have tended to stress the role of the *professional* during the assistive technology decision-making processes, with less emphasis on *family* participation (Parette & Angelo, 1996). It appears that the actual implementation of family-centered services as they relate to assistive technology devices and service delivery has not yet been fully realized (Angelo, 1996). The innovative approaches and skills now required by law for working with families of young children still need to be translated into practice.

In a review of current practices, it has been reported that family involvement during assistive technology assessment and prescription was often limited to that of information provider and trainer as opposed to decision-maker (Parette, 1995). When family members were involved in assessment processes, it was sometimes limited to completing forms and providing basic information about the child to enable professionals to make more informed decisions. For example, Parette (1995) identified a range of roles reported across states for family members who participate in assistive technology assessment and prescriptive processes. This study suggested a continuum of roles that are typically assumed by families. At one end of the continuum are families who are *passive recipients* of services. Their involvement is characterized by minimal participation in assistive technology decision-making and is limited to activities such as allowing programs to transport their children to intervention sites, completing forms, providing information to professionals, and observing strategies deemed to be important by professionals.

At the other end of the participation continuum are families who are *proactive* and exhibit ongoing involvement in assistive technology processes (Parette, 1995). These families display such participatory behaviors as pursuing and initiating referrals for augmentative and alternative communication (AAC) services, participating in evaluation conferences, directing evaluation strategies used with their children, participating in decision-making regarding specific devices that might be used with their children, and participating in training related to the use of assistive technology devices for their children.

Other reports have suggested that states tend to involve families in more passive roles for specific types of assistive technology assessment processes (i.e., AAC), as opposed to the active roles they may assume during IFSP and Individual Education Plan (IEP) service plan development activities (Parette, 1998). This type of participation diverges from family-centered practices, in which families maintain or acquire a sense of control over their family life and attribute positive changes resulting from early intervention to their own strengths, abilities, and actions (Dunst, Trivette, & Deal, 1988). Family-centered assistive technology practices place family members "in the driver's seat" and make them both the beginning and end points for determining and implementing intervention goals (Hanson & Lynch, 1995).

Given the relatively recent increase in assistive technology service delivery to young children with disabilities and their families, little research has been conducted to examine the impact of devices and services on the family. Qualitative reports and empirical studies of child outcomes subsequent to the provision of assistive technologies to children have been well-documented (see, e.g., Angelo et al., 1995, 1996; Hutinger, 1994; Kinsley & Langone, 1995). These reports, however, reflect a noticeable absence of attention to the effects of assistive technology on families, indicating the timely need for an insightful examination of this issue.

The Family as a System

In order to fully appreciate the potential impact of assistive technology devices on families, professionals must give consideration to the family as a *system*. Numerous family systems theories have emerged during the past two decades (e.g., Bronfenbrenner, 1979; Minuchin, 1974; Turnbull, Summers, & Brotherson, 1984; Turnbull & Turnbull, 1990). In general, these theories describe the family as a system with many subsystems. Events or interventions involving one family member are likely to have effects on other members of the family. The relationship of these theories to actual families of children who use assistive technology devices is reflected in personal narratives and third-person accounts which reveal that immediate family members—

especially parents—are most influential in the lives of their children with disabilities (Angelo, 1996; Huer & Lloyd, 1990). Accounts provided by adult assistive technology device users recognize family members as the most significant assistive technology partners for young children, and family members are credited with helping young children achieve their developmental potentials. Successful child developmental outcomes are almost always attributed in some way to the support and commitment of family members over time (Huer & Lloyd, 1990; Parette, Brotherson, Hoge et al., 1996).

Thus, from a systems perspective, family members can positively and negatively influence the course of assistive technology interventions. Several investigators have reported that family acceptance of assistive technology devices is an important variable in predicting intervention outcomes (Margalit, 1990; Silverman, 1989; Van Dyck, Allaire, & Gressard, 1990). Unfortunately, family influences have been underestimated by professionals who often find, to their dismay, that family members fail to carry out prescribed interventions (Angelo, 1996). This often signals a failure to understand family dynamics as well as the concerns, priorities, and resources of family members (Angelo, 1996; Hanson & Lynch, 1995).

Given the growing importance and use of assistive technology devices in the context of more family-centered intervention practices for young children with disabilities (Angelo et al., 1995; Brotherson, Cook, & Parette, 1996; Parette & Brotherson, 1996), an examination of emerging issues seems warranted. This chapter provides a discussion of family expectations for assistive technology and the resulting nature of change that may result in families once assistive technology devices are selected and provided to the child and family.

Family Expectations for Assistive Technology

The expectation is that *both* the child and the family will enjoy benefits from assistive technology devices that may not be achievable without technology. Anticipated benefits take many different forms (e.g., functional communication skills, computer access, environmental control) but have in common the potential for creating meaningful differences in the lives of children with disabilities and their families. The value that families place on these technology-related benefits is determined by a number of issues that extend beyond the needs of the child, which determine how receptive the family will be to a recommendation for an assistive technology device and contribute to the family's expectations and "readiness" for assistive technology devices and services. More importantly, they shape and define the role of the family as decision-makers in the process (see Table 6-1, pp. 154-157).

Family Resources, Priorities, and Needs

An underpinning of family-centered practice is that professionals give deference to resources, priorities, and needs identified by families during the decision-making processes. Planning for the delivery of appropriate assistive technology devices and services cannot be accomplished successfully without information related to what is valued and needed by the family. This requires an understanding of family needs. Of particular importance is the need for *information.*

Several studies have reported family needs for information about assistive technology–related services. For example, Angelo et al. (1995) surveyed a small sample of two-parent households to develop a profile of families having children who use assistive technology devices. Among the priority needs for both mothers and fathers was the need for *increasing their knowledge* of assistive devices, as also reported by Parette and VanBiervliet (1990a, 1990b). Like other parents of young children with disabilities (cf. Brotherson & Goldstein, 1992), both mothers and fathers in this study reported the need for informational supports, suggesting that professionals should provide ongoing opportunities for family members to learn about assistive technology devices and services (Angelo et al., 1996).

The families also expressed a strong need for information about *future* child services, like other families of young children with disabilities (cf. Cooper & Allred, 1992). Professionals should make every

Table 6-1. Family goals and expectations for assistive technology, with implications for potential positive and negative outcomes

Goal or Expectation	Potential Positive Outcomes	Potential Negative Outcomes	Implications
Preconceived idea that child will be able to immediately use assistive technology	• Child may quickly adapt to device/service usage • Family self-esteem may be enhanced • Caregiver time may be freed to pursue other activities • Family members may become more involved with child • Professionals may be intensely involved in training child and family • User-friendly training and support materials may facilitate rapid progress in child and family use of device/service	• Child and all family members may be unable to use device/service without initial and ongoing training • Intensive training may be required • Intervention personnel may have little or no interest in assistive technology • Commitments of family time required to use assistive technology in natural settings • Changes in family routines to accommodate device usage with child • Family must transport device and be available for effective use • Increased levels of stress • Technology abandonment	• Provide information regarding anticipated training, maintenance, and transportation needs • Share information regarding device/service demands; determine family willingness to use devices/services across settings • Identify training needs of all family members to effectively implement device/service and provide direct training with user-friendly materials • Use support groups to provide training and information

* From *Family-centered augmentative and alternative communication issues: Implications across cultures*, by H.P. Parette, M.J. Brotherson, D. Hoge, and S.A. Hostetler, 1996, December. Paper presented to the International Early Childhood Conference on Children with Special Needs, Phoenix, AZ. ©1996 by Howard P. Parette. Reprinted with permission of the author.

Table 6-1 (*continued*).

Goal or Expectation	Potential Positive Outcomes	Potential Negative Outcomes	Implications
That child's functioning will change on receipt of assistive technology	• Child developmental functioning may show rapid improvement • Increase in child's skills in other developmental areas • Family satisfaction with device or service may develop	• Family may have to choose between quality of life issues and implementing the assistive device or service • Progress may be slow • Progress may increase and plateau • Child and family may become frustrated • Episodes of illness may result in setbacks in child's ability to use device or service • Increased levels of stress • Technology abandonment	• Help family to celebrate small changes in behavior related to device usage • Provide information regarding anticipated family commitment of time to use device or service appropriately with child • Assist families in problem-solving regarding organization of time for device or service implementation • Provide direct training to family to enable them to work effectively with child • Use support groups to help families deal with stresses related to assistive technology

Table 6-1 (*continued*).

Goal or Expectation	Potential Positive Outcomes	Potential Negative Outcomes	Implications
That child will have immediate and ongoing access to device/service	• Funding source may secure device/service promptly once a decision is made • Loaner device may be available to child and family during funding and repair intervals	• Funding source may require inordinate period of time, resulting in frustration and anxiety for family • Loaner devices may not be available for child and family use during repair and funding intervals	• Ensure availability of loaner devices or other alternatives • Clearly communicate timelines required for funding and repair intervals
That child will be more like other children	• Child may interact more effectively with others in natural settings • Child will demonstrate skills and abilities that were previously not possible without the use of assistive technology	• Child may be perceived to be different from other children • Reduced interactions with others • Family and others must assume responsibility for availability of device/service for child's participation in activities • Increased levels of stress • Technology abandonment	• Inform and train other children with whom child will interact regarding nature of device/service and how to use appropriately • Determine responsibility for transportation of devices across settings
That device/service usage will lead to ability to use other devices (e.g., computers)	• Use of devices/services may help child develop prerequisite skills important for use of other devices (e.g., fine motor control, tracking skills, keyboarding)	• Device/service may require use of splinter skills unrelated to use of a computer or other devices deemed important to families	• Identify and communicate the features of devices/services and the relationship of skills developed to family preferences, priorities, and needs

Table 6-1 (*continued*).

Goal or Expectation	Potential Positive Outcomes	Potential Negative Outcomes	Implications
That child will be accepted in community	• Greater access to services and activities available in the community • Heightened independence of the child in the community • Less dependence of child on family for successful interactions in community • Heightened self-esteem on part of child and family • Community members may display willingness to learn to use device/service with child	• Family may be unable to predict how and in what instances devices/services will be used in community settings • Others in community may not understand how to interact with child who uses the device/service • Undue attention may be drawn to child and family • Family may refuse to use device/service in social settings • Family must transport device across settings for child • Realities of financial responsibility for device/service may inhibit family willingness to use in the community • Increased levels of stress • Technology abandonment	• Clearly identify contexts in which device/service will be used and demands for effective usage • Clarify family responses to social usage of the device/service before making recommendations related to usage in community settings • Provide training to child, family, and others in natural settings on appropriate use of device/service • "Plan for success" by anticipating how device/service may be potentially used in community • Identify easily transportable devices • Clarify financial responsibilities for devices/services with families and develop solutions to optimize use in community

* From *Family-centered augmentative and alternative communication issues: Implications across cultures*, by H.P. Parette, M.J. Brotherson, D. Hoge, and S.A. Hostetler, 1996, December. Paper presented to the International Early Childhood Conference on Children with Special Needs, Phoenix, AZ. ©1996 by Howard P. Parette. Reprinted with permission of the author.

attempt to minimize the demands on families by helping coordinate service delivery systems across the child's life span. Linking families with parent support groups, advocacy groups, professional organizations, volunteer services, and social service agencies helps them identify and access resources and educate themselves to meet both present and future needs related to assistive technology devices. Professionals also need to help them focus on transitions across service systems and settings, and develop transition plans and strategies to ensure the effective use of assistive technology devices and services.

The mothers in the Angelo et al. (1995) study indicated such priorities as developing community awareness and supports for their children for using assistive devices in the community, obtaining computer access for their children, and finding advocacy groups for parents of children using assistive technology devices. The fathers expressed priority needs for funding of assistive devices, finding volunteers to work with their children, teaching their children how to use the assistive technology device, and integrating the device at home.

Parette, Brotherson, Hoge et al. (1996) reported that family members from various cultures across the country who participated in focus groups and structured interviews identified numerous issues related to assistive technology decision-making. Presented in Figure 6-1 (pp. 159-161) are needs identified by families related to working with professionals. These reported needs are different in many respects from professional perceptions of family expectations of professionals. As noted in Figure 6-2 (pp. 162-163), families consistently reported needs for *more extensive information* about assistive devices to effectively participate in decision-making processes. This may be due to the *technical orientation* of many professionals who are working with families to identify and select appropriate assistive technology devices and services. Professionals in early childhood special education, particularly related service personnel, are often not trained to deal with the human aspects of assistive technology service delivery.

Also noteworthy in Figures 6-1 and 6-2 are differences between professionals' and families' perceived needs for family teaming with professionals. Family members frequently do want to be *more in-*

Figure 6-1. *Family issues related to working with professionals**

Communication Style. *Families want professionals to:*

- minimize use of jargon that limits communication with families
- communicate their discomfort with assistive technology to families
- communicate the extent of their involvement in learning to use assistive technology if families are uncomfortable with technology being considered

Specific Information Needs. *Families want professionals to:*

- provide more information regarding devices and services (e.g., range, critical features, maintenance, support, funding process, warranties)
- clearly communicate information regarding device ownership
- allow the family to see other children using an assistive technology device prior to purchase
- clearly communicate information regarding short-term assistive technology alternatives during repair periods and while waiting for receipt of devices

Family Values. *Families want professionals to:*

- be sensitive to family expectations for a child
- demonstrate recognition of and sensitivity toward immediate and future needs of the child and family
- recognize that families have no background in parenting children with disabilities
- understand the realities of family life, demands, routines, or combination of the three
- recognize that some children and families will have had a range of past experiences using assistive devices and that these experiences influence their needs and priorities
- consider compact and easily transportable devices for smaller children

---

* From *Family-centered augmentative and alternative communication issues: Implications across cultures,* by H.P. Parette, M.J. Brotherson, D. Hoge, & and S. A. Hostetler, 1996, December. Paper presented to the International Early Childhood Conference on Children with Special Needs, Phoenix, AZ. ©1996 by Howard P. Parette. Reprinted with permission of the author.

Figure 6-1 *(continued).*

- examine the child's home environment before prescribing devices and services
- be sensitive to terminology that is used in discussing children
- recognize that child and family preferences for devices differ from those of professionals
- understand that children with similar symptoms are unique individuals from different families and should not be discussed collectively as a group
- recognize the child's need for "personal space" during assistive technology interventions

Teaming. *Families want professionals to:*
- recommend devices and services based on objective rather than subjective experiences (biases)
- be experienced and comfortable with the use of assistive technology devices and services
- be sensitive to and provide options for child and family during repair intervals
- value family ideas and preferences for assistive technology devices and services
- recognize that professional recommendations are based on short-term contact with the child (versus the lifetime contact of the family)
- consider the age-appropriateness of recommendations
- validate family concerns
- include family members in meetings and ensure ownership of the process
- ensure that new team members are familiar with the past work of the team
- communicate their concerns regarding the child and assistive technology devices and services
- acknowledge family members for their work in identifying resources
- provide guidance in making better decisions
- recognize that a child may refuse to participate in evaluations as a defense mechanism in response to new team members
- understand the importance of the primary caregiver in developing child and team member rapport during evaluations
- adapt child testing procedures and establish rapport with the child before testing

Figure 6-1 *(continued).*

- clearly understand that insurance companies base decisions on evaluation information provided by teams
- provide information regarding timelines in assistive technology assessment process
- ensure continuous access of the assistive device or service to the child from time of rental to actual delivery to family
- ensure that an assistive device or service is not taken away after the child has had hands-on experiences with and shows a preference for and ability to use the device or service
- ensure that a particular device or service is not selected for use by many children, but rather, that selection is individualized to meet a child and family's needs

Training. *Families want professionals to:*
- provide opportunities for hands-on experiences
- be trained in the use of assistive technology devices and services
- be sensitive to the inordinate time families must wait to receive toll-free technical assistance callbacks
- be sensitive to family needs in receiving repeated training to learn how to use a device or service effectively
- recognize that vendors provide varying levels and quality of family support
- provide user-friendly and accessible training and support materials prior to purchase of device or service and thereafter
- create parent support groups for dissemination of information and training
- ensure continuity of assistive technology programming across natural and community settings (e.g., ordering, getting, and learning to use)
- work with siblings in family to appropriately use assistive technology devices and services intended for home usage
- clearly communicate the extent to which professionals will train families (including siblings and extended family) and children to use devices and services
- teach families how to teach their children to use assistive devices and services

Figure 6-2. *Professional concerns related to working with families** *

Communication Style. *Professionals should:*
- not use jargon
- gear language to listeners

Families and professionals should:
- maintain open lines of communication across settings
- be open-minded
- not assume defensive postures

Specific Information Needs. *Professionals should:*
- communicate the role of the family in assistive technology decision-making

Values. *Professionals should:*
- share with families the common value of wanting the child to learn
- value family insights
- value family members as team participants
- value insights of all persons who work with the child on a daily basis
- recognize that child and family bonds exist even in absence of regular contact
- recognize that families are limited by financial, educational, and physical constraints

Families should:
- accept the reality of disabilities and their children's limitations
- be patient and not demand rapid results after an assistive technology device or service is implemented

* From *Family-centered augmentative and alternative communication issues: Implications across cultures,* by H.P. Parette, M.J. Brotherson, D. Hoge, and SA. Hostetler, 1996, December. Paper presented to the International Early Childhood Conference on Children with Special Needs, Phoenix, AZ. ©1996 by Howard P. Parette. Reprinted with permission of the author.

Figure 6-2 *(continued).*

Teaming. *Professionals should:*

- consider family needs to ensure appropriate selection of devices and services
- respect family needs, concerns, and priorities
- recognize that families will display varying degrees of willingness to participate in assistive technology implementation across time (acculturation)
- build trust with family members
- collaborate with family members and build consensus
- meet regularly with family members
- celebrate with family members the positive daily changes resulting from assistive technology implementation

Families should:

- recognize that for some children, child factors may be more important for assistive technology success than family commitment
- recognize that the evaluation process may have unfair elements: optimum devices and services may not be feasible due to funding constraints
- clearly communicate their expectations regarding assistive technology
- not have preconceived ideas regarding assistive technology
- clearly specify goals for children
- examine a range of devices and services
- be matched to the demands of assistive technology devices and services
- be aware that technology options are increasing in the midst of decreasing funding availability

Implementation and Training. *Professionals want families to:*

- commit time to assistive technology implementation
- understand that assistive technology success is linked to the time commitment given by families

Families want professionals to:

- provide social support through family support groups
- train family members in use of assistive technology in community settings
- make loaner devices available after evaluations
- provide training, targeting integration of device into home and community

volved in team decision-making. They desire to be effective in their level of participation; this idea is reinforced by family-reported needs to be included, having their concerns validated, and having their ideas and past information-gathering efforts valued by the team. Families often will have invested a great deal of time working with personnel across a range of agencies to secure necessary services for their children. These experiences affect family expectations of team members and for assistive technology devices that might be considered for their children.

Having professionals who are knowledgeable about assistive technology devices is also highly desirable to families. When professionals do not have expertise in or information about assistive technology devices, this should be clearly communicated to family members. Such information may assist families in decision-making related to which professionals they might choose to work with their child in the use of the assistive device.

Families have a broader range of training needs than has been traditionally provided by service systems. Families express concerns that assistive technology training provided to the primary caregiver fails to consider that family members are *not* educators—they need to know how to teach their children, siblings, and others to use assistive technology identified and prescribed by the team. Training that is sensitive to family routines and that can easily be used by the family is also preferred. Support groups generally appear to be a highly desirable mechanism for training family members (Alper, Schloss, & Schloss, 1994), for the delivery of information about assistive technology devices, and for informal exchanges regarding experiences with devices.

Consideration of home issues is also identified by families as a need prior to receipt of devices. Recent surveys of Part H Coordinators and P.L. 100-407 state project directors (Parette, 1995; Parette & Hourcade, 1996) have found that professionals report less consideration of family issues than of more traditional child, technology, and service system issues (see Chapter 5) during assistive technology decision-making. Families especially note concerns that professionals do not give thought to home-environment concerns during team decision-making processes. Brotherson et al. (1996) have provided an insightful review of family and assistive technology issues related to the home environment. Generally, it is recommended that both *physical* and *social* dimensions of the home setting be examined, which gives the family a key voice in making decisions about assistive technology that will fit their own family, home, and culture. Presented in Figure 6-3 (pp. 166-167) is a listing of questions that may assist professionals in working with families to identify concerns related to the use of assistive technology devices in the home environment.

The value of these studies was in verifying that parents have specific needs for their children related to assistive devices and technology services. They also lend support to the importance of identifying family needs as part of the assistive technology assessment process. Clearly, a family's own values and needs do not always coincide with those determined for them by professionals. Differing concerns and priorities for assistive technology devices and services can result in parent-professional dissonance, family and child dissatisfaction, and unsuccessful assistive technology outcomes (Angelo, 1997; Angelo et al. 1995, Parette, 1994; Parette & Angelo, 1996). It is extremely important that the recommendations proposed by professionals be congruent with the priorities identified by the family.

Linking assessment and evaluative information

Recognition of the importance of family values and needs underscores the significance of linking assistive technology team-generated *assessment* and child and family *evaluative information* (Parette & Angelo, 1996). The assistive technology assessment process determines eligibility for and identification of appropriate assistive technology services and provides information that enables team members to select specific devices and services to consider for a particular child and family. The evaluation process also provides information regarding the quality and impact of assistive technology.

Peterson (1987) noted that *formative* evaluation from family mem-

Figure 6-3. *Home-centered questions to facilitate the identification of assistive technology for young children with disabilities and their families*

Influence of family characteristics (culture, values, and needs):

- What are your child's needs and preferences for technology?
- What are your family's desires and needs for technology?
- What has been done in the past to meet your child's needs and how was this successful?
- Do you perceive that the technology makes your child or family more visibly disabled?
- How, if at all, does the technology improve your family's quality of life?
- How will this technology help your child to be part of your normal family life?
- Can you describe any barriers your family might experience in using this technology?
- How, if at all, is this device in harmony with your family values or culture?
- Will the use of the technology give your child greater access to his or her environment?
- What, if anything, about this technology concerns or frightens you?

Impact on family interactions and relationships:

- What persons in your family do you want consulted about the technology decision?
- Who in the family will be able to comfortably use the technology?
- How easy will it be to take care of the device from day to day?
- How easy will it be to repair the device?
- Will you have to train anyone in your extended family or friends to use the technology?
- How will use of the technology change or disrupt your family routine?
- How will the technology add tasks to your family routine (e.g. battery charging, cleaning, programming, training)?

---

* From "A home-centered approach to assistive technology provision for young children with disabilities," by M.J. Brotherson, C.C. Cook, and H.P. Parette, 1996, *Focus on Autism and Other Developmental Disabilities, 11*, pp. 86-95. ©1996 by PRO-ED. Reprinted with permission of the author.

Figure 6-3 *(continued).*

- How will it increase or decrease caregiving demands for any one family member?
- Will use of the technology make it easier for your child to interact with friends and family?
- How, if at all, will siblings have to change to be able to use this technology?

Impact on family resources and functions:

- How will your home need to be modified to accommodate this technology?
- Who else in your family could help with these ideas?
- How will this technology place transportation demands on your family?
- Can the device be easily moved or transported?
- How much will this financially cost your family?
- How much time will be required for the child and others to use the technology?
- How much training will be required to learn to use the technology?
- Can your home accommodate the size or space needed for this technology?
- Where will you store the technology?
- How will this technology change how your family communicates with each other?

Dreams and desires for the future:

- What would you like to accomplish in the next several months with technology?
- How would you see this happening in your everyday life?
- Describe what you would like to see happen as a result of using this technology.
- Describe what you dream the future will hold for your child?
- How will you know when this assistive technology has been successful?
- How will you know if it is time to change the technology?
- Describe how the school or program can help you to meet your desires.
- How long before you foresee your child will outgrow this technology?
- Will this technology support your child in building friendships for the future?
- Will this technology help your child in the next environment?

bers and children who use assistive technology devices provides feedback as decisions are being made about an appropriate device. This type of evaluative information may best be provided when hands-on opportunities to use devices are available to children and family members, enabling them to report the efficiency with which an assistive technology solution can be used prior to purchase. Since professionals in the field of special education have recognized that assessment and evaluation are ongoing team processes (Behrmann & Schepis, 1994; Ray & Warden, 1995), formative feedback from family members and children with disabilities should be an integral component of the assistive technology assessment processes.

If collaboration does not occur between family members and professionals in assistive technology decision-making, or if formative feedback from children with disabilities and families is not obtained, lack of consensus regarding the appropriateness of a particular device may occur. When consensus about a device cannot be reached, even the most comprehensive service plan may be undermined, resulting in limited device use by the child and family (Allaire, Gressard, Blackman, & Hostler, 1991; Culp, Ambrosi, Berniger, & Mitchell, 1986) and abandonment of devices (Batavia & Hammer, 1990; Dillard, 1989).

Several researchers have described assistive technology abandonment as a pattern exhibited by children and families, which is characterized by: (a) provision of the device following an evaluation or personal selection process; (b) use of the device followed by recognition that it fails to meet the needs of the child even after attempted modification; (c) continued use of the device, remaining dissatisfied with it until it is no longer usable, or abandoning the device at an early stage; and (d) choosing *another* device that more appropriately meets needs not met by the previous device (but often fails to meet other needs) (Batavia & Hammer, 1990). Family values, routines, needs, and resources must be collaboratively considered in assistive technology assessment processes if service plan implementation is to be effective and device abandonment avoided.

Cultural and Ethnic Factors

In recent years, the importance of the family has been advanced by a growing appreciation for cultural-diversity issues in service delivery. Professionals need to gain a better understanding of the influence of cultural diversity and develop basic principles and practices that address multicultural family needs, priorities, and preferences in a technology-oriented society (Blackstone, 1993). In working with culturally diverse populations, it is important that professionals respect the values, beliefs, traditions, expectations, experiences, and priorities of families. Undoubtedly, awareness of cultural and ethnic factors will be an important variable in determining whether individuals with disabilities will gain competence through assistive technology applications.

Public Law 99-457 specifies that early intervention programs for children with disabilities must not only be family-centered but also culturally competent and that services must be provided within the context of the lifestyle and values of the family (Anderson & Battle, 1993). Cultural competence refers to the need for professionals to honor the cultural diversity of families by respecting the beliefs, interpersonal styles, attitudes, and behaviors of the families receiving services (Roberts, 1990). This philosophy should promote the use of nonbiased, culturally sensitive decision-making in assistive technology service delivery.

While cultural and ethnic concerns have, until recently, been relatively ignored in decision-making processes, there is clear evidence that they play a significant role in family willingness to participate in the implementation of assistive technology device interventions (Parette, Brotherson, Hoge et al., 1996). A more comprehensive discussion of these issues is presented in Chapter 7.

Technology Enculturation

Depending on the extent to which families have been exposed to technology over the course of their lives, professionals may expect varying levels of acceptance of assistive technology devices during the decision-making process. Some families will have expectations based on seeing other children use specific types of devices in the past. If these observations demonstrated that other children were successful in using the assistive technology device or service, or if other positive benefits were observed, there may be a tendency for the family to also want that device or service for their child. Similarly, negative observations of a particular device or service might result in a family bias against its use. Other families will have previously used assistive technology, and their personal experiences and histories with technology will likewise influence their perceptions and future recommendations. It is important for professionals to honor and understand these past experiences in order to understand each family's preferences for specific devices and services.

Family Perception of Disability

It has been widely recognized that family responses to children's disabilities vary markedly (Alper et al., 1994; Harry, Grenot-Scheyer, Smith-Lewis, Park, Xin, & Schwartz, 1995), and may affect how families perceive professionally recommended interventions (Lian & Aloia, 1994; Roos, 1985). These perceptions are deeply embedded in the cultures of families. African-American and Native American families for example, may be more accepting of children's disabilities than Euro-American families, and be more sensitive to the use of labels such as *retardation* and *disability* (Harry, Allen, & McLaughlin, 1992; Smith, Osborne, Crim, & Rhu, 1986). Likewise, different religious beliefs may encourage or discourage acceptance. The use of family-sensitive language acknowledges and respects the family's perception of the child and results in greater family receptivity to assistive technology interventions.

Perceptions of Professionals

A powerful determinant of successful assistive technology decision-making processes and readiness for technology is the family's perception of the professional. Families may view the judgments of professionals to be more important than their own (McBride, Brotherson, Joanning, Whiddon, & Demmitt, 1993). This feeling of loss of power or transfer of decision-making power to professionals who are viewed as knowing "what is best" for the family may contribute to the loss of much valuable information during assistive technology decision-making. Information which might potentially be lost includes the identification of family resources and solutions that have been successful to address child needs (Parette & Brotherson, 1996). This information is critical during the assessment process since it can identify family solutions *that may be better than any solutions technology might provide.* It may also result in a failure to address specific needs that families have related to assistive technology decision-making. In short, a parent who takes a dependent, agreeable stance may not ultimately be the best or most successful client.

Parette, Brotherson, Hoge et al. (1996) asked family members to discuss their perceptions of the roles of professionals and how professionals might more effectively work with them. Figure 6-1 (pp. 159-161) presented the values and teaming needs that were expressed by family members; those expressed by professionals were presented in Figure 6-2 (pp. 162-163). There are differences in the perceptions of the two groups regarding the nature of involvement of professionals and families (Parette, Brotherson, Hoge et al., 1996). While professional values suggest an acknowledgment of the importance of families, *less sensitivity* to family concerns is often articulated when professionals must identify their roles with families in the teaming process. This reduced sensitivity is supported by previous examinations of perceptions of state assistive technology assessment processes (Parette, 1995; Parette & Hourcade, 1996). Generally, families want professionals to be more understanding of family issues and concerns and to recognize that families generally have no prior experience in raising children with disabilities. They also want their efforts in obtaining information prior to or during decision-making processes to be acknowledged and valued. Assistive technology implementation recommendations from professionals should be sensitive to the realities of family life, such as time constraints of family members and demands of the home environment (Brotherson et al., 1996).

Team recommendations should be developed with the understanding that they have far-reaching implications for families. For example, once a team decides that a particular need is present and a specific assistive technology solution is appropriate for the need, funding for the device will be driven by the team recommendation. Funding agencies and insurance companies will rely on the team recommendation, and devices desired at a later date might not be funded without additional team recommendations.

Families also need the team to be more sensitive toward the child during decision-making processes. Children may be given hands-on experiences in using devices prior to purchasing them. When the trial yields immediate improvement in functioning in a particular developmental area, the family experiences great excitement and anticipation. But the family then has to wait for the device while funding is sought—or worse, never receives the device because funding is denied. Either instance will be disappointing to the family and adversely affect the family's trust of the professional members of the team. The family and child are tempted with the proverbial "carrot" of a desired assistive technology device but denied access to the device even though the child might benefit from its use. Granted, it might be argued that most consumers in our society have regular experiences with appealing technologies that they would like to own but do not have access to; nonetheless, professionals should be sensitive to how such experiences affect family perceptions of them. Many families see the denial of assistive technology devices as unfair and insensitive to their hopes and aspirations for their children and themselves. In simpler terms, they may come to question the system and perhaps the helping stance of the team.

Implementation of Assistive Technology Devices

Clearly, the family's expectations of assistive technology devices and services are influenced by a number of variables, all of which may shape a family's readiness or receptiveness for technology. When families actively participate in the decision-making, they are more likely to support the final recommendations because of their belief in anticipated benefits for the child and family. Once technology is prescribed and intervention begins, other issues arise that must be taken into consideration in the implementation process. As with any change within a family system, there is a need for ongoing contact and evaluation as the effects of assistive technology devices and services on the family system and on the child become evident. Effective implementation requires professionals and family members to both monitor change and engage in constructive problem-solving when implementation issues arise. As with assessment, it requires that families be part of this ongoing process, providing feedback and continuing their roles as team decision-makers with professionals.

Recently, studies have attempted to describe how assistive technology devices and services impact on the family. Researchers have investigated a number of issues or factors (e.g., stress) that can potentially have either a positive or negative impact on the outcome of technology interventions. These issues emerge as each family acquires its own *history* with technology. Because each family is unique, it is difficult to anticipate which factors will shape intervention outcomes. However, professionals need to be aware of contributing factors, particularly those that contribute to stress within families, stemming from implementation of the technology.

The impact of assistive devices on families is realized as family members attempt to integrate the technology in the home and community (Brotherson et al., 1996). Many assistive technology devices, particularly more sophisticated ones (e.g., electronic communication devices, environmental control systems), require a considerable time investment by family members to ensure effective use by young children with disabilities as they learn to operate, program, and use a device (Parette, 1994). Carrying out prescribed interventions can be time-demanding and, consequently, preempt or restrict more typical family activities. Accommodating the technology may complicate or prolong daily family routines.

Over time, technology often causes families to assume additional roles and responsibilities beyond those of primary caregivers (Angelo, 1995). Family members frequently become teachers, therapists, technology programmers and problem-solvers, transporters, transition coordinators, program evaluators, and advocates. These families need to accommodate assistive technology devices and equipment, technology services, assistive technology specialists, and agencies within their existing tasks, roles, and responsibilities. Demanding daily tasks, roles, and responsibilities for parents can be overwhelming and result in family stress or burnout.

Family Stressors Associated With Assistive Technology Devices

Considerable attention has focused on stresses experienced by families of children with disabilities (e.g., Beckman, 1991; Hanson & Hanline, 1990). Research has suggested a possible relationship between levels of stress and (a) increased caregiving demands placed on families (Haddad, 1992; McNaughton, 1990), (b) time required for family members to provide intervention services (Brotherson & Goldstein, 1992), and (c) the introduction of assistive technology devices (Donahue-Kilburg, 1992; McNaughton, 1990). Family stress has been described as an important outcome and mediator of early developmental outcomes (Hanson & Hanline, 1990). However, there appears to be considerable variability in the extent to which family members report stress (Beckman, Robinson, Rosenberg, & Filer, 1994).

Parenting stressors were reported for a limited sample of white, middle-class, educated, two-parent families with children between the ages of 3 and 12 years who used augmentative and alternative communication (AAC) devices (Jones et al., 1996). Approximately 40% of the mothers and 37% of the fathers had extremely high stress levels, as measured by the *Parenting Stress Index* (Abidin, 1986). Both parents reported the three highest child-related parenting stressors were acceptance, demandingness, and adaptability of the child. Differences were found between mothers and fathers on parent-related stressors. The highest parent-related stressors for mothers included relationships with their spouse, health, and social isolation. For fathers, attachment to the child, social isolation, sense of competency, and parent health were associated with greater levels of stress (Jones et al., 1996).

Because the parents who participated in this study were not representative of more diverse families, it is difficult to generalize these results to all families with young children using assistive technology devices. However, the study lends support to the notion that there are many potential sources of stress for mothers and fathers of children using certain types of devices and services. But not all families experience significant stress emanating from these sources, due to their ways of coping used to buffer the stress (Parette & Angelo, 1996). Parents and family members cope in a variety of ways, depending on the child's disability and needs as well as the family's needs, resources, and supports (Zipper, Weil, & Rounds, 1991). Professionals should be sensitive to these stressors and provide individualized assistance as needed to the family. As noted by Donahue-Kilburg (1992), "Without special awareness of families and their needs while adapting to a child with an impairment or disability, it is easy for professionals, even with the best of intentions, to increase the stress that family members feel" (p. 81).

Caregiving demands

Among the many potential sources of stress are demands of time and energy on the caregiver. Some studies have reported increased caregiving demands being placed on families by aspects of disability (Haddad, 1992; Harris, 1988). The introduction and use of assistive technology can potentially contribute to caregiving demands or stresses for families, even as it reduces some of those demands and stresses (Brotherson, Oakland, Secrist-Mertz, Litchfield, & Larson, 1995).

Increased levels of family stress may be related to these increased caregiving demands (Beckman-Bell, 1981). Professionals should examine the caregiving demands often required by additions to family routines (e.g., daily battery charging or cleaning), restrictions of family activities (e.g., hindrance on travel due to the size and/or portability problems of a powered wheelchair), and modifications to the home environment (e.g., setting aside "protected" space for a computer). Major changes in family structure and environments may severely disrupt family functioning. Such changes may diminish a family's ability to cope with stress and, thereby, adversely affect the child's development (Murphy, 1988).

Training requirements and technical support

For a substantial number of parents and primary caregivers, inadequate training in the use of their children's devices may cause problems (Church & Glennen, 1992; Parette & Brotherson, 1996). Training is an essential support service that ensures that technology provided to families and children will be appropriately used and maintained.

In assessing any need for technology, professionals must give careful consideration to the demands that will be made on families for learning to use, maintain, and repair the particular device. Training provided should be *user-friendly* at each phase of assistive technology implementation and be sensitive to family needs for strategies to teach their children and other family members how to use the device appropriately. Based on interviews with family members in focus groups, Parette, Brotherson, Hoge et al. (1996) found that families want professionals to realize that varying levels of support are available from manufacturers of devices (see Figure 6-1, pp. 159-161). Families must sometimes wait inordinate periods of time to receive callbacks from technical support services provided by manufacturers, contributing to stress and frustration.

Changes in family roles, responsibilities and routines

Doernberg (1978) noted that the vast majority of services for children with disabilities involve the child's mother as therapist, teacher, trainer, and transporter for the child—leaving little time, money, or energy for the development of normal interpersonal relationships for family members. If use of assistive technology causes severe disruption to a family's normal activities, support that helps the family redefine their quality of life in relation to assistive technology could be offered. An understanding of daily routines is important when planning interventions because it offers insight into the feasibility of the intervention. If the major impact falls on the women, then the stress for mothers, daughters, and other female caregivers should be addressed (Brotherson et al., 1995). Professionals must be cautious and work with the family to assure that the assistive technology device or service interfaces well with the daily activities and demands of the individual family and child (Jones et al., 1996).

Quality of life concerns

Several investigators have previously advocated caution in the use of assistive technology with families for which there has been an inadequate research base. Campbell, Bricker, and Esposito (1980) emphasized that the indiscriminate use of new technologies may not necessarily result in improved services to children with severe disabilities and their families. Cavalier and Mineo (1987) suggested that the rush to technologize without an adequate knowledge base may at times impede a child's progress. Some families experience a delicate balance between their quality of life and the specific needs of the child (Brotherson et al., 1995). The introduction of assistive technology may improve mobility or communication, but if it limits family interactions or leads a family to become more isolated, the tradeoff becomes questionable. Practitioners must be aware of when technology can assist parents in meeting identified child needs and when positive family outcomes are doubtful or uncertain (Lahm, 1989).

Several studies (Brotherson et al., 1995; Parette, Brotherson, Hoge et al., 1996) have found that families of young children who received assistive devices sometimes chose between maximizing a device's benefits for the overall development of their child and preserving the quality of life for the entire family. These choices arise when demanding roles and responsibilities, elaborations of routines, restrictions of activities, drained family resources (e.g., money, time), strained family and social relationships, compromised health and well-being, and increased stress levels become important issues. This may account for parent reports of limited assistive technology device usage by children in the home and the community (Allaire et al., 1991; Angelo, 1996; Culp, 1987; Culp et al., 1986; Parette, Brotherson, Hoge et al. 1996). These and other studies suggest that stressors can undermine the family's efforts to use assistive technology devices in the home and community. Stressors can alter the family's role as decision-maker and compromise interventions if professionals ignore the potential impact of stress following implementation. More important, it can lead to technology abandonment if the stressors are overwhelming from the perspective of the family.

Monitoring stressors and impact of assistive technology on the family following introduction of a device or service is necessary since resources are expended for support and maintenance. It is important that ethical issues guide the decision-making processes (e.g., family's ability to use a device vs. professional perceptions regarding the most appropriate device for a child vs. availability of resources for purchase of the device) (Holder-Brown & Parette, 1992). Failure to consider child and family issues can result in technology abandonment, particularly if assistive technology impact across environments and cultures is not considered (McNaughton, 1990; Parette, 1994).

Consequences and Outcomes of Assistive Technology Usage

Once assistive technology is implemented, careful monitoring should begin. An important role of the team is to identify and minimize any negative consequences associated with devices and services. This is essential to avoiding unsuccessful intervention outcomes, such as technology abandonment or underutilization. Similarly, it is equally important to identify positive consequences that contribute to successful intervention outcomes, such as increased independence, self-confidence, and communication. This is necessary to validate the original team decisions based on anticipated benefits as well as to suggest future technology recommendations. As seen in Table 6-1 (pp. 154-157), a number of potential consequences may result from intervention, and implications for change are indicated.

In a recent study, Angelo (1996) conducted in-depth interviews with families of children from various cultures using augmentative or alternative communication (AAC) devices. For these parents, technology was implemented based on the benefits they anticipated—primarily improved communication skills for their children. Parents were asked to identify, from a family perspective, both positive and negative consequences of their child using an AAC device for a period of at least one year. Many of the consequences listed in Table 6-1 were reported by parents affected specifically by AAC devices and services.

In terms of positive consequences, parents most often reported that technology devices provided a *voice* that increased communication opportunities for their child. Many participants expressed the belief that the device enhanced communication more with others (e.g., teachers, peers) than with immediate family members who had already developed usable means of communicating even without the device. Given increased communication opportunities, parents reported that children enjoyed greater participation and inclusion in educational and social environments. These interactions seemed to encourage friendships and personal relationships outside the family. Parents also indicated that the *voice* enabled the child to reveal his or her personality, which is often masked by the disability, to others.

It was also reported that the device offered a means to tap the child's current and future educational or academic potential. For many parents, technology enabled the child to demonstrate existing abilities that were not easily detected without the device and, subsequently, increased their expectations of the child. These raised expectations resulted in a more stimulating and challenging environment for the child with more opportunities to communicate his or her current and future abilities. Parents often linked technology with educational or academic success and the key to future employment opportunities. Technology was seen as playing an important role in building the child's self-confidence and self-esteem.

Other positive consequences included gains in the child's independence and control over his or her environment. The device appeared to reduce the child's dependency on the family to anticipate communication needs and interact socially with others. Many parents expressed a sense of relief that their children could enjoy more communication partners, which reduced the isolation associated with limited communication opportunities. The importance of being able to communicate was tied to improved quality of life for the child and the family.

Some parents reported enjoying the success of negotiating an extremely challenging journey involving a host of professionals, agencies, and service delivery systems. Parents shared a sense of personal growth and accomplishment in confronting an often insurmountable task and realizing their own strength as a family. Partnerships which developed as a result of networking with other families, professionals, and service agencies were noted. Other positive outcomes included the roles children and families assumed in advocating for themselves and other families of children with severe communication disabilities.

Of course, not all reported consequences were positive ones. Parents often expressed negative consequences associated with technology breakdowns. Lack of access during repairs was identified as a major source of frustration and stress for children and families. During extended repair periods, the benefits of communication, participation, and environmental control were disrupted.

Some parents expressed disappointment with technology because anticipated benefits were not realized immediately. For them, the magic and enticement of technology was tempered by the reality of the child's slow progress in mastering the device and developing communication skills. The need to adjust their expectations of the power of the device was not communicated by the team prior to receipt of the device.

Parents also reported frustration regarding the time lag from the initial assessment to the arrival of the technology, as well as the fact that necessary adaptations to existing devices, upgrades, or replacements were slow to materialize. Parents expressed concerns that children forfeited valuable instructional time and social opportunities during these intervals. Lack of adequate training and follow-up after the arrival of the technology also created stress for many parents. This was coupled with problems associated with a lack both of trained professionals and of continuity of services, forcing families to assume the search for devices and services alone.

Families also reported restricted or limited device use as negative consequences. This was related to lack of support, lack of training, and demands on family members to integrate the device in the home and community. Some parents indicated stigmatizing effects of using technology. Because members of the community are not trained in how to communicate with individuals using technology, isolation in social situations may continue to occur.

To minimize negative consequences, professionals should solicit formative feedback to make necessary changes throughout implementation. Being cognizant of potential consequences can ultimately determine positive and negative intervention outcomes. The time invested by teams to problem-solve and convert negative consequences into positive ones will make the difference between successful and unsuccessful outcomes.

Summary

The process of family-centered assistive technology decision-making deviates from current practices in that assessment, planning, implementation, and evaluation are interrelated. This comprehensive approach attempts to deal with the dilemma of providing appropriate services within existing resource constraints. Inherent in the evaluation component of these interrelated dimensions is that feedback from the system is necessary to assist in identifying and providing appropriate assistive technologies and services to families. This feedback is vital so that systems changes may be accomplished on an ongoing basis (Parette & Brotherson, 1996).

Measures of satisfaction are important as an avenue for family input, enabling families to be valued contributors to the assessment process. The nature and extent of satisfaction associated with the services being provided to families should be incorporated into assessment strategies (see, e.g., Mann & Lane, 1995; Parette & VanBiervliet, 1990a, 1991). Families may report satisfaction with services, regardless of whether the child's needs are being met. Conversely, services may appropriately address the child's needs but still cause dissatisfaction or stress within the family. Open communication with the family is extremely important to understanding the dimensions of family satisfaction with services received (Parette & VanBiervliet, 1990a, 1991; Winton & Bailey, 1990). Another important factor affecting family responses may be the degree to which families feel that professionals are intruding on the family unit (Dunst et al., 1988). Many times the strategies used to gather information can be intimidating to families; caution must be exercised to involve family members in assessment processes in a nonthreatening manner. Families have indicated that they prefer open-ended conversations that give an opportunity for friendship and rapport to develop with professionals, rather than standardized measures (Summers, Dell'Oliver, Turnbull, Benson, Santelli, Campbell, & Siegel-Causey, 1990).

Frequent follow-up is needed to examine whether both child and parents are succeeding with the assistive technology and coping with the demands of the device, or whether changes are needed. Many times families are provided with regimens of services (e.g., physical or occupational therapy strategies) and assistive technologies that are difficult to use in the home setting. For example, a family might have received an apnea monitor that is cumbersome and difficult to move from room to room. A therapist might recommend specific seating and positioning devices for a child with cerebral palsy, but their use may require more time than the family has available.

Stress may result when assistive technology becomes "early intrusion," not early intervention, for a child and family (Brotherson et al., 1995; Condry, 1989; Doernberg, 1978). It may be that the *greatest need* of the family is for less frequent time demands or for *alternative and user-friendly forms of information* regarding devices or services. It may also be that the family needs training to help them adapt to the demands of the device or service. For those families that report satisfaction, it is important to examine what devices, services, and strategies the family is presently using and how these result in satisfaction. The future and changing needs of the family and child could be discussed based upon what is most satisfying and successful.

CHAPTER SEVEN

Cultural Issues and Family-Centered Assistive Technology Decision-Making

Howard P. Parette
Southeast Missouri State University

Current practices in assistive technology decision-making are influenced by both research and practice. On the one hand, medical and rehabilitation research studies are providing explanations of human behavior among diverse target populations. Implications from these studies are being drawn to explain cultural and family influences on assistive technology usage. On the other hand, direct experiences with families and persons with disabilities are also providing direction for the helping professions (Angelo, Jones, & Kokoska, 1995; Hutinger et al., 1994; Parette, Brotherson, Hoge, & Hostetler, 1996). These experiences include the use of culturally sensitive information-gathering methodologies within the context of the family (Parette, Brotherson, Hoge et al., 1996; Smith-Lewis & Ford, 1987).

This chapter is supported in part by Grant No. H029K50072 from the U.S. Department of Education. Opinions expressed herein are those of the author alone and should not be interpreted to have agency endorsement.

This shift in current practice presents tremendous challenges to professionals in the field of early childhood special education. The importance of family-centered, culturally sensitive practices is widely acknowledged in the professional literature. Numerous descriptions of characteristics of family members across cultures have been provided (see, e.g., Alper, Schloss, & Schloss, 1994; Darling & Baxter, 1996; Lynch & Hanson, 1992a; Peterson & Ishii-Jordan, 1994). A growing body of professional literature also suggests that cultural and ethnic factors have become increasingly important considerations in assistive technology decision-making (Hetzroni & Harris, 1996; Soto, Huer, & Taylor, 1997). Similarly, the influence of acculturation, developmental expectations, social influences, and life experiences on the process of assistive technology decision-making may become critical components of future decision-making (Luborsky, 1993). Figure 7-1 below presents the relationship among these variables in the context of family-centered assistive technology decision-making. Child, technology, and service system issues are discussed in Chapter 5. Specific

Figure 7-1. *Culture-related influences on family-centered assistive technology decision-making*

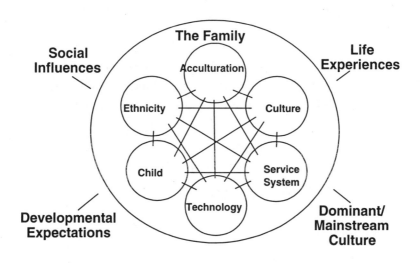

©1997 by Howard P. Parette, Jr. Reprinted with permission of the author.

family issues are addressed in Chapter 6. Each of the remaining issue areas that are culturally based are discussed in the following sections, with their implications for professionals who work with families.

Cultural Influences

The importance of cultural influences in family-centered assistive technology decision-making has emerged because of huge changes in the American population in the past half-century. By early in the next millennium, one-third of the U.S. population will consist of African-Americans, Native Americans, Hispanic-Americans, Asians/Pacific Islanders, and other cultural minority groups (Chan, 1990; Kundu & Dutta, 1995). When considering both the size and the age of these ethnic and minority populations, it seems reasonable to assume that they will contain a substantial number of potential recipients of intervention services, especially as minorities in our society have a disproportionately higher rate of disability-related conditions (Asbury, Walker, Maholmes, Rackley, & White, 1991; Clay, 1993; Thornhill & HoSang, 1988).

Toward a Definition of Culture

Culture has been defined as a set of common beliefs, values, behaviors, and communication patterns that are shared by a particular group of people and learned as a function of social membership (Soto et al., 1997). It has also been described as a *lens* through which individuals see themselves in relation to others and the world (Battle, 1993). Culture exerts a strong influence on the way in which professionals behave toward family members when providing services and the manner in which family members perceive and respond to these services (Misra, 1994).

The cultural uniqueness of the various American ethnic and cultural groups and the importance of having an understanding of various cultural groups are generally recognized by many professionals in the field of early childhood special education. Without an understanding of cultural diversity and related value systems, professionals cannot begin to serve these young children and families appropriately (Baruth & Manning, 1992; Hetzroni & Harris, 1996). Cultural understanding is vital to an expanded view of assistive technology assessment processes that are family-centered.

Unfortunately, family members from minority cultures are often less informed about and participate less in service plan development and implementation processes than family members from the dominant or mainstream culture (Bennett, 1988; Harry, 1992). Exacerbating this problem is an ongoing lack of respect demonstrated by many professionals for families from non-mainstream backgrounds (Harry, 1992), frequently resulting in alienation of family members from participation in early childhood special education processes.

Many professionals in early childhood special education and related disciplines, as well as many family members, are *monocultural;* that is, their interactions with others tend to be based on their own individual cultural backgrounds or their perceived similarity to others (Lynch & Hanson, 1992b). Family members with whom these professionals interact may also be *bicultural,* identifying with two cultural groups and interacting comfortably with both (Hanson, Lynch, & Wayman, 1990), or *multicultural,* identifying with the value systems of more than two different groups.

Professionals clearly need to become sensitive to the cultural identities of families with whom they are striving to develop partnerships. Examples of family values across cultures and their relationship to assistive technology decision-making are presented in Tables 7-1–7-3 (pp. 188-193). For example, *familialism* is a cultural value in which persons have a strong identification with and attachment to their nuclear and extended families and share values of loyalty and solidarity (Marin & Marin, 1991). *Allocentrism* is a value that emphasizes the objectives and needs of one's in-group rather than an emphasis on competition and individualism (Marin & Marin, 1991). Such values as those presented in Table 7-1 may place families in conflict with professionals who adhere to value systems markedly different from their own.

Table 7-1. Family characteristics and values which may influence family-centered assistive technology decision-making

Perspectives on Disability

Euro-American	African-American	Asian-American	Hispanic-American	Native American
Families may: • View disability as having multiple causes • Believe that disability may be prevented with proper health care and living conditions • Accept labeling of children to attain educational opportunities and access to other services • Differ in their reactions to disabilities	Families may: • Believe that disabilities are due to punishment from God, influence of evil spirits or the devil, bad luck, or some combination of the above • Accept children's disabilities due to supports from extended family and strong ties to church • Prefer milder, less stigmatizing labels in reference to their children	Families may: • Believe disability is a function of fate • Believe disability results from sins committed by parents, ancestors, or both • Consider only children with physical disabilities to be worthy of receiving services, treatment, or both • Believe disabilities are objects of shame for families • Assume full responsibility for children with disabilities	Families may: • Attribute visible disabilities to external, nonmedical causes (witchcraft) • View disability as part of incomprehensible divine plan or as punishment for wrongdoing • Have difficulty accepting nonvisible disabilities • Differ in their acceptance of disabilities • Tend to keep children with disabilities at home	Families may: • See children as gifts from God who should be shared with others • Attribute disability to both natural or supernatural causes • Be more inclined than any other group to integrate children with disabilities without seeking external assistance • Prefer use of less stigmatizing words to describe children (e.g., "slow" or "incomplete" to "mental retardation" or "disability")

Source: From "Family, vendor, and related service personnel perceptions of culturally sensitive augmentative and alternative communication service delivery," by H.P. Parette, 1997, paper presented to the Symposium on Culturally and Linguistically Diverse Exceptional Learners, New Orleans. ©Howard P. Parette, 1997. Reprinted with permission.

Table 7-1 (*continued*).

Perspective on Health Care

Euro-American	African-American	Asian-American	Hispanic-American	Native American
Families may: • Value the use of technology (drugs, surgery, testing) in medical and health care practices • Value preventive campaigns • Base health care practices on available scientific information	Families may: • Prefer a variety of health care approaches, depending on income and educational level • Have limited access (quality and quantity) to health care services and information regarding health practices • Not have medical insurance • Prefer holistic approaches to health care	Families may: • Be hesitant to seek intervention to "save face" • Believe caring for child with disabilities is a family responsibility • Rely on folk and established Eastern medical procedures (e.g., acupuncture, herbs, massage, and baths in hot springs) • Visit religious shrines and temples to seek healing • Consult/seek approval from community leaders before seeking assistance from external resources	Families may: • Believe in healing processes involving folk medicines • Rely on spiritualists to heal their children or dispel evil spirits • Prefer small clinics or service settings to larger facilities • Seclude and deprive children of treatment if vitality and health are highly valued • Have negative perceptions of institutionalization and prefer to treat children at home	Families may: • Accept information from professionals regarding causation of disability but rely on tribal healers or practitioners to determine why disability occurred • Rely solely on traditional tribal healing procedures or ceremonies to heal children and protect families • Jointly employ Western and tribal treatment approaches

Table 7-1 (continued).

		Perspective on Family Life		
Euro-American	African-American	Asian-American	Hispanic-American	Native American
Families may: • Value equality of partners in decision-making regarding children • Be very diverse and reflect varying configurations • Emphasize autonomy, independence, and self-reliance of children in daily life activities • Expect children to leave home to establish separate residences on completion of educational experiences (high school or college) • Prefer for elders not to live with their children • Place high value on efficient use of time	Families may: • View blood relatives and friends as members of the "family," and may not reside together • Rely on extended family members for child care • Value aggressive pursuit of individual goals in life but expect reasonable sharing of private gains with the community • Respect and value the wisdom and experiences of elders • Emphasize socialization, guidance, and inspiration for children	Families may: • View the family as the basic unit of society, which serves as a model of the larger society • Value loyalty, obligation, mutual cooperation, interdependence, and reciprocity of family members • Value elders, ancestors, and the past • Include an extended family of three generations, with varying roles for each family member • Encourage children's emotional and economic dependency on parents into early adulthood	Families may: • View the family unit as the most important institution in Hispanic-American society • Indulge children with disabilities, with no expectations for child participation in treatment and care • Teach children that cooperation is more important than competition and individual achievement • Teach children to respect adults and not to question authority • Restrict females and teach them that they should be protected • Value the wisdom and experiences of grandparents	Families may: • Believe the tribe and extended family are of greater importance than the individual • Believe that child-rearing roles rest with many family members • Teach children to be self-sufficient at an earlier age than Euro-American peers • Teach children to learn through observation • Honor elders and value their wisdom • Place great value on harmony with nature • Differ in their understanding and use of time for daily life activities

Table 7-1 (*continued*).

Perspective on Education/Intervention				
Euro-American	*African-American*	*Asian-American*	*Hispanic-American*	*Native American*
Families may: • View education as a primary determinant of professional and social opportunity • Value freedom and informality in the public education process • Value achievement, action, work, and materialism • Place emphasis on directness and assertiveness in the pursuit of educational goals • Value efficiency and optimum use of time	Families may: • View the acquisition of education, life skills, and personal competence as major goals for children • Not place their trust in school systems • Feel that educators over-identify African-American children as having disabilities • Hide their real feelings toward professionals • Reveal hostility toward professionals through verbal responses that indicate misperceptions and fears	Families may: • Encourage their children to excel in education and place high value on achievement (esp. Chinese & Japanese) • Not view education as being important (esp. Laotian & Pacific Islanders) • Prefer informal and formal liaisons or entry points with the Euro-American professional community to get and provide information • Give great deference to educators	Families may: • Entrust the education of their children to professionals • Consider direct disagreement to be disrespectful • Be hesitant to assume a dominant role in intervention decision-making for children • Encourage children to assume responsibility for learning and only offer support if provided with specific instructions by professionals	Families may: • Mistrust school officials, given the history of forced residential schooling for Native Americans • Be hesitant to share private information about children and families • Resent the superior attitudes of Euro-American professionals • Prefer observation as a learning technique • Value role models in the learning process • Fail to value intervention settings that are dissimilar from the home

Table 7-2. Communication styles of families that may affect assistive technology decision-making

	Providing Information and Meetings				
	Euro-American	African-American	Asian-American	Hispanic-American	Native American
	Families may: • Prefer direct eye contact • Value privacy and prefer not to discuss personal matters • Prefer an informal interaction style • Be direct and assertive, and rely on verbal rather than nonverbal messages • Prefer professionals to be open when giving information • Prefer turn-taking during conversations • Prefer moderated voice tones • Prefer to work as partners in team processes • Prefer to be informed and have a voice in intervention processes • Expect scheduled and punctual meetings • Prefer that individual differences be accepted	Families may: • Not prefer direct eye contact • Prefer observational and nonverbal cues during conversations to understand the perspective of others • Be direct in stating opinions and not restrict emotions • Actively participate in discussions and view turn-taking as restrictive • Use extended family system as a supportive and therapeutic base • Fail to participate in assessment processes due to scheduling and transportation problems, and lack of knowledge regarding service plan development process • Be more oriented to situations than to time	Families may: • Avoid direct eye contact • Rarely express feelings or show emotions in facial expressions • Prefer one-way conversations • Exhibit modesty in discussing the family, personal matters, or expressing opinions • Maintain silence to show respect • Rarely engage actively in group discussions and tend to minimize attention to themselves • May be unfamiliar with the educational system and be reluctant to attend meetings • View questions as a challenge to authority • Prefer to engage elders during conversations • Enjoy refreshments at meetings	Families may: • Prefer direct eye contact except with authority figures • Use tact and diplomacy to avoid children's problems • View time as being unimportant • Prefer not to feel hurried by professionals • Encourage cooperation rather than competition • Need information about locations of sites for evaluations and require transportation assistance • Enjoy refreshments at meetings	Families may: • Prefer eye contact for direct observations to get information • Not participate in conversations unless they feel contribution is valued • Choose words carefully and pause longer between "turns at talk" • Not respect interruptions during conversations • Feel that oral questions reflect incompetence to acquire information independently, or a diminished intelligence, or a denial of rights • Fail to use greetings when entering or leaving a room to denote respect for activities taking place • Give subtle cues using body language and voice tone regarding needs • Prefer meeting in comfortable, informal settings

Source: From "Family, vendor, and related service personnel perceptions of culturally sensitive augmentative and alternative communication service delivery," by H.P. Parette, 1997, paper presented to the Symposium on Culturally and Linguistically Diverse Exceptional Learners, New Orleans. ©Howard P. Parette, 1997. Reprinted with permission.

Table 7-3. Family reactions to assistive technology across cultures

Euro-American	African-American	Asian-American	Hispanic-American	Native American
Families may: • Prefer devices that do not make children look different to grandparents • Want to minimize stress of integrating devices into home life, forcing them to choose between quality of life issues and technology usage • Want to be taught how to teach their children to use devices • Desire specific and ongoing training to ensure that they can use assistive technology with children effectively • Want community to use devices with their children • Want assistive technology that makes children more independent and socially accepted • Change their perceptions of assistive technology after receipt and implementation in home and community	Families may: • Prefer assistive technology that does not draw attention in social settings • Prefer electronic speech devices that use dialect of culture • Prefer assistive technology that allows for rapid use during communication with multiple partners • Prefer assistive technology that allows children choices or independence across environmental settings of children's choosing • Prefer assistive technology that is simple to use • Prefer assistive technology that is easy to transport and maintain • Prefer assistive technology that enables children to be accepted by others	Families may: • Want devices that do not increase child independence, that are functional, and do not replace traditional family caregiving roles • Want assistive technology that does not draw attention in social settings • Prefer assistive technology that provides direct, immediate benefits vs. long-term benefits • Prefer that professionals assume responsibility for training in use, maintenance, and support of assistive technology • Desire ongoing support for family usage of assistive technology • Desire to see assistive technology used by other children and families before accepting its utility	Families may: • Prefer electronic speech devices that use dialect of culture • Have high expectations for children to be able to use the assistive technology at important family celebrations • Desire to have training provided to siblings who may assume responsibility for maintenance of certain assistive technology • Prefer not to use assistive technology in home setting if children's basic needs are being met • Prefer assistive technology that allows some degree of independence at home • Prefer not to have training/support services provided in home settings • Prefer collaborative implementation of assistive technology	Families may: • Prefer assistive technology that is easily transportable and facilitates interactions with extended family members • Prefer assistive technology that uses colors and symbols reflective of children's culture • Prefer electronic speech devices that use language of family's culture • Prefer assistive technology that allow children's personalities and social needs to emerge, thus allowing families to "know children as persons" • Be fearful of using sophisticated assistive technology • Prefer assistive technology that facilitates children's identification and interaction with members of clan

Source: From "Family, vendor, and related service personnel perceptions of culturally sensitive augmentative and alternative communication service delivery," by H.P. Parette (1997). Paper presented to the Symposium on Culturally and Linguistically Diverse Exceptional Learners, New Orleans. ©Howard P. Parette, 1997. Reprinted with permission.

Professionals in early childhood special education who embrace a family-centered philosophy have often reported difficulty in working with families whose beliefs and values are strongly linked to one group but who have adopted the values or practices of another group—for instance, those of the dominant culture (Lynch & Hanson, 1992b). This can result in situations in which certain values like early educational experiences may be perceived favorably by the family, while other seemingly related values, such as technology usage, may be viewed negatively (Luborsky, 1993; Smith-Lewis, 1992). The goals and perceptions of professionals who make decisions about assistive devices often diverge markedly from those of the people who use the devices (Becker & Kaufman, 1988; Ory & Williams, 1990).

The referral and assessment paradigm in American culture has developed almost exclusively from the perspectives and values of the dominant Euro-American culture (Blackstone, 1993). Early childhood special education services must work within this dominant culture. Smart and Smart (1992) noted that the Euro-American culture is characterized by three prominent barriers that may affect assistive technology service delivery: (a) that prejudice and discrimination still exists against minorities, (b) that equality of advantages (e.g., training, education) does not equate with equality of rewards, and (c) that professionals view themselves as different from family members and children with disabilities with whom they work.

Luborsky (1993) suggests that the bright promise of technology is not yet fulfilled for many persons with disabilities due to persistent use of assessment and intervention approaches based on ideals and values of Euro-American culture. For example, in Euro-American culture, there is an emphasis on (a) individualism and privacy; (b) equality; (c) informality; (d) the future; (e) human goodness; (f) time, action, work, and achievement; and (g) directness and assertiveness (Althen, 1988; Hanson, 1992). Such values influence the expectations that professionals have for young children with disabilities and their families when assistive technologies are prescribed during team processes. Many of these values are in conflict with those of Native American, African-, Hispanic-, and Asian-American families.

Some studies have suggested that families may refuse to use assistive technology devices due to the stigmatizing effects of using them in public or to fears that the child will not attain important developmental skills if they rely on a device (Allaire, Gressard, Blackman, & Hostler, 1991; Berry, 1987). However, few studies have examined this issue from a *cultural* perspective. Smith-Lewis (1992) reported that African-American and Hispanic-American family members of children with severe disabilities often resisted the use of augmentative and alternative communication (AAC) devices, since these families perceived such systems to be unnatural and more stigmatizing than spontaneous communication efforts. Similarly, African-American family members have reported that they prefer not to use devices in public settings when they draw attention to the family (Parette, Brotherson, Hoge et al., 1996). Such values held by family members may markedly influence how resources in the existing service system are utilized.

In a recent study of assistive technology needs in North Carolina (Trachtman & Pierce, 1995), the average cost of assistive devices reported for young African-American children was one-third that for Euro-American children. The investigators concluded that the difference might be attributable to (a) differences in the prevalence of primary disorders reported for the various ethnic groups participating in the study, (b) greater reported needs for high-cost devices by Euro-American respondents, and/or (c) more frequent reports by African-American respondents for "no equipment" needs. It may be that African American children are underidentified for early childhood special education and assistive technology services due to family resistance to the use of labels and to their preferences not to have devices that call attention to the families (Parette, Brotherson, Hoge et al., 1996).

Ethnicity

Ethnic factors have important implications for professionals working with young children with disabilities and their families. For example, self-esteem, identity formation, isolation, and role assumption have all been shown to be affected by ethnic influences (Chin, 1983; Cross, Bazron, Dennis, & Isaacs, 1989; Kumabe, Nishida, & Hepworth, 1985). Such factors may affect responses to assistive technology intervention recommendations, team processes, and usage of devices (Blackstone, 1993; Luborsky, 1993). Ethnic differences have also been reported to affect family members' responses to disability (Chan, 1986; Hanline & Daley, 1992) and their willingness to receive interventions from professionals who use interaction styles that differ from their own (e.g., authoritarian or non-authoritarian) (Harry et al, 1995).

However, despite the recognition of differences among families from varying ethnic backgrounds, professionals in special education have historically expected families to adapt to the expectations of the Euro-American culture (Correa, 1987). For example, electronic AAC devices are typically designed to produce Euro-American voices (Parette, 1996). Some families may prefer to have their child speak in a particular dialect, such that the child can clearly be associated with their ethnic group (Parette, Brotherson, Hoge, et al., 1996).

Such findings may suggest a need for professionals—and manufacturers—to develop a better understanding of the familial and ethnic heritages that affect family perceptions of disability (Luborsky, 1993). How ethnicity influences family and child concerns and professional beliefs about treatment effectiveness and assistive technology must also enter into the decision-making process.

Acculturation

Damen (1987) defined *acculturation* as internalization of the knowledge necessary to function in a particular societal group. This process entails disengaging from the previously held world view, learning new ways to meet old problems, and shedding ethnocentric evaluations. A more recent definition suggests that acculturation is the degree to which people from a particular culture display behavior which is more like the behavior exhibited by persons in the dominant culture (Torres-Davis & Trivelli, 1994). Wide ranges of individual acculturation effects have been demonstrated with regard to various health-related attitudes and social behaviors (Kunkel, 1990; Pomales & Williams, 1989). The influences of such factors must be considered by team members during assistive technology decision-making, as family members may be distributed along an entire continuum, from strong affiliation with their own unique culture and its values and beliefs to alignment with Euro-American culture.

The degree of acculturation influences the extent to which family members are familiar with and may be responsive to particular devices and services developed or provided by Euro-American professionals. In contemporary American society, people have increasingly become acculturated to the daily use of technology. From turning off the electronic alarm clock in the morning to operating the videotape recorder (VCR) by remote control at night, family members have become more accustomed to the use of technology in their lives. Many people are also not as fearful of computers and other sophisticated devices as they might have been a decade ago. The influence of such "technology acculturation" cannot be underestimated.

Discomfort with technology can place significant stress on family members when approaching assistive technology. For example, families from very rural areas may not have been exposed to information about assistive devices or seen assistive devices used by young children prior to meetings with professionals. This lack of technology acculturation may have a significant effect on their willingness to use assistive technology.

Families from diverse cultural backgrounds will also have been affected to varying degrees by their exposure to technology. Hence it is useful for professionals to understand how family members *currently* use technology. This understanding will (a) provide insights into the comfort with which the family may be able to discuss specific assistive technology solutions considered during team processes; (b) assist the team in understanding the priorities, concerns, and resources of families during assistive technology decision-making; and (c) enable the selection of devices from a more culturally sensitive perspective.

Social Influences

Professionals who work with families must also recognize that cultural factors are influenced by situational or *social factors*. This often results in family members agreeing with professionals during a meeting that certain types of interventions are appropriate, yet behaving very differently when they are in natural settings such as their own home, school, or the public community (Lynch & Hanson, 1992b; Parette, Brotherson, Hoge et al., 1996).

The cultural and psychosocial aspects of assistive technology usage have, until recently, been understudied. Qualitative reports of technology usage with adults with disabilities indicate a dynamic interaction between devices and user factors. These factors include (a) differences in assistive device acceptability due to the person's age-related normative psychological and physical capabilities, (b) life cycle changes, and (c) family life stage (Luborsky, 1991; Murphy, 1987; Smith-Lewis & Ford, 1987). Also, the presence of a disability often results in emotional issues that influence motivation to use a device (Scherer, 1996; Turner & Noh, 1988). These same factors may be relevant to families of young children with disabilities, though they have not been empirically examined.

Luborsky (1993) noted that the social and personal stigma associated with persons who are visibly different in appearance or behavior is a major factor in decisions to use devices. While professionals may desire the use of technology, the family may feel that its use will result in increased social stigma. The need to preserve their self-esteem and prestige may be more important than the potential of assistive technology to increase their child's independent functioning. For example, several studies have noted the social consequences of assistive device use among African-American family members in public settings. Generally, these studies strongly suggest that many families prefer *not* to have attention directed towards themselves by assistive technology devices (Parette, Brotherson, Hoge et al., 1996; Smith-Lewis, 1992). When attempting to identify appropriate assistive technology devices, professionals should be sensitive to the needs of families to feel accepted in community settings.

Sometimes family members report reluctance to initiate professionally-prescribed interventions when changes in family routines are anticipated (Lund, 1986). Other studies have described consumers or family members opting not to use specific assistive devices due to quality of life issues (Brotherson, Oakland, Secrist-Mertz, Litchfield, & Larson, 1995; Parette, Brotherson, Hoge et al., 1996) or increased visibility of the disability (Kaufert & Locker, 1990), even though improved functioning would result from device usage. As Ainlay, Becker, and Coleman (1986) noted, such motivational factors are not inherent traits of the assistive technology or of the disability but are a function of the *social contexts* of device usage. Sensitivity to these factors does not mean ignoring them out of deference, but rather talking about the family's concerns, checking them out, and helping family members weigh the benefits for the child against the social costs.

Furthermore, social contexts have important implications for professionals during the assessment process, because sensitivity to the cultural background of family members should suggest varying the way in which information is communicated during team decision-making. High-context cultures, such as Native American, Asian-, Hispanic-, and African-American, place greater emphasis on the amount of information transmitted through the context of situations; the relationship of persons involved in the interaction; and physical and/or nonverbal cues (Hall, 1974; Lynch, 1992). Conversely, Euro-American families typically display low-context backgrounds in which direct, concise verbal communication is perceived as being important. Less importance is given to communications that do not get to the point quickly (Hecht, Anderson, & Ribeau, 1989). Professionals should determine which communication style most appropriately matches the preferences of the family and use that style to convey information and facilitate family participation throughout the decision-making processes (Parette, Brotherson, Hourcade et al., 1996).

Developmental Expectations

The *life course* of the child and family also influence the type and level of participation that may be expected in assistive technology decision-making. The life course refers to the culturally defined expectations of stages and transitions for the socially defined individual (Luborsky, 1993). Miller (1979) reported that developmental milestones across Euro-American, African-American, and Native American cultures vary markedly. Developmental expectations across the life span may influence the responsiveness of children with disabilities and family members when assistive technology devices are prescribed (Harry et al., 1995). For example, if the expectation for independence for young children in the area of dressing themselves is almost a year earlier for a Native American family than for Euro- or African-American families, greater importance may be placed on assistive technology devices that lead to increased independence in this area of functioning. If the professional is working with an Asian-American family that encourages dependence beyond the period deemed appropriate for Euro-American children, discussions of assistive technology that facilitate greater independence in the environment may not be viewed favorably by the family.

Life Experiences

Life experiences in using assistive technology devices also influence family perceptions of and willingness to use assistive technology (Luborsky, 1991, 1993; Soto, 1995). As described by Luborsky (1993), personal experiences in using assistive devices result in a unique perspective and set of themes developed by the person with a disability over time, which affects the focus of evaluations and interventions provided and resulting experiences. Luborsky's (1993) central premise is that users of assistive devices evaluate and use equipment based on their objective and subjective social, cultural, and lifetime contexts. Many families have had previous experiences with assistive technologies and have a considerable experiential base from which to participate in decision-making processes. They may have clearly perceived desires for specific types of devices based on their past experiences. Conversely, family members who have not had such experiences may tend to rely more on the recommendations of professionals. This will be particularly true for many families from Native American, Asian-, and Hispanic-American cultures who see professionals as authorities and give them great deference in making decisions about interventions (Parette, Brotherson, Hoge et al., 1996). Such observations support the position taken by Nespor (1987) who claimed that beliefs and attitudes gain their power from past experiences that influence the comprehension of subsequent events.

The challenge to professionals in early childhood special education, then, is to recognize that the provision of *appropriate* assistive technology first begins with a sensitivity to the influence of culture and ethnicity (Buzolich, Harris, Lloyd, Soto, & Taylor, 1994), since these influences help to shape the positions of persons toward the use of assistive technology devices. Once a professional achieves heightened sensitivity to cultural factors, it is easier for him or her to understand how social factors, child and family life course, and life experiences have contributed to a family's perception of or willingness to become involved with assistive technology devices.

Issues for Future Consideration

Proponents of multicultural special education emphasize the characteristics of the environments in which persons function, since these are the contexts for individual characteristics to be formed (Bennett, 1990; Nieto, 1992). Harry et al. (1995) noted that "every family is a unique blend of its own cultural heritage, acculturational and social status, and idiosyncratic style" (p. 101). This framework "guides and bounds life practices" (Hanson, 1992, p. 3). Thus, it may be expected that cultural beliefs and practices in the U.S. lie along a continuum on which all groups interact to some degree (Harry et al., 1995).

Professionals in early childhood special education who work with families should adopt a holistic view that recognizes that all parts of any particular culture must be seen *within the larger context* in which they operate. This challenges professionals to develop individualized and open-ended strategies for discovering what families believe, enabling them to develop appropriate intervention approaches.

In Chapter 5, important traditional factors to be considered in assistive technology decision-making processes were discussed. These factors *cannot* be considered outside the framework of the family, with cultural and other influences being viewed as exerting an influence on family willingness to accept and use assistive technology.

Within the framework of the family, young children with disabilities and family members are affected by the dominant or mainstream culture, social influences, life experiences, and developmental expectations across the life span. Embedded within the complex family framework are additional influences related to assistive technology decision-making, which include the unique cultural background of the family, ethnicity, and acculturation factors. More traditional domains within the family that influence assistive technology decision-making include child characteristics, device features, and service systems issues.

Interaction Within Spheres of Influence

The various factors presented in Figure 7-1 (p. 185) are interrelated (Parette & Brotherson, 1996) and cannot be viewed as having isolated influences on the process of assistive technology decision-making. From a systems perspective, Euro-American culture must be seen as a system with numerous interacting subsystems. One event within the dominant culture system has an impact on other components within the system. Such a perspective builds on Bronfenbrenner's (1979) "ecology of human development" model, which describes the multiple systems that impact the family: (a) the *microsystem*, consisting of relations and roles within the family; (b) the *mesosystem*, consisting of the settings and persons with whom the child and family interact; (c) the *exosystem*, consisting of settings that influence the child and family but with which the family does not directly interact;

and (d) the *macrosystem*, consisting of belief systems and specific elements within societal systems. Professionals must begin to develop a broader understanding of these related and interacting systems to more fully understand family willingness to receive and use assistive technology for young children with disabilities.

Pragmatics of Culturally Sensitive Practices

Implementing family-centered assistive technology approaches must acknowledge the influence of the various domains noted above. The review presented in this chapter should provide a broad understanding of the potential contributory influences of interrelated domains that impact assistive technology decision-making. Once professionals have developed a better understanding of the importance of these sources of influence, efforts can be directed toward determining (a) the nature of the changes expected in each domain, and (b) the timeline anticipated for each of these outcomes during decision-making processes (Parette, Brotherson, Hourcade et al., 1996). For example, if an expensive AAC device were to be provided to a child, it would first be important to project *all probable outcomes* of that technology and the length of time anticipated for the child and others to learn to use the device. This might require giving thought both to the nature, extent, and timing of training that would be required for family members, the child, and others in the community to use the device well, and to the impact of the training requirements on changes in family routines.

A particularly useful way to gather this information is simply to ask families what they think will happen if certain interventions are provided. These "What do you think might happen if ... ?" questions can result in information useful to planning an overall strategy for services (Parette, Brotherson, Hourcade et al., 1996). Presented in Figure 6-1 (pp. 159-161) were sample values and teaming concerns expressed by families across five cultures regarding their expectations of professionals during assistive technology decision-making. These concerns are heavily influenced by cultural factors.

Professionals must exercise caution in using probing questions with many families, because families may not be able to project how they might feel about certain hypothetical circumstances. This is particularly true of families who have not used assistive technology devices in the past and have not been exposed to the demands placed on families in learning to use or maintain devices. This will require professionals to provide examples of specific situations in which devices might be used and to clearly describe what the family may be required to do to use and maintain the device both in the short term and the future.

Chapter 6 provides a more insightful discussion of the impact of assistive technology devices on families. Examples of additional questions that cut across the various sources of influence are presented in Figure 7-2 (pp. 205-208). Although these questions have been arbitrarily assigned to particular areas, they may also fit into other categories. For example, numerous assessment design questions address cultural considerations. While these questions are not exhaustive, they should provide a pool of family-centered and culturally sensitive items that might potentially be asked by professionals when examining existing assistive technology assessment and prescriptive processes (Parette, Brotherson, Hourcade et al., 1996).

Implications for the Future

The outcome of an effective and *comprehensive* technology assessment process is to generate a unique set of recommendations that ensures appropriate delivery of assistive technology to young children with disabilities without adversely affecting family functioning. The process of assistive technology assessment described in Chapter 5 must be individualized to each child with a disability and his or her family to ensure relevance and appropriateness (Anderson & Goldberg, 1991). Given the many possible variations for assistive technology assessment, even within a particular cultural group, professionals should, at the least, become competent in *both* family-centered strategies and culturally competent intervention approaches. Such a

Figure 7-2. *Questions for professionals working with families across cultures*

Assessment Design

- Have I individualized the assistive technology assessment process for the family and the child?

- Have I taken the time to develop a trusting relationship with the family before starting the assistive technology assessment procedures?

- Have I identified strategies for involving the family in the assessment process?

- Have I observed the child in a variety of naturalistic settings with and without caregivers?

- Do I conduct assistive technology assessments in an environment that is familiar to the child?

- Have I included the extended family in the assistive technology assessment process?

- Have I examined the assistive technology assessment process for cultural biases?

- Has the assistive technology assessment protocol or procedures been reviewed by members of the cultural group being served?

- Do I know how or where to find cultural information that will help me during assistive technology assessment processes?

- Have I been trained in cultural competence during assistive technology assessment processes?

Professional Collaboration

- Have I always made translators available to maintain communication with family members?

- Am I flexible when meeting with family members?

- Do I provide necessary assistance to the family members to ensure their participation in the assistive technology assessment process?

- Is it possible to meet with the family members in their home prior to the assistive technology assessment?

Source: Adapted from Anderson, M., & Goldberg, P. (1991). *Cultural competence in screening and assessment: Implications for services to young children with special needs, ages birth through five.* Chapel Hill, NC: National Early Childhood Technical Assistance System, pp. 22-23. ©1991 by NECTAS. Adapted with permission.

Figure 7-2 *(continued)*.

- Have I informed family members of their rights in the assistive technology assessment process?
- Have I told family members about local assistive technology support groups?
- Do I understand how the family feels about making direct contact with professionals involved in assistive technology decision-making?
- Am I networking with other professionals to address cultural issues in assistive technology assessment?

Cultural Issues

- Have I done a self-assessment of my own cultural background, experiences, values, and beliefs?
- Do my experiences, values, and beliefs allow me to interact with people from various cultures?
- Do I understand the family's values, beliefs, customs, and traditions?
- Have I modified the assistive technology assessment process to ensure cultural competency?
- Do I try to achieve professional cultural competence?
- Can I train other staff members about cultural competence in assistive technology assessment?
- Do I communicate regularly with the cultural communities that I serve through the provision of assistive technology?
- Do I provide information and printed materials related to the assistive technology assessment process in the language spoken by the family?
- Am I aware of the cultural rules regarding body language, eye contact, and proximity for the family?
- Have I determined whether a community liaison would be the most appropriate contact through which to provide information to or receive information from the family?

Values

- Am I aware of what the family expects out of me in the assistive technology assessment process?
- Do I understand how family members may perceive a translator?
- Do I understand the family's attitude regarding disabilities?
- Do I know who is the key decision-maker of the family?

Figure 7-2 *(continued)*.

- Do I understand the family's expectations of me as a professional?
- Do I understand the importance of the extended family?
- Am I aware of the family's approach to discipline?
- Have I determined whether the family is willing to receive formal assistive technology services?
- Do I understand the responsibilities of other siblings in the family setting?
- Does the family accept the idea of assistive technology as a tool to help their child?
- Does the family's religious affiliation influence their willingness to participate in or perceptions of the assistive technology process?

Family Factors

- Have I asked family members about their concerns for their child?
- Am I willing to pick up or arrange transportation for family members?
- Do I provide assistance to help family members when filling out forms necessary for assistive technology assessment?
- Do I allow family members to share cultural information about their child?
- Have I identified the family's primary caregiver?
- Does the socioeconomic status of the family impact on the child for whom assistive technology is being considered?
- Have I examined the home setting and determined how it might facilitate or inhibit the use of assistive technology?
- Have I clearly identified the family's willingness to use assistive technology in daily life activities?
- Does the family clearly understand the demands of the assistive technology device with regard to training (both short-term and ongoing), use, maintenance?
- If the family will be expected to participate in training their child to use the device, is the family willing to assume this responsibility?

Acculturation

- Do I understand how acculturation has influenced the family's perceived need for or receipt of assistive technology?

Figure 7-2 *(continued).*

Ethnicity

- Have I examined ethnic factors that might affect the child or family's perception or use of assistive technology?
- Do the assistive devices being considered for the child and family reflect ethnic features that might make the devices more acceptable within the ethnic settings in which they will be used?

Social Influences

- Have I identified important social influences that might affect child or family perception and use of assistive technology?
- Do I understand whether the child and family wish to have attention drawn to themselves in public settings when using assistive technology?

Past Experiences

- Have I identified past experiences in child or family use of assistive technology that could influence their current perception and use of assistive technology?

Developmental Expectations

- Have I determined the family's expectations regarding developmental milestones for the child that might influence perception and use of assistive technology?

---

process may require professionals and family members to jointly engage in a process of "mutual adaptation" (Correa, 1987) or "bending" (Harry, 1995) in which both family members and professionals change through the process of collaboration.

Roberts (1990) indicated that professional competence requires more than beliefs, attitudes, and tolerance of individuals who are different. Competence also requires skills that help professionals "translate beliefs, attitudes, and orientations into action and behavior within the context of daily interaction with families and children" (p. 1). Such competencies are not components of personnel preparation programs nationally, though some innovative practices have been initiated, particularly in the area of augmentative and alternative communication (AAC). The American Speech-Language-Hearing Association (1995) has developed a series of inservice education approaches designed to help professionals provide quality services to linguistically and culturally diverse preschool children with disabilities and their families. A project to train graduate students in speech-language pathology, with special emphasis on AAC and multiculturalism, will culminate in the preparation of 30 qualified professionals trained to enter the field of speech-language pathology with skills enabling them to work with families across cultures during AAC decision-making (Huer, 1994).

Parette and VanBiervliet (1995) examined the impact of AAC devices on families from a cultural perspective. This project conducted focus groups with vendors of AAC devices, related service personnel involved in assessment and prescription of devices, and family members across five cultures (African-, Asian-, Euro-, Hispanic-, and Native American). The data suggests that there are marked differences in the ways that persons from various cultures perceive assistive technology assessment processes (Parette, Brotherson, Hoge, et al., 1996). This project will also be used to develop a bilingual, interactive CD-ROM that can be used by professionals and family members when making decisions about AAC devices.

Innovative approaches to training personnel to be culturally sensitive during assistive technology decision-making have also been developed. Rehabilitation Engineering Society of North America's (RESNA) *Technology Training Project: Project Reaching Out* (Torres-Davis & Trivelli, 1994), provides Hispanic-Americans with low-incidence disabilities an overview of information on assistive technology in a culturally sensitive manner.

These examples of innovative projects reflect the growing interest in a broader assistive technology assessment paradigm than has been used in the past by professionals working with young children having disabilities and their families. Teachers, related service personnel, family members, and others involved in assessment and prescriptive processes must develop new competencies that will enable them to address the assistive technology needs of children and families from a more family-centered and culturally sensitive perspective.

CHAPTER EIGHT

Inservice in Assistive Technology: A Necessity in Early Childhood Special Education

Mary Beth Bruder
The University of Connecticut Health Center

The use of assistive technology as a tool for young children with disabilities is a growing area within early childhood special education. Research with this population was conducted in the early 1980s, using adapted computer systems to enable young children with disabilities to control their environment through movement of hands and feet (Brinker & Lewis, 1982). The movement-activated switches produced a variety of environmental consequences, such as turning on lights. The children learned to use the switches to indicate preferences. Behrmann and Lahm (1983) expanded this research to demonstrate with infants and toddlers with disabilities the use of switches, speech synthesis, and graphic representations of objects. Since then, other research in this area has supported the use of assistive technology to facilitate learning with a range of young children with disabilities (Hutinger, 1987; Hutinger & Ward, 1988; McCormick, 1987; Spiegel-McGill, Zippiroli, & Mistrett, 1989; Sullivan & Lewis, 1990). It has, therefore, been suggested that a greater emphasis on assistive technology be incorporated into early childhood intervention (Behrmann, Jones, & Wilds, 1989; Daniels, Sparling, Reilly, & Humphry, 1995; Hutinger, Robinson, & Clark, 1990; Odom & Warren, 1988; Sullivan & Lewis, 1993) because technology expands a child's options and independence (Dunst, Cushing, & Vance, 1985; Reed & Bowser, 1991; Sullivan & Lewis, 1990).

In addition, medical assistive devices are a necessity for many young children with special health needs. These devices replace or augment inadequate bodily function (Baroni, Tuthill, Feenan, & Schroeder, 1994; Levy & Pilmer, 1992). The frequency with which children require medical technology assistance is rather low, occurring in about 1 in 1,000 children (Palfrey et al., 1991). The Office of Technology Assessment (1987) defines a child who receives medical technology assistance as one who uses such a device and requires substantial daily skilled nursing care to avert death or further disability. These devices include:

- respiratory technology assistance (e.g., oxygen supplementation, mechanical ventilation, positive airway pressure devices),
- surveillance devices (e.g., cardiorespiratory monitors, pulse oximeters),
- nutritive assistive devices (e.g., tube feedings, ostomies),
- intravenous therapy (e.g., nutrition, medication infusion), and
- kidney dialysis.

Approximately half of children who need medical technology assistance require some form of respiratory technology assistance.

The field of early childhood special education must be prepared to use any technology necessary to enhance a child's learning. For this to occur, early childhood special educators must be skillful in assessing a child's current use, or need, for assistive technology for survival or enhanced learning and, subsequently, must be able to use the most appropriate technology for each child's need. This requires that early childhood special educators have the opportunity to learn about and become proficient in the various applications of assistive technology for young children with disabilities. This usually occurs through inservice training.

The term "inservice" refers to professional development activities undertaken to assist the more experienced professional in expanding and growing with the profession, while the term "preservice" refers to professional development efforts that prepare individuals to perform the entry-level functions of their disciplines or professions (Winton, McCollum, & Catlett, 1997). These distinctions blur in fields in which content and strategies keep changing as a result of research and consumer input. The field of early childhood special education and, in particular, the area of assistive technology are examples in which new practices are being adopted at a very fast pace, therefore necessitating the design, development, and implementation of inservice programs at both an entry level and an advanced level for the practicing professional. The purpose of this chapter is to describe inservice training methods and models as they apply to early childhood special education and the use of assistive technology.

Early Childhood Special Education

Part H of the *Individuals with Disabilities Education Act* (IDEA) has created a service delivery system that requires a number of components unique to infants, toddlers, and their families. These components have also been applied to children age 3 to 5 receiving preschool services under IDEA. These components include the development of an Individual Family Service Plan (IFSP): (a) use of a team approach; (b) delivery of services in natural environments, such as the home and other places in which typical children participate; and (c) formalized collaboration across agencies. Because of these required mandates, state and local service agencies are struggling with the development of early childhood intervention systems that encompass these components.

Many recent articles have attempted to respond to the changes in service delivery created by the law by proposing specific training recommendations across professional disciplines for those serving young children with disabilities. These disciplines include special education (McCollum & Stayton, 1996; Thorp & McCollum, 1994), occupational therapy (Hanft, Burke, & Swenson-Miller, 1996; Hanft & Humphry, 1989), physical therapy (McEwen & Shelden, 1996), nursing (American Nurses Association, 1990; Cox, 1996), social work (Nover & Timberlake, 1989), nutrition (Kaufman, 1989), psychology (Drotar & Sturn, 1989; Mowder, 1996), speech and language (Losardo, 1996) and medicine (Wachtel & Compart, 1996). The content proposed includes discipline-specific skills in infancy, early childhood, and families as well as interdisciplinary and interagency skills necessary for the implementation of the law (Bailey, 1996; Fenichel & Eggbeer, 1990; Lowenthal, 1996; Winton, McCollum, & Catlett, 1997). For example, all disciplines should have thorough knowledge of early development, identification and assessment strategies, intervention techniques, family systems, and communication strategies. The interdisciplinary skills would include functioning within a team by sharing and utilizing other members' expertise for both assessment and program planning (Briggs, 1996; Widerstrom & Abelman, 1996). All disciplines should also have a working knowledge of interagency coordination and service coordination strategies as required by IDEA (Bruder & Bologna, 1993; Harbin & McNulty, 1990). It must be noted that many of these skills will require supervised practical application to ensure the trainee has acquired competence in these areas (Bennett & Watson, 1993; Bruder, Brinckerhoff, & Spence, 1991).

A growing awareness of the need to expand inservice opportunities in early intervention and early childhood special education has evolved from both legislation and research documenting a lack of content specific to early childhood special education within preservice preparation programs. First, IDEA requires the development of a Comprehensive System of Personnel Development (CSPD) that must include an inservice component (Kontos & File, 1992). Second, a number of surveys have identified gaps in preservice training content in early childhood special education, both within discipline-specific programs and across disciplines (Bailey, Simeonsson, Yoder, & Huntington, 1990; Courtnage & Smith-Davis, 1987). For example, few personnel preparation programs report any training content on team process or infant and family assessment and intervention, both areas of importance in early childhood special education. As a result, a number of articles and chapters have recommended the development of comprehensive inservice programs for those providing early intervention and early childhood special education (e.g., Bruder & Nikitas, 1992; Klein & Campbell, 1990; McCollum & Bailey, 1991; McCollum & Yates, 1994; Miller, 1992; Sexton et al., 1996; Trohanis, 1994; Winton, 1990). The content for these inservice activities reflects the needs of the field for both discipline-specific skills and cross-disciplinary competencies, as well as the addition of newly identified content in areas such as assistive technology. In particular, skills and knowledge in assistive technology have not been widely addressed by preservice programs, resulting in the need for effective inservice opportunities for early interventionists and early childhood special educators.

Inservice Education

Inservice has been described as the process by which service personnel are provided experiences designed to improve or change professional practice (Bailey, 1989). A more extensive definition has been proposed by Trohanis (1994): "Inservice is an ongoing and systematic enterprise that consists of diverse educational and training activities to support improvement, capacity building, and change, and that is focused on the accomplishment of organizational and individual goals" (p. 312). Generally, the objectives of inservice training include the changing of attitudes, the acquisition of new knowledge, and the development and enhancement of technical skills (Bernstein & Zarnick, 1982; Laird, 1985). The desired outcome of inservice training is for the participants to internalize new knowledge and apply what they learn to their specific professional needs (Barcus, Everson, & Hall, 1987).

A number of specific inservice methodologies have been identified in the literature. These include modeling, practice, and feedback to trainees as they learn new skills (Joyce & Showers, 1980; Sparks, 1986). Still, most of the literature on inservice training reflects a foundation grounded in principles of adult learning. These principles have been articulated throughout Malcolm Knowles' (1978, 1980) work on adult education. In particular, Knowles (1978, pp. 78-79) has outlined a set of characteristics of adult learning, including the following.

The need to know. Adults will learn more effectively if they understand why they need to know certain information or why they must have the ability to perform particular skills. Adult learners must be able to see that the benefit of learning a skill will outweigh the cost of the time and effort it takes to learn it. The more clearly adults can see the benefit of learning, the more strongly they will feel the "need to know."

The need to be self-directed. As people mature into adulthood, they have a deep psychological need to be responsible for their own lives. Cultural conditions will obviously enhance or retard this process, but there comes a time in the psychological development of adults when they "feel like an adult." At this point in time, adults will resent being told what to do and having decisions made for them. Adult learners are more successful if they can take responsibility for their own learning.

The importance of experience. Adults, by virtue of their age and life experiences, bring a vast amount of knowledge and a wide variety of experiences with them to the classroom. This wealth of life experiences can result in the following consequences for the training program:

(a) Groups of participants will have wide and varied backgrounds; therefore, the training staff must individualize instruction.
(b) Adults are a rich source of information for themselves and for other trainees because of their experiences. The training staff

should take advantage of these experiences by using techniques such as group discussion and brainstorming.

(c) Adults may have some rigid ways of thinking that consequently interfere with learning. The training staff may need to "unfreeze" these ways of thinking through activities such as sensitivity training or values clarification.

The readiness to learn. Adults will learn the things that they perceive will bring them greater satisfaction or success in life. As adults move through various stages of psychological and social development, their readiness to learn is reflected accordingly. For example, adults are interested in learning specific job skills when they acquire a job. As a result, it is important for the training staff to understand that learning opportunities should be offered in a timely fashion on topics of immediate value.

Orientation to learning. Adults see the reason for learning as acquiring competencies that will enable them to cope more effectively with life, perform life tasks, and solve real problems. Training staff will need to organize training programs around real-world issues that confront adults from day to day.

Knowles (1978) also suggests that successful, adult learning models utilize techniques and methods to enhance the acquisition of new knowledge (see Table 8-1 on the next page). It has further been identified that different methods can bring about different types of learning. For example, lectures, videos, stories told by families and service providers, and readings could all result in a raising of participants' awareness. Knowledge about a specific content area or intervention procedure requires a more in-depth approach to learning. Methods to upgrade knowledge could include problem-solving exercises, demonstrations about procedures, readings about the area with the opportunity to either individually or in a group reflect on the reading, completion of projects, and discussions about the area. To impact application of skills, more participatory learning is required. This usu-

---

Table 8-1. *Adult learning techniques and methods*

- The establishment of a climate that is conducive to learning (both psychological and physical) for participants
- Mutual planning between the trainer and trainee prior to any training
- Diagnosis of individual training needs
- Joint formulation of learning objectives by the trainer and trainees
- The implementation of training through a variety of techniques
- The evaluation of training on a continuous and multidimensional basis
- The provision of follow-up for all participants

---

ally occurs during a practicum situation where practice of the skill and feedback or coaching is provided. Role playing is another way to practice skills, as is self-assessment and guided reflection on the implementation of a skill. The last type of learning, mastery, usually occurs by teaching someone else the content or procedure. (For more information about the methods appropriate for different types of learning, see Catlett & Winton, 1997).

Effective inservice training relies on many different things: the effectiveness of the instructor, the experience level of the students, the difficulty level of the content, the method of presentation, and the ease of application on the job. Each of these aspects of training combines to create a systematic approach to inservice activities, as illustrated in Figure 8-1 on the next page. As with early intervention and early childhood special education, a planning process is key to an effective inservice system (Trohanis, 1994). The following describes phases of such a system.

Phase 1: Analysis

The first phase when designing an inservice training is to define the true needs of an organization or group. Information on perceived needs should be collected from all stakeholders at all levels of an

Figure 8-1. *The five components of an effective inservice system*

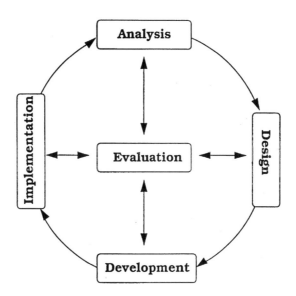

organization or group (administrators, providers, parents). After the needs analysis is conducted, a problem analysis should articulate the defined problem from the needs analysis, then identify possible solutions. Once the solutions are identified, a population analysis should be conducted to identify the inservice participants' characteristics, including educational levels, experience levels, physical needs, cultural differences, language skills, and motivation levels. A resource analysis should then be done to determine what types of training materials are available. The training constraints (e.g., time, motivation, timing) should be identified. Finally, a job analysis creates the opportunity to decide how best to translate training content into job application.

Phase 2: Design

The design phase of training is the phase in which the actual planning for training is done. This includes the design of objectives and the sequence and methods to be used in the training. The sequence usually takes into account the degree to which the new information is to be embedded within learning activities. The new information should be logically sequenced to enable the participants to understand the relevance of the new information. The methods to be designed include a variety of formats in which the participants may gain information. These range from didactic presentations to demonstration, practice and feedback, and on-the-job coaching. A variety of training media should also be used during training, including workbooks, transparencies, videos, and actual materials.

Phase 3: Development

During this phase of training, all training and evaluation materials are produced. All materials should support the objectives and design of the training. These materials should include: an instructor's guide that outlines the content and sequence of the training; participants' manual, which should include information for the participants on the training content and activities; resource materials to supplement what is taught in the course; and evaluation materials to assess the acquisition of training content by the participants.

Phase 4: Implementation

The actual teaching of the inservice content and the ongoing evaluation of the participants' learning constitute this phase of training. The training methodology should be monitored during this phase, as should the use and effectiveness of the training materials. Modifications should be made at any point during the implementation phase as determined by the ongoing evaluation.

Phase 5: Evaluation

Evaluation is an ongoing process. At the end of any inservice training, however, a thorough evaluation of the training and the participants' acquisition of the training content should occur. Multiple methods of evaluation are recommended, including a self-evaluation of content acquisition by the participants. The most important evaluation should be an evaluation of the participants' use of inservice content to on-the-job applications.

Inservice and Early Intervention Childhood Special Education

Unfortunately, inservice models in early intervention and childhood special education have been criticized as being ineffective (Bailey, 1989; Sexton et al., 1996). A number of reasons may be responsible, including a lack of awareness of adult learning principles on the part of the inservice trainers and a lack of awareness about the need for a systematic planning process. These critical components of the inservice training may also be overlooked because of the immediate and important need to implement training on critical early intervention and early childhood special education skills to service providers (Sexton et al., 1996). As a result, early intervention and early childhood special education inservice activities are often implemented by using procedures that contradict principles of adult learning and effective training methods (e.g., large didactic workshops without follow-up).

There are, however, instances of inservice practices that have been successfully implemented in early intervention and early childhood special education. These practices include the use of training teams that represent different professional disciplines (Bruder et al., 1991; Bruder, Lippman, & Bologna, 1994), the use of parents as co-training instructors (Bruder et al., 1991; Bruder et al., 1994; Capone, Hull, & DiVenere, 1997; McBride, Sharp, Hains, & Whitehead, 1995), the use of case vignettes to illustrate training content (Fallon, 1996), and the use of videoconferencing and distance education models (Collins, Hemmeter, Schuster, & Stevens, 1996; Ludlow, 1994; Rowland, Rule, & Decker, 1996). Training has proven effective when delivered to teams representing different disciplines (Bailey, McWilliam, & Winton, 1992), delivered in small groups (Bruder & Nikitas, 1992), and delivered over time—including contacts after initial training—using follow-up support and coaching (Bailey, Palsha, & Simeonsson, 1991; Bruder & Nikitas, 1992; Wischnowski, Yates, & McCollum, 1996). Sexton and his colleagues (1996) surveyed 242 early childhood special educators in Louisiana on their perceptions about the most effective inservice methods that allowed them to change practices. The methods identified included observation and actual practice, small group discussion, demonstration and modeling by a trainer, and follow-up job assistance.

Inservice and Assistive Technology in Early Intervention and Early Childhood Special Education

The area of assistive technology is relatively new to the field of early childhood special education. As such, few preservice training programs have incorporated knowledge and skills about this area into their personnel preparation programs. The result has been an overwhelming need for the development of inservice training models to teach early interventionists and early childhood special educators about assistive technology devices and services. While a number of training materials have been developed in assistive technology (e.g., American Speech-Language-Hearing Association, 1995; Parette & Van-Biervliet, 1990, 1991; Reinhartsen, 1995), there is still a major shortage of inservice training models in assistive technology for early interventionists and early childhood special educators.

Few model inservice programs for early intervention and early childhood special educators in assistive technology exist. One exemplary model is the Technology Inservice Project (TIP) at Western Illinois University. TIP personnel developed, demonstrated, evaluated, and disseminated a competency-based technology inservice model for staff and families who work with young children with disabilities, ages birth to 8 (Hutinger, 1995).

TIP offered a wide variety of menus of both content and methodology to training participants. The content ranged from awareness workshops to application sessions. These are listed in Table 8-2 on the next page. Participants chose to attend the workshop that had the

Table 8-2. *Technology Inservice Project (TIP) menu of training contents*

	Child Applications	**Adult Productivity**
Awareness sessions	• Assessing the Child with Severe Disabilities • Children and Computers: What Does It Take?	• Overview of Graphic Applications • Getting Started in Multimedia • Software Overview
Hands-on workshops	• Getting To Know Your Computer • Peripheral Devices • Birth to 3 Technology Applications • Preschool Technology Applications • Switch Workshop • Logo in Early Childhood Curriculum • Adaptive Firmware Card • Applications for Children with Severe Disabilities	• Finance Management • Database and Spreadsheet Applications • Getting to Know Your Mac • Word Processing and Desktop Publishing • Graphic Applications

most application to themselves, their sites, or both. The TIP inservice model was based on initial awareness training and was followed by hands-on workshops on various technology topics, follow-up training sessions, and continued support through monthly or bimonthly visits by a TIP staff member. TIP staff also were available for technical assistance via telephone or fax.

TIP also offered many other training options, including preservice classes at Western Illinois University and workshops at international, national, regional, state, and local conferences. TIP also used interactive satellite television to broadcast an inservice program that was attended by 78 teachers. The program was then available on videotape for individuals who were interested.

Inservice events were attended by 1,971 participants over 3 years. Ratings and comments made by those participants completing evaluations determined the strengths and weaknesses of TIP's training. Changes in training format, content, and presentation were made based on that feedback. Follow-up evaluations were also sent to training participants 6 months after training to determine if TIP training had had the expected impact on the participant. Overall, presentations and training sessions were rated highly (either 4 or 5, with 5 being the highest rating) across such areas as: organization; content; knowledge of TIP staff; helpfulness of TIP staff; quality of handouts and materials; and most important, usefulness of training to participants' activities or programs.

Training participants also competed self-evaluation forms of their competencies both before and after participating in TIP hands-on training. Competency forms were related to specific topics of the training. For example, the competencies for the *HyperStudio* workshop (1993) related to skills involved in creating stacks, adding buttons, adding sound, and creating animation. The competencies for the peripheral workshop pertained to connecting and using various peripherals, such as a TouchWindow™, PowerPad™, IntelliKeys™, and printer. In all cases, prior to training, no more than one or two people in a training event indicated they felt competent or had many computer-related skills. Following training, self-perceived competency levels more than doubled in every case. While a participant might have marked that she felt competent in only one or two skills areas prior to training, following training usually all but one or two skills were marked.

Another inservice model project was developed at the University of Connecticut (Bruder, 1996). The inservice component on assistive technology was one component of a broader training project focused on collaborative skills in early childhood special education (for children birth through 2 and their families). Multisession institutes on assistive technology were held over 2 years of the 3-year project. Each institute contained 5 sessions, 2 hours each. Special emphasis was placed on cultural sensitivity and collaborative relationships within the early childhood special education system, and hands-on practical use of assistive technology was highlighted. To demonstrate the types of collaborative relationships that need to take place in early childhood special education, the institute was team-taught by an early childhood special educator, an occupational therapist, a parent, a speech and language pathologist, and a technology consultant.

Institutes were held regionally throughout Connecticut, and participants were required to be delivering early childhood special education. The content of the institute sessions was held constant, that is, all institute participants over the two years received the same content. This was to allow comparison among types of training and follow-up methodologies. Follow-up support was provided to all participants to facilitate the completion of program competencies.

Participants were recruited for the institute through advertisements by the Part H statewide program office. Participants chose to participate in training, and they were randomly assigned to a training condition. Eighty-two participants finished the course. Training was available to any family, provider, or administrator providing, coordinating, or enhancing (e.g., day care or early childhood program) early childhood special education in Connecticut. Twenty-five service coordinators, 3 program directors, 3 speech and language pathologists, 3 early childhood teachers, 12 occupational therapists, 17 special education teachers, 9 physical therapists, 5 occupational therapy aides, 1 assistive technology consultant, and 4 parents enrolled in the institutes. Institute groupings of participants were made geographically and heterogeneously (across disciplines and backgrounds).

Training took place during five 2-hour sessions. The topics for each session were derived from two pilot trainings on assistive technology. The topics for each session are contained in Table 8-3 on the next page. Each training session had a written outline that contained agendas, objectives, readings, and references for specific topics. In addition, each session consisted of a variety of activities, including problem-solving tasks, case studies, discussions, video demonstrations, and practice. Flexibility within each session's agenda allowed adaptation to trainees' concerns, interests, and immediate issues. Each class revolved around a story of a child with a disability who could benefit from assistive technology.

Two variations of the training model were used: traditional training, in which the group of trainees met with the trainers, and teleconferencing, in which two groups of students at two different sites attended training conducted by the team, using an interactive videoconferencing system. An interactive videoconferencing system is voice-activated; sound activates a camera to switch to different participat-

Table 8-3. *Inservice model institute topics (University of Connecticut Health Center)*

Session	Content
1. Technology Options for Families and Children in Natural Routines and Environments	• What is Technology? (1) Definition (2) Range of Technology for Young Children (3) Legislation • The Role of Technology in Early Intervention • Toy Adaptation
2. Technology and Communication	• Principles of Family-Driven Technology Use • Range of Technology, Resources, and Funding for Communication • Intervention in Natural Environments Using Technology • Application to Case Study
3. Technology and Mobility and Self-Care	• Range of Technology, Resources, and Funding for Feeding, Positioning, and Mobility • Intervention in Natural Environments • Application to Case Study
4. Technology Across Development	• Overview of Switch Access and Interface for Computers • Use of Computers for Skill Development in Young Children • Early Childhood Software Review • Application to Case Study
5. Technology Across the Life Span	• Funding Issues • Resources in Connecticut • Family Role in Using Technology • IFSP Development: (1) Assessment (2) Intervention in Natural Routines • Case Study

ing sites. All sites can be heard, however, allowing full participation between the trainers (at one site) and participants. The content for both types of training remained the same.

Follow-up was held for up to 6 months after the institute was completed. The content of the institute was translated into a series of competency tasks that were implemented by all participants during this follow-up phase. The follow-up consisted of observations of the participants at their work site, by project staff, and individual or group meetings for the purpose of providing consultation or support and assistance in implementing training content.

A variation of supervised follow-up methodology has been the use of peer supervision or mentoring models (Fenichel, 1992; Wischnowski et al., 1996). This technique consists of allowing participants to assist each other in the acquisition of new knowledge and skills. The peer-mentoring model may be implemented in many ways; in this project, trainees chose at least two partners, and each was responsible for helping the others complete the individual task competencies. Both forms of follow-up were used during training.

There were no differences at either entry or posttraining between those who took the institute in the traditional mode and those who took the institute via videoconferencing. Participants reported an average number of 5.95 years experience serving children in early childhood special education. Of the 16 possible reasons for taking the course, more than half indicated the highest level of importance was "to become more informed about assistive tech" and because "I think the information will be useful." Both the in-person and interactive video institute were well received. The average of all 17 questions on the training satisfaction questionnaire for the five sessions was 4.49/5.00 for the in-person and 4.31/5.00 for the interactive videoconference. Participants also completed a pre- and postknowledge test. There were significant gains made by both groups on the test after training. Participants were also asked to rate themselves on 18 competencies both before and after the course. The categories for self-rating were "No Awareness," "Awareness," "Knowledge," "Application," and "Mastery." After the institute, there were significant changes on these results also. A last measure on the participants' use of assistive technology also showed a significant difference both before and after training.

During follow-up, participants completed competency tasks. Interestingly, there were also no differences between those participants who chose a supervisory model and those who chose a peer-mentoring model on "number of follow-up contacts" and "number of competencies acquired." Table 8-4 on the next page contains a sample follow-up record completed by participants, regardless of condition.

Table 8-4. Sample assistive technology inservice follow-up log

Objective:

Team Members:

Type of Contact	September	October	November	December	January	February	March		
Formal Session									
Peer Contact									
Material Request									
Material Review									
Resource Contact									
Technical Assistance									
Other									

Conclusion

The use of assistive technology in early intervention and early childhood special education is an area that warrants inservice training, since many service providers have not received preservice training in this relatively new area. As with any new technique or strategy, service providers will need opportunities to effectively acquire knowledge and skills on the use of assistive technology to better serve children and families. As states begin incorporating training on assistive technology into the statewide CSPD, a few recommendations can be made for planning effective training models. These recommendations include:

Have Families Participate as Both Trainers and Trainees

Family-centered care is an accepted concept in early intervention and early childhood special education. As such, families should be integral to any training that is conducted for this age group. Training audiences that include families will benefit from the inclusion of a family-centered point of view during training activities. Partnerships between providers and families can be established at this learning stage, thus promoting a model for equality that can prevail during all family-provider interactions. Families have identified a need to learn how to teach their children to use assistive technology (Parette, 1993). As with any inservice activity, families must be participants in the planning and evaluation of an inservice on assistive technology which they attend. In particular, inservices that include families must help the family learn assistive technology applications specific to their child. An additional contribution of families during training can be their inclusion as co-instructors of inservice. Families have much to offer service providers, and their addition to the training team ensures a family perspective.

Have Cross-Disciplinary Representation on Both the Training Team and in the Training Audience

Early intervention and early childhood special education is delivered by many disciplines. Assistive technology should be used by many disciplines. Therefore, the training team should be represented by persons of multiple disciplines to demonstrate how discipline-specific interventions should be implemented across technology and learning domains (e.g., motor, communication, cognition). This model demonstrates to audiences the cross-disciplinary application of assistive technology devices and services. It also provides an opportunity for the training team to model a collaborative problem-solving process across disciplines. It is also recommended to have a diverse training audience representing multiple professional disciplines and perspectives.

Plan Learning Activities That Require Collaborative Problem-Solving Across Professional Disciplines and Families

This type of methodology gives participants the opportunity to learn collaborative skills during training in a unique content area (assistive technology). Methods that require active learning across participants (usually in small groups) can result in acquisition of knowledge-based content on both team problem-solving and assistive technology. Training should result in the participant becoming more comfortable with problem-solving technology issues. Both professionals and families benefit from open communication around a child's needs in assistive technology and the ability to use a problem-solving process to continue to meet those needs. By emphasizing problem-solving, the training activity allows participants to practice these skills during training, insuring the likelihood of continued use of technology after the training has been delivered.

Use Competencies as a Way to Ensure Breadth and Depth of Learning

Competency-based learning is an accepted practice in early intervention and early childhood special education. Using assistive technology requires both breadth across technology applications and in-depth knowledge about such applications. Competency-based learning provides a way to be sure that participants can demonstrate relevant objectives ranging from adapting a toy using a battery switch (entry level) to designing a computerized system for a child's speech and language, to continued problem-solving around a child's needs. This latter skill requires the use of such resources as the Internet and state and national databases (e.g., Abledata, CO-NET). Again, competency-based training ensures acquisition of knowledge and skills, decreasing the opportunities for abandonment of the use of the assistive device.

Provide Supervised Application of Competencies

For participants to acquire skills in the assistive technology area, application of the content activities must occur. Skills in assistive technology require hands-on manipulation of devices in conjunction with a child in need of such a device. Participants should demonstrate collaboration about the device, service, or both with the child's family. Participants will also have to demonstrate the ability to problem-solve with other professionals from other disciplines on a service delivery team to select the most appropriate device, services, or both that all team members and the family can use. Supervision, coaching, feedback, and encouragement by another is essential as participants learn skills in assistive technology. It is also important that this supervision occur over time, as training participants learn to increasingly use technology in their jobs. All too often, ineffective inservice activities (e.g., one-shot workshops) result in the abandonment of the content and skills taught (Parette, in press). Only through effective long-term training that includes supports, such as ongoing supervision and coaching, can we expect to see increases in the availability of appropriate assistive technology devices and services for young children and their families.

As inservice models in assistive technology begin to expand, it is hoped that these recommendations help to ensure the success of such efforts.

CHAPTER NINE

Expanding the Vision of Assistive Technology with Young Children and Families: Future Directions and Continuing Challenges

Howard P. Parette, Jr.
Southeast Missouri State University

Sharon Lesar Judge
University of Tennessee

Given the growing emphasis placed on family-centered practices in early childhood special education, professionals have increasingly acknowledged the necessity of promoting and maintaining family involvement in assistive technology decision-making and implementation processes. Acquiring new family-centered competencies is a prerequisite to ensuring that these processes are more effective in the years ahead. This is particularly important in light of recent shifts in policies at the national level suggesting the possibility of greater fiscal constraints being imposed on service systems in the future.

Chapter 1 of this text provided the reader with a rationale for accessing assistive technology for young children, while Chapters 2-

4 described the types of devices and applications that enable infants and young children to participate in family and school activities. Chapter 5 described the process of selecting appropriate assistive technology for young children with disabilities and their families. Chapter 6 described potential impacts of assistive technologies on family functioning, issues which have *not* typically been considered from a family systems perspective during team decision-making processes. Similarly, newly emerging issues relating to the *cultural influences* on a family's relationship to assistive technology service delivery were described in Chapter 7. In these discussions, readers should recognize that early childhood special education (ECSE) professionals, families, and other team members must consider this wider array of issues if assistive technology devices and services are to be provided in a truly family-centered approach. When this array of issues is comprehensively considered, it is anticipated that children and their families will more reliably receive such benefits as enhanced functioning and ability to engage in play, mobility, communication, and learning activities, from the types of devices described in Chapters 2-4.

Admittedly, involving family members in the assessment process often presents a challenge for professionals, though maintaining family collaboration throughout assistive technology decision-making may continue to be problematic (Crais, 1991). Greater success in such collaborations may be facilitated through the provision of ongoing and effective inservice training opportunities for both family members and professionals (see Chapter 8). Inherent in the recommendations for inservice is that family members participate *both* as trainers and trainees, though careful consideration must be given to the goals and philosophical underpinnings of the training provided.

Designers of training experiences for students and practitioners must acknowledge that family and cultural issues are significant sources of influence on a family's willingness to participate in the training and to use the competencies acquired during the training to support the child's use of the device. For example, clinical experience has revealed a decline in parental involvement once the newness of an assistive device fades (Angelo, 1997). The time demands required to maintain and accommodate an assistive technology device in the home may restrict more typical family activities or prolong daily routines (e.g., choice-making during mealtimes; making clothing selections during dressing routines). The demands of these tasks and responsibilities for parents may negatively affect family routines, interactions, and levels of stress (see Chapter 6 for an in-depth discussion of the impact of assistive technology on family functioning). When this occurs, families may not have the time, resources, or energy to carry out support for the device.

As noted in Chapters 6 and 7, assistive technology has the potential to improve the quality of life for all children with disabilities; but its *success* is linked to parent/professional cooperation, sensitivity to cultural and family factors, and time commitment to the goals of intervention. If professionals maintain a collaborative relationship with families throughout the assessment and intervention process, family satisfaction is a likely result. To ensure ongoing family satisfaction with family-centered assistive technology practices, two additional sets of issues must be considered by practitioners: *training* and *funding*. We will consider these issue areas in turn.

Training Issues

Inadequate training and inappropriate application of strategies for using a device are increasingly becoming a concern of professionals (Augusto & Schroeder, 1995; Cramer, 1992; Phillips & Zhao, 1993). Several studies conducted early in this decade have reflected substantial needs for training professionals involved in the delivery of assistive technology services (see Chapter 8). Parette (1991) reported results of a survey of 529 professionals across a range of service sectors in one state, many serving infants and toddlers with disabilities. Approximately 68% of the respondents reported that they received *insufficient training* in college regarding assistive technology and its applications for persons with disabilities. Among the top-reported topical needs for training in this study were (a) matching needs of persons with disabilities to technology, (b) conducting assessments and evaluations, (c) navigating legislation and funding, and (d) using computers. The most important finding to emerge from the Parette (1991) study was the consistently reported *needs for information by professionals.*

Needs for additional professional training have also been reported in other states. The Illinois Department of Rehabilitation Services (DORS) collected data from 264 DORS staff members regarding their assistive technology needs (Dederer et al., 1991). The survey was designed to solicit information on (a) training needs in assistive technology, (b) types of assistive technology services provided or purchased by service providers, (c) difficulties in the delivery of technology services, and (d) recommendations for improving the provision of assistive technology services. The data revealed that professionals in all departments were equipped with relatively few training opportunities related to assistive technology (M = .94 sessions; Range = 0 - 5 sessions) on an annual basis. Approximately 82% of the professionals participating in the survey reported that they needed additional training to more appropriately serve their client populations.

A recent study by Lesar (1998) examined early childhood special educators' knowledge, training, and perceived barriers to the use of assistive technology for young children with disabilities. The results revealed that 68% of ECSE professionals felt unprepared in the use of assistive technology. It was noted that the majority of the respondents reported significant deficits in their knowledge and ability to utilize assistive technology as well as limited usage and hands-on experiences with various assistive devices. These findings suggest that ECSE professionals lack the training and knowledge to make informed decisions about the selection and use of appropriate assistive technology. Such deficiencies in the practical knowledge bases of ECSE professionals may adversely affect their effectiveness in meeting the assistive technology needs of young children with disabilities. Similar findings have been reported in a three-state study of assistive technology application practices by school personnel in Indiana, Tennessee, and Kentucky (Derer, Polsgrove, & Rieth, 1996). In this study, only 19% of the 405 participants indicated that most or all of their training needs were being met.

Experts who often attest to the importance of training needs believe that a major reason for inappropriate training is due to a shortage of experts who can provide families and related service personnel with technology-related training. Studies have indicated a need for more qualified service providers with specialized skills in assessing technology needs and knowledge of appropriate methods for service delivery (Dederer et al., 1991; Somerville, Wilson, Shanfield, & Mack, 1990). Such topical areas should be increasingly targeted in the development of inservice training approaches for both professionals and family members.

Professionals who have been trained to use various assistive devices and training strategies find it extremely difficult to keep abreast of the rapid growth of technological devices and effective strategies for their use. In addition to increased availability, the newer products are more complex and sophisticated and often require more training for professionals to use them effectively (Augusto & Schroeder, 1995; Parette, 1994; Parette, in press; Thorkildsen, 1994).

The need for more qualified assistive technology service providers has not only been recognized by rehabilitation professionals but also by users of devices and family members. Families of children with disabilities are discovering that they often know as much or more about assistive technology as the related service personnel who are supposed to be supporting them (McNutty, 1988). While families do understand that professionals will have varying levels of training in assistive technology, the majority of training on specific implementation of assistive devices is often provided by professionals who have little or no experience in this area (Behrmann, 1995). This inadequate training and the resulting failed attempts at device integration are both emotionally and financially frustrating for children with disabilities and their families.

At the least, appropriate preparation could offset some of the barriers professionals are likely to face in providing assistive technology services to young children with disabilities. Future early childhood special education personnel would benefit from course content and hands-on experience that familiarizes them with the uses and benefits of assistive technology. The challenges for teacher preparation are twofold. First, preservice preparation programs need to provide assistive technology training in evaluation, identification of devices, training in specific assistive technology applications, maintenance, and funding as part of the preservice teaching competencies. This is important since currently there are few professional preservice training standards for personnel needing to provide assistive technology services. Second, formal training programs need to be established to train leadership personnel and specialists for the roles of trainer, supervisor, consultant, and technical assistant.

Based on an examination of funding and service practices in North Carolina, Trachtman and Pierce (1995) estimated that the per capita dollar amount expended on technology equipment for young children with disabilities is approximately $508 for children under age 1 year, $732 for children between ages 1 and 2 years, $952 for children between 2 and 3 years, $1,788 for children between 3 and 4 years, and $3,000 for children between 4 and 5 years. Thus, substantial fiscal resources are allocated for specific devices for children and families, though adequate training in the effective use of such devices may be infrequently provided (Hutinger, 1995; Lesar, 1998; Thorkildsen, 1994; Trachtman & Pierce, 1995). We can only conjecture what percentage of these devices will be abandoned over time due to family frustration resulting from lack of training and other needed supports (see Chapter 6 for a discussion of technology abandonment).

Though the emphasis on assistive technology training has increased over the last few years, it is evident that professionals and families both still need additional training. Until technology training is significantly improved, young children with disabilities may often continue to be mismatched with devices that do not meet their communicative, educational, and independent learning needs. However, enhanced educational opportunities and training programs can better prepare professionals and families to make appropriate device choices during the decision-making process.

Dimensions of Training for Future Inservice

Families of children with disabilities express needs to be well-informed and knowledgeable about devices available to their children and about related service personnel (Angelo, 1997; Angelo, Jones, & Kokoska, 1995; Angelo, Kokoska, & Jones, 1996; Parette, Brotherson, Hoge, & Hostetler, 1996; Parette & VanBiervliet, 1990, 1991). Many families express frustration with inadequate training and a lack of other assistive technology support services. They recognize that professionals vary with regard to their competency levels and abilities to work effectively with families across cultures; however, many feel that *most professionals* need more information relating to availability and use of devices. When professionals have an adequate assistive technology knowledge base, they can (a) provide needed family training, (b) assist families in planning for their children's future needs, and (c) help families implement intervention strategies that will improve children's quality of life in home and community environments.

Several criteria for effective training approaches have been developed in the literature, including: (a) relevance and specificity, (b) family and cultural sensitivity, (c) duration and intensity, and (d) user-friendliness.

Training should be relevant and specific. While the selection and application of assistive technology should be individualized and have specific relevance to all aspects of the child's home, school, and other natural settings (see Chapter 5), careful consideration should also be given to customizing training to meet the needs of individual families. Families have reported that they want professionals to recognize the uniqueness of their children and family units, and *not* to provide interventions designed for generic groups of individuals (Parette et al., 1996). All too often, parents are provided with core content that has been identified *by professionals* as being important, but the family has had little or no input into selecting the information that is provided. When this occurs, some families fail to see the relevance of the training and view professionals as insensitive to their needs. Development of future training should include strategies to empower families to be involved in all aspects of the selection and provision of assistive technology. Empowering families to choose a leadership role in making decisions fosters their sense of control and provides a basis for partnership in parent-professional relationships. When professionals promote increased involvement and a sense of empowerment in families, then families build the competence and confidence that will carry them successfully through the life span.

Training should be family- and culture-sensitive. Historically, professionals have determined goals for families of children with disabilities based solely on their own assessments of family needs (Angelo, 1997; Angelo et al., 1995; Garshelis & McConnell, 1993). However, service providers must recognize that family members may belong to a variety of cultural systems that hold differing perspectives on disease, disability, and need for services than those of professionals from Euro-American backgrounds. As noted in Chapter 7, families often perceive their training needs differently from professionals, and have different communication styles and preferences for interacting with trainers.

To provide a culturally diverse clientele with appropriate training opportunities, professionals must establish a knowledge base about different cultural value systems and related issues and their influence on families, and sensitize themselves to these influences. Professionals can learn about various cultural value systems from other individuals in the family's community, through observations of and interactions with the child who uses assistive technology and the family, and by asking questions to acquaint themselves with the family's views. Such information can provide valuable insights that will assist in the design of more meaningful training opportunities for families. For example, many families express an interest in receiving training from family support groups which include other members of their particular culture.

It may be that the use of information technologies (e.g., CD-ROM) will also assist professionals and families to obtain information needed for future training in assistive technology. Using an extensive knowledge base formed from focus groups and structured interview conversations with family members from Euro, African, Hispanic, Asian, and Native American cultures, Parette and VanBiervliet (1995) have developed an interactive, bilingual CD-ROM designed to enable family members and professionals to examine important family and cultural issues prior to making decisions about augmentative and alternative communication (AAC) devices for children with disabilities. Such user-friendly resources, which can be used across cultures, may become increasingly employed in conjunction with training opportunities for families.

Culturally valid training should consider the rules of social and communicative interaction as defined by the family's cultural group (Soto, Huer, & Taylor, in press; Taylor & Clarke, 1994). Training strategies designed to increase a family member's ability to implement assistive technology in natural settings should respect cultural norms of participation and customary ways of interaction. For example, communicative interactions in African-American families often consist of several individuals speaking simultaneously. This is very different from the typical style of presenting information in training formats developed by Euro-American professionals whose values dictate that turn-taking occur in communication interactions. Both the training strategies and the assistive technology intervention must be tailored to the communication style of a family and their culture to ensure full participation.

Training should be of appropriate duration and intensity. Since the implementation of assistive technology requires families to assume additional roles, training should target the identification of *reasonable expectations* of families. Families often feel they must sacrifice the quality of life of their family to invest the needed time in learning how to implement an assistive device (Parette et al., 1996). Training requires families to be away from the home environment, resulting in changes in established routines. Hence, professionals who provide training often place family members in the tenuous position of having to choose between implementing training recommendations that might enhance the development of their child and maintaining quality of life for the entire family. Professionals must consider new ways in which training can be provided to minimize the possibility of adverse consequences when families are requested to attend training sessions. Reasonable timelines that indicate the nature, extent, and length of the training program required of family members should be established, with provisions for child care and other supporting services when needed.

Because families will need to make decisions regarding technology throughout their lifetime, Phillips and Zhao (1993) recommend that training in assistive technology be available during important transition periods. Families of young children who use assistive technology devices want the security of a continuous intervention process that will enable successful transitions from early intervention to school to higher education to vocational placement (Angelo et al., 1996), and for adulthood: community living, career changes, and health status.

Training should be user-friendly. When training is provided to family members, materials and approaches should be user-friendly. Information presented should be in formats that are easily accessible to and usable by family members. Support materials and family-sensitive approaches should also be available to families after the training has been given. For example, the information presented during training is often not "family-friendly" because it has been designed for professional audiences rather than for family members (Parette et al., 1996). Terminology that is understood and commonly used by professionals may not be easily comprehended by family members. Adequate textual information that is sensitive to the reading levels of family members, and/or orally presented information that is free of excessive jargon, should be used during both training and follow-up activities. Opportunities should be provided for family members to obtain clarification of terms used and content provided in the training. For families from different cultural or linguistic backgrounds, use of trained interpreters may be necessary to ensure understanding.

Typical training approaches used in the United States target family members and other professionals as the end recipients of information. Information is provided with the expectation that all participants in the training will know how to use and implement the information. However, families often express concerns that they are not prepared to teach their children how to use assistive devices. While the training provided to families may, in fact, enable caregivers and extended family members to use devices, it does not necessarily mean that they, in turn, can teach their children to use the devices. If family members are expected to teach their children to use and maintain assistive devices, professionals should provide the time and the necessary follow-up supports to assist families who are charged with such responsibilities. Otherwise, the family may experience stress and frustration with the assistive device, culminating in its minimal use or total abandonment. In addition, professionals should provide training to families on how to integrate assistive technology devices into naturally occurring activities and routines.

One family-friendly approach with great credibility is the use of family support groups to exchange experience-based advice, help one another with problem-solving, and provide assistive technology follow-up information. Groups may be organized to meet formally at designated, mutually convenient times. Informal contacts will also develop from these groups, with support group members calling one another as needed for information and support. Having information provided by other families who use assistive technology is often a much more powerful way to provide supportive services to families who have specific questions regarding assistive technology device usage and maintenance. Of course, access to a professional for technical or other questions should still be made available.

Funding Issues

Funding for assistive technologies remains one of the biggest obstacles to acquiring needed devices and services. Funding is available from a variety of public and private sources. However, finding and paying for the right assistive technology can be difficult for families. This may be due to the high cost of equipment (Hofmann, 1988), the restrictive or vague eligibility criteria imposed by potential public and private sources of funding (McGuiness, 1982; Ward, 1989), professionals' lack of knowledge about finding funding options (Lesar, 1998), or difficulty locating and accessing third-party payment sources (Church & Glennen, 1992).

As assistive technology use among young children with disabilities becomes more widespread and as technologies continue to become increasingly sophisticated, both their total cost and the demand for them rises. For example, alternative and augmentative communication (AAC) devices, such as the *Macaw* by Zygo, cost up to $2,200; a *Dynavox* device, which, through software, provides synthesized speech via direct touch, joystick, auditory or visual scanning modes, costs $5,300. Very few families can afford to pay for high-tech assistive devices—or even many low-tech devices—on their own. Without financial alternatives to help families obtain these devices, young children with disabilities will be denied the ability to play, learn, communicate, and interact with family and friends.

Even though the Technology Related Assistance for Individuals with Disabilities Act (Tech Act) of 1994 increased the availability of and the provisions for funding these mechanisms, there are still three major funding issues that must be addressed by service providers and families: (a) the costs of delivering assistive technology services, (b) locating and acquiring funding sources, and (c) the training of professionals and family members about funding options available through third-party payment sources.

Costs of Delivering Assistive Technology Services

The costs associated with delivering assistive technology services generally fall into two areas: equipment and personnel (Church & Glennen, 1992). The cost of assistive devices will vary with the focus of the program and the functional needs and preferences of the child.

Schools and human services agencies should have access to demonstration try-out centers and "loaner" equipment to allow young children and families the opportunity to try devices in time frames and environments that would permit informed choices. Considering the rapid pace of new and changing technology, the use of demonstration try-out centers in which families can borrow devices could help lower the cost of purchasing new devices. Demonstration try-out centers could be implemented through partnerships with assistive technology vendors and human service agencies.

Personnel costs will vary with the focus of the assistive technology program; programs that provide assistive technology services in more than one area will need more professionals on the team to provide a wider array of services. Overall personnel costs will be related to the total number of children served and the extent of the services provided. In addition to personnel costs, professionals working with young children with disabilities need continued training and technical support in the uses, adaptations, and applications of assistive technology.

Locating and Acquiring Funding Sources

Professionals in early intervention programs and families need to become knowledgeable about the most feasible sources of funding for assistive technology. Funding under IDEA and the Tech Act is available for use in supplying technology-related needs; but with shrinking budgets and limited resources, it is increasingly difficult for funding sources to process all the requests for assistive devices. As a result, the application process may require substantial energy expenditure and advocacy in finding a source for funds. Although financial resources are often scarce, funding does not limit a child's need for assistive technology. Professionals must assist families in becoming resourceful and actively involved in accessing funding mechanisms for needed assistive technology. The following is a brief overview of some of the major assistive technology funding sources that exist at the federal, state, and private levels.

Medicaid. Medicaid is a jointly funded federal and state medical insurance program for individuals and families with low income. The Medicaid program has a durable medical equipment category that covers some devices if that device is considered medically necessary and a physician's authorization is obtained. Each state develops its own regulations for program participation according to specified federal guidelines, and each state may provide additional services at their own discretion. Thus, there are wide variations in the scope of state services offered. In addition, assistive technology services (e.g., occupational, physical, and speech therapy) are covered under federal Medicaid law.

The Early and Periodic Screening, Diagnosis, and Treatment (EPSDT) program for children from birth to age 21 requires that states cover regular and periodic exams for eligible children. This program specifically states that any medically necessary services or durable medical equipment prescribed by EPSDT must be provided, even if that service is not covered in that state's Medicaid program. This includes assistive devices that may have been excluded under the regular Medicaid program.

CHAMPUS. The Civilian Health and Medical Program of the Uniformed Services (CHAMPUS) is a federally funded medical benefits insurance program for spouses and children of active duty, retired, and deceased active duty and retired uniformed services personnel. CHAMPUS provides funding for assistive technology if it is deemed medically necessary. This federal program is operated by contracts through various insurance companies to provide health coverage in a designated region.

Public school programs. Local school districts are required by law to provide assistive technology for children with disabilities if it is shown to be necessary to allow the child to receive an education in the least restrictive environment. Need for assistive technology devices and services must be included in the Individual Education Plan (IEP). Once the assistive technology need is determined by the IEP committee, the school system must actively pursue funding to obtain the device for the child.

Private insurance. Some individual health insurance policies will fund assistive technology, but private insurance plans vary greatly in terms of insurance coverage and the degree of payment. Most private insurance will fund only assistive technology that is considered medically necessary and prescribed by a physician.

Private funding. Private funding sources include nonprofit disability associations (e.g., United Cerebral Palsy Association, United Way, March of Dimes), private foundations, service clubs and organizations (e.g., Lions Club, Shriners, Rotary Club), and national advocacy groups. Most private funding will assist in the purchasing of devices if other sources of funding have been unsuccessful. These organizations usually have specific guidelines and eligibility requirements. It is often useful to contact these organizations by telephone for information about the process for obtaining funding and specific agency forms.

Loan programs. Credit financing provides another option for families who are not eligible for other third-party payment programs. A variety of loan financing programs operate in some of the state Tech Act projects that provide low- or no-interest loans to help buy assistive technology. Information about credit financing of assistive technology can also be obtained from the manufacturer of the equipment.

Funding assistive technology for young children with disabilities may be one of the most important challenges facing professionals and families. Some funding streams may take a considerable amount of time to access, and other funding requests may be denied. Parette, Hofmann, and VanBiervliet (1994) suggest a series of steps for professionals and families to follow to ensure the likelihood that applications for assistive technology will be funded. If a denial for funding is issued, they recommend that families be encouraged to participate in an appeal. Often denials are reversed at the appeal level due to errors in the paperwork or the reviewers in the funding agency's lack of understanding of the assistive technology.

Training in Funding Issues

The increasing number of assistive devices available for young children with disabilities should alert us to the need for ECSE professionals and families to understand how to find and pay for assistive technology. No two states will approach in the same way the problems inherent in developing comprehensive systems of assistive technology service delivery. Policy makers are confronted with the task of identifying appropriate and potential sources of funding, followed by developing a system of entry points for a particular funding source, developing bridges to other funding sources, and identifying barriers to the use of these sources. Such challenges must, of necessity, involve the input of many different persons, including families of young children with disabilities, service providers, professionals, technology manufacturers and dealers, and state agency officials.

The use of Medicaid, for example, as a primary source of funding for equipment and devices is undergoing close scrutiny by all states. Early studies have suggested that it is essential for all persons dealing with the Medicaid system to develop lines of communication with *state* Medicaid personnel, particularly those who handle prior authorization and policy decisions (Markowicz & Reeb, 1989). Such decisions are amenable to local influence, parental and advocacy pressure, and smaller-scale political processes in ways that federal processes are not (Mendelsohn, 1989; Morris, 1990). Professionals must also understand the federal and state laws and policy guidelines that shape the Medicaid program in their particular states. The better families and professionals comprehend the legal and policy framework within which Medicaid personnel work, the better prepared they will be to communicate with those officials in advocating for the child's rights under the program and federal law.

Personnel preparation programs should address the extent to which information is disseminated in states regarding Medicaid and the understanding of the system demonstrated by those who are using it. Also, the relationship between greater understanding of the Medicaid system, its utilization, and long-term outcomes, such as integration into community settings, should be given careful consideration in research studies and in curriculum development in personnel preparation settings.

Information about alternative funding sources for assistive technology, particularly credit-based systems, may become an integral component of personnel preparation programs in the future as well as inservice training for both professionals and family members. The ability for families to acquire credit financing for assistive technology is an option that has not been adequately pursued (Parette & Van-Biervliet, 1990; Reeb, 1987; Wallace, 1995). This is particularly interesting in light of the frequently expressed need for credit alternatives. Since the financial resources available to individuals vary greatly, the efficacy of a range of credit options in states must be more closely examined by professionals. This information should then be integrated into the curricula of training programs.

Data is needed to determine the financial needs of families of young children with disabilities within existing service delivery systems, and training strategies are needed to train professionals to meet these needs. Of particular importance is the development of programs having revolving loan funds that provide opportunities for persons with disabilities to demonstrate responsibility for repaying loans, such as those programs developed in New York, Maine, Vermont, Illinois, and Nevada (Wallace, 1995). Specific curriculum issues which would evolve in the development of such loan funds across the states would include (a) the critical features of the loan fund, (b) the application processes, (c) identification of the person(s) or group responsible for controlling the fund and authorizing financing, (d) repayment monitoring, and (e) personnel requirements for developing and implementing the fund.

A national study reported by the Virginia Assistive Technology System (1993) identified three phases that were determined to be crucial to developing successful loan programs. In the first phase, critical components include: (a) identifying the target population to be served, (b) formulating a needs assessment, (c) identifying barriers to securing traditional funding, and (d) developing a mission and general program components. In the second phase, other activities receive emphasis: (a) soliciting funding, (b) soliciting external partners (if necessary), (c) seeking approval from state legislatures (when necessary), (d) developing critical program elements, and (e) negotiating any necessary agreements. A final phase involves (a) developing and implementing a marketing strategy, (b) hiring and training staff, and (c) operating the loan program.

With regard to the use of private insurance for funding technology, it is important for personnel preparation programs to begin to develop curriculum strategies that teach future professionals basic information regarding private insurance (e.g., obligations of the insurance company and the types of technology and related services that are covered under policies). Information relating to the identification of key decision-makers within private insurance companies might be provided along with recommendations for developing a rapport with those persons. Such basic information can facilitate an understanding of the perspectives of those persons as well as expedite payments for technology needed by persons with disabilities that are consistent with insurer constraints (Galvin, 1990).

Subsidies are one form of funding mechanism for the assistive technology and the services presently being offered to persons with disabilities. Although there are few innovative programs available at this time, there has been a significant growth in such financing strategies (Ward, 1989). In this area, personnel preparation programs might assume the leadership in developing strategies to explore the impact of subsidy programs on the longitudinal development of persons with disabilities. For example, it is unknown to what extent persons with disabilities and families who are subsidy recipients accomplish what they desire through the use of assistive technology, since they are typically not followed over time. It is also unknown to what extent information is available regarding subsidy programs for this population. Data regarding who and how a person with a disability obtains information about these programs or what inhibits their application for subsidized assistive technology appears to be nonexistent. Finally, the effectiveness of specific models of subsidy provision have yet to be examined. Comparisons should be made of existing models to determine which programs facilitate the use of procured technology most effectively and how appropriate matches between individuals and technologies can be assured to insure the highest level of functioning possible.

Conclusion

As we prepare to enter the 21st century, we must all recognize that the young children of today are the adults of tomorrow. The authors acknowledge the potential of assistive technology to enhance the quality of life for many young children with disabilities and their families. In the new world that is rapidly emerging, all individuals must be better prepared to access, manipulate, and control information and their environments through the use of technology. However, the mere provision of assistive technology to young children with disabilities and their families is admittedly *not an end* in itself. The full potential of devices and services for a particular child or family cannot be realized unless several operational assumptions are met.

First, children with disabilities, their families, and professionals must develop *trust in* and *respect for* one another. Greater understanding of family systems and recognition of family concerns, priorities, and resources are essential to developing such trust and understanding. Once a level of trust and mutual respect has been achieved, a solid foundation for more effective assistive technology decision making may be present. Second, professionals and families must learn to *work together* in meaningful and potentially different ways than they have in the past. Unilateral decision making on the part of professionals who are "proficient" in aspects of assistive technology service delivery may not result in the types of outcomes anticipated. Family members who are willing and able *must* have greater presence and involvement in all aspects of decision making. Third, pro-

fessionals and families must effectively identify, acquire, and implement effective assistive technology devices and services. This assumes
that appropriate supports will be provided to families during all phases
of decision-making, acquisition, and implementation. We believe that
these more truly family-centered assistive technology practices can
and will produce the kinds of real changes that make a difference in
the lives of children with disabilities and their families.

APPENDIX A

Software Resources

Commercial Sofware Resources*

7th Level, Inc.
P.O. Box 832190
Richardson, TX

Academic Software, Inc.
331 W. 2nd Street
Lexington, KY 40507
(606) 231-2332

ahead media AB
P.O. Box 24135, S-104
51 Stockholm, Sweden

Bit Jugglers, Inc.
785 Castro Street
Mountain View, CA 94041
(415) 968-3908

Brøderbund Software, Inc.
500 Redwood Blvd.
P.O. Box 6121
Novato, CA 94948-6121
(800) 521-6263

Byron Press Multimedia
175 Fifth Avenue
Ste. 2122
New York, NY 10010

C & C Software
5713 Kentford Circle
Wichita, KS 67220
(316) 683-6056

CD-ROM Warehouse
1720 Oak St.
Lakewood, NJ 08701
(800) 237-6623

Computer Curriculum Corp.
5718 Huron Street
Vermilion, OH 44089-1009
(216) 967-1000

Creative Communicating
P.O. Box 3358
Park City, UT 84060
(801) 645-7737

Cyan, Inc.
P.O. Box 28096
Spokane, WA 99228
(509) 468-0807

Davidson & Associates
19840 Pioneer Ave.
Torrance, CA 90503
(310) 793-0600

Digital Impact, Inc.
6506 S. Lewis, Ste. 250
Tulsa, OK 74136
(800) 755-4232

Digital Pictures
212 N. 2nd Street
Minneapolis, MN 55401
(612) 371-4515

---

* ©1997 by Macomb Projects. Used with permission.

Discis
90 Sheppard Ave. E., 7th Floor
Toronto, Ontario, Canada M2N 3A1
(800) 567-4321

Discovery Channel
7700 Wisconsin Avenue
Bethesda, MD 20814

DK Multimedia
95 Madison Avenue
New York, NY 10016
(800) DKMM-575

Don Johnston Incorporated
1000 N. Rand Rd., Bldg. 115
P.O. Box 639
Wauconda, IL 60084
(800) 999-4660

Dr. Peet's Software
4241 Aldrich Ave. S.
Minneapolis, MN   55409
(800) 354-2950

Dunamis, Inc.
3423 Fowler Blvd.
Lawrenceville, GA 30244
(800) 828-2443

EA*Arts (Electronic Arts)
1450 Fashion Island Blvd.
San Mateo, CA 94404
(800) KID-XPRT

Edmark
P.O. Box 97021
Redmond, WA 98073-9721
(800) 426-0856

Educational Resources
1550 Executive Drive
Elgin, IL 60123
(800) 222-2808

Edutainment
932 Walnut Street
Louisville, CO 80027
(800) 338-3844

Egghead Software
22011 SE 51st St.
Issaquah, WA 98027-7299
(800) EGG-HEAD

Exceptional Children's Software
2215 Ohio
Lawrence, KS 66046
(913) 832-1850

Great Wave Software
5353 Scotts Valley Dr.
Scotts Valley, CA 95066
(408) 438-1990

Gryphon Software Corp.
7220 Trade Street, Ste. 120
San Diego, CA 92121-2315
(619) 536-8815

GT Interactive
16 East 40th Street
New York, NY 10016

HACH
P.O. Box 11754
Winston-Salem, NC 27116
(800) 624-7968

HarperCollins Interactive
10 E. 53rd Street
New York, NY 10022

Hartley
9920 Pacific Heights Blvd.
San Diego, CA 92121-4330
(800) 247-1380

Humongous Entertainment
13110 N.E. 177th Place
Woodinville, WA 98072

IntelliTools, Inc.
55 Leveroni Ct., Ste. 9
Novato, CA 94949
(800) 899-6687

Judy Lynn Software
278 Dunhams Corner Rd.
East Brunswick, NJ 08816
(908) 390-8845

Knowledge Adventure, Inc.
1311 Grand Central Ave.
Glendale, CA 91201

Laureate Learning Systems
110 E. Spring St.
Winooski, VT 05404
(800) 562-6801

Lawrence Productions
1800 S. 35th St.
Galesburg, MI 49078
(800) 421-4157

Learning Company
6493 Kaiser Dr.
Fremont, CA 94555
(800) 852-2255

Macomb Projects
27 Horrabin Hall
Western Illinois University
Macomb, IL 61455
(309) 298-1634

Macromedia, Inc.
600 Townsend Street
San Francisco, CA 94103

MarbleSoft
12301 Central Ave. NE, 205
Blane, MN 55434
(612) 755-1402

Mayer-Johnson Co.
P.O. Box 1579
Solana Beach, CA 92075
(619) 550-0449

MECC
6160 Summit Dr. N.
St. Paul, MN 55430-4003
(800) 685-6322, ext. 529

MediaVision, Inc.
47300 Bayside Parkway
Fremont, CA 94538

Memorex Software
N-TK Entertainment Technology, Inc.
18000th Studebaker Road, Suite 200
Serritos, CA 90703

Merit Software
13707 Gamma Road
Dallas, TX 75244
(800) 238-4277

Micrografx
1303 Arapaho
Richardson, TX 75081
(214) 234-1769

Mindplay
160 W. Ft. Lowell
Tucson, AZ 85705
(800) 221-7911

Mindscape
88 Rowland Way
Novato, CA 94945-5000
(415) 897-9900

ModernMedia Ventures, Inc.
1317 Hyde Street, Ste. 4
San Francisco, CA 94109

Nordic Software, Inc.
P.O. Box 6007
Lincoln, NE 68505
(402) 488-5086

Optimum Resource Inc.
5 Hiltech Ln.
Hilton Head Island, SC 29926
(800) 327-1473

Packard Bell Interactive
1301 3rd Avenue, Ste. 2301
Seattle, WA 98101

Phillips Media, Inc.
10960 Wilshire Blvd.
Los Angeles, CA 90024
(800) 340-7888

Poor Richard's Publishing
P.O. Box 1075
Litchfield, CT 06759
(860) 567-4307

R.J. Cooper and Associates
24843 Del Prado, Ste. 283
Dana Point, CA 92629
(800) RJ-COOPER

Ringling Multimedia Corp.
1753 N. Gale Blvd.
Sarasota, FL 34234

Roger Wagner Publishing
1050 Pioneer Way, Ste. P
El Cajon, CA 92020
(800) 421-6526

Scholastic, Inc.
2931 East McCarty Street
P.O. Box 7502
Jefferson City, MO 65102
(800) 541-5513

Simon & Schuster Interactive
c/o StarPak Inc.
P.O. Box 1230
Greeley, CO 80631

Simtech Publications
134 East St.
Litchfield, CT 06759-3600
(860) 567-1173

SoftTouch/kidTECH
4182 Pinewood Lake Dr.
Bakersfield, CA 93309
(805) 837-8774

Soleil Software
P.O. Box 50664
Palo Alto, CA 94303

Sunburst Communications
101 Castleton St.
Pleasantville, NY 10570
(800) 321-7511

T/Maker Company VroomBooks
1390 Villa Street
Mountain View, CA 94041
(415) 962-0195

Terrapin Software, Inc.
10 Holworthy Street
Cambridge, MA 02138
(617) 547-5646

UCLA Intervention Program for Children with Disabilities
1000 Veteran Ave., Room 23-10
Los Angeles, CA 90095
(310) 825-4821

Voyager
1351 Pacific Coast Highway
Santa Monica, CA 90095
(310) 541-1383

William K. Bradford Publ. Co.
16 Craig Rd.
Acton, MA 01720
(800) 421-2009

Internet Software Resources*

A+ Discount Software http://www.aplusbooks.com/software.html
Offers discount pricing on software from major publishers

Lawrence Getz's Shareware for Children
http://pages.prodigy.com/VDJW65A/
Offers shareware for MS Windows

Children's Software http://www.nerdworld.com/nw429.html
Lists sites that offer children's software and/or reviews of children's software

---

Kids Connection http://kidsconnection.com/computers/software/sfchil.html
Offers information about children's software

Children's Software and More! http://www.gamesdomain.ru/tigger
Offers shareware and freeware for Macintosh and PC, freeware from Disney, demos of commercial products, reviews, graphics, and programming for kids

Kids First http://www.cybersuperstores.com/kidsfirst/cover.html
Lists CD-ROMs endorsed by the Coalition for Quality Children's Media

Children's Software Archives
http://qv3pluto.leidenuniv.nl/steve/reviews/archives.htm
Provides a list of Internet archive sites that include children's software

Kids Korner Wiz Kids http://www.wizkids.com./dshults
Teaches parents, teachers, and kids about the Internet

Children's Software Archives
http://qv3pluto.leidenuniv.nl/steve/reviews/garbo.htm
Provides resources for public domain and shareware

Kids Shareware PC http://www.gamesdomain.com/tigger/pc/pc-sites.html
Offers shareware to download for your PC

Children's Software on the Internet
http://ois.lemuria.com/martin/chidr.htm
Provides links to and descriptions of children's software sites on the Internet

Look Out World http://www.lookoutworld.com/
Offers free demos of the company's early childhood software

Children's Software Review—All Star List
http://microweb.com/pepsite/Revue/allstar.html
Lists top choices of educational software by age group and subject matter

Mac Downloads 4 Kids http://gamesdomain.com/tigger/sw-mac.html
Offers shareware and freeware for the Macintosh plus reviews and demos

Creative Wonders http://www.cwonders.com/
Gives descriptions and ordering information for CD-ROMs for home and school

Maplehurst Productions http://www.maplehurst.com/
Features children's software on CD-ROM and free activities to download

Family Surfboard http://www.familysurf.com/depot.htm
Features software reviews and demos

Media-Pro http://www.widdl.com/MediaPro/
Describes two CD-ROMs in the Magic Carpet series

Newsweek's Parents' Guide to Children's Software
http://www.newsweekparentsguide.com/
Contains over 600 software reviews

Totware—Benjamin's Favorites
http://www.het.brown.edu/people/mende/totware.html
Lists and describes various Mac and PC shareware and freeware programs

Planet Fun http://www.davd.com/fun.html
Features previews and downloadable samples

Wierenga Software http://www.novagate.com/~wierenga/index.html
Features educational shareware to download

Random House Children's CD-ROMs
http://www.cyberstores.com/rh/cover.html
Gives descriptions and ordering information for Living Books, Humongous Entertainment, and Knowledge Adventure CD-ROMs

Zia's Software Page http://www.zia.com/kids/games/ksoftware.htm
Offers shareware and freeware plus links to other children's software sites

Software Publishers Marketplace
http://www.spmarket.com/spm/spmcat.html
Provides a catalog of software titles produced by independent software developers

Ziff Davis Software Library http://www.hotfiles.com/educate.html
Rates shareware and offers software demos that can be downloaded

The Children's Software Company http://www2.childsoft.com/childsoft
Offers on-line software guide, catalog, and programs at discount prices

*Information is continually being added to Internet Sites. We suggest a search using "children's software" to find more information.

Public Domain Software Resources*

Center for Adapted Technology
5755 W. Alameda Avenue
Lakewood, CO 80226
(303) 233-1666

Lekotek of Georgia, Inc.
1955 Cliff Valley Way, Ste. 102
Atlanta, GA 30329
(404) 633-3430

Easter Seals of the Lehigh Valley and the Poconos
2200 Industrial Drive
Bethlehem, PA 18017
(610) 866-8092

Technology for Language and Learning
P.O. Box 327
East Rockway, NY 11518
(516) 625-4550

EDUCORP
7434 Trade St.
San Diego, CA 92121
(800) 843-9497

APPENDIX B

Voice Output Devices

Listed are a number of voice output devices appropriate for young children. For more information, see *The Guide to Augmentative and Alternative Communication Devices (1996 Edition)*, $25, Rehabilitation Engineering Research Center on AAC, Applied Science and Engineering Labs, University of Delaware/A.I. duPont Institute, P.O. Box 269, 1600 Rockland Road, Wilmington, DE 19899-0269.

Action Voice
Membrane surface keyboard with 10 cells and 60 or 120 seconds of digitized speech.
Ability Research
P.O. Box 1721
Minnetonka, MN 55345
(612) 939-0121

Alphatalker
Membrane surface keyboard with 4-, 8-, or 32-location options and 3 minutes of digitized speech.
Prentke Romich Company
1022 Heyl Road
Wooster, OH 44691
(800) 262-1984

BigMack
A one-shot message device offering up to 20 seconds of digitized speech.
AbleNet
1081 Tenth Avenue, S.E.
Minneapolis, MN 55414
(800) 322-0956

Blackhawk
Provides 16 message cells and four levels, with 4 minutes of digitized speech.
AdamLab/Wayne Co.
RESA
33500 Van Born Rd.
Wayne, MI 48184
(313) 467-1415

CheapTalk 4 and 8
Provides up to 5 seconds of digitized speech on each of four or eight message cells.
Enabling Devices
385 Warburton Avenue
Hastings-on-Hudson, NY 10706
(800) 832-8692

DeltaTalker
Can be set up with 8, 32, or 128 locations using one of the ten DEC-talk voices with digitized speech.
Prentke Romich Company
1022 Heyl Road
Wooster, OH 44691
(800) 262-1984

Digivox
Offers 1-48 keys, using up to 8 levels, recording 4.5-18 minutes digitized speech.
Sentient Systems Technology, Inc.
2100 Wharton St.
Pittsburgh, PA 15203
(800) 344-1778

DynaVox
Portable AAC device with DECtalk speech. Features a customizable dynamically changing picture symbol screen with symbols categorized into pages or layers.
Sentient Systems Technology, Inc.
2100 Wharton St.
Pittsburgh, PA 15203
(800) 344-1778

Hawk
Membrane surface touchpanel with 9 locations, with each location recording up to 5 seconds of digitized speech.
Adamlab
33500 Van Born Rd.
Wayne, MI 48184
(313) 467-1415

Light Activated Switch Panel
Allows child to have direct selection capabilities using a light beam.
Creative Communicating
P.O. Box 3358
Park City, UT 84060
(801) 645-7737

Link
Membrane keyboard that features written output plus DECtalk speech for voice output. Comes with 8 different voices. Instant phrases accessed with minimal keystrokes for output to the speech synthesizer.
Mayer-Johnson
P.O. Box 1579
Solana Beach, CA 92075
(619) 550-0084

Lynx
Presents 4 message cells, each with 4 seconds of digitized speech.
Adamlab
33500 Van Born Rd.
Wayne, MI 48184
(313) 467-1415

Macaw II
Membrane keyboard offers 2- through 32-choice selection, with 9 minutes of digitized speech. Models available with either direct selection only or both direct selection and scanning.
Zygo, Inc.
P.O. Box 1008, Portland, OR 97207
(800) 234-6006

Megawolf
Membrane keyboard with 1-36 squares using synthesized speech output.
Adamlab
33500 Van Born Rd.
Wayne, MI 48184
(313) 467-1415

Messagemate
Keyboard offers 20 membrane squares with 20 seconds of digitized speech.
Words+, Inc.
P.O. Box 1229, Lancaster, CA 93584
(800) 869-8521

Parrot
Keyboard offers up to 16 brief messages using digitized speech.
Zygo, Inc.
P.O. Box 1008, Portland, OR 97207
(800) 234-6006

Pockettalker
Handheld device offers access to digitized speech messages through direct selection.
Attainment Co.
P.O. Box 930160, Verona, WI 53593
(800) 327-4269

Sayit
Two versions of 20-second speech prerecorded on a built-in, solid state tape recorder.
Enabling Devices
Toys for Special Children
385 Warburton Ave.
Hastings-on-Hudson, NY 10706
(800) 832-8697

Say It Simplyplus
Uses text-to-speech synthetic speech with messages arranged into 28 message levels.
Innocomp
33195 Wagon Wheel Drive
Solon, OH 44139
(800) 382-8622

Speakeasy
Includes up to 12 message cells on membrane keypad accessing up to 4 minutes of digitized speech.
AbleNet
1081 Tenth Avenue, SE
Minneapolis, MN 55414
(800) 322-0956

Superhawk
Membrane keyboard with 1-48 squares, in a variety of configurations and digitized speech.
Adamlab
33500 Van Born Rd.
Wayne, MI 48184
(313) 467-1415

Switchmate 4/Voicemate 4
Permits recording of 4 phrases, with 4 seconds time for each.
TASH
Unit 1, 91 Station St.
Ajax, Ontario L1S 3H2 Canada
(416) 686-4129

Talk Back VI
Presents 6 cells with digitized speech.
Crestwood Company
6625 N. Sidney Place
Milwaukee, WI 53209
(414) 352-5678

Voice Pal Plus
Can record up to 60 seconds of digitized speech that can be accessed by either direct selection or scanning. Can be activated by onboard keyboard, external switches, or Taction Pads.
Adaptivation
ISU Research Park
2501 N. Loop Drive, Ames, IA 50010
(800) 723-2783

Wolf
Inexpensive, portable voice-output device that uses synthesized speech.
AdamLab
33500 Van Born Road
Wayne, MI 48184
(313) 467-1415

APPENDIX C

Computer Peripherals

Described below are some widely-used peripherals for young children. These peripherals consist of special keyboards, interfaces that offer numerous access options, and a variety of other input options.

All-Turn-It, Jelly Bean, Big Red (AbleNet)
Single switches in a variety of sizes that are responsive across entire surface when pressed. Available in different colors.

Big Keys Keyboard (Don Johnston)
Alternate keyboard offers large, 1-inch keys with even larger spacebar and return keys. The keyboard attaches through the standard keyboard and works with all regular software.

ClickIt! (IntelliTools)
Software program that allows the user to point and click without a mouse. "Hot spots" can be chosen for places where the user needs to point and click.

Concept Keyboard (Hach Associates)
Alternate membrane keyboard which includes overlay making software. Two *Concept Keyboards* can be active on the same computer at the same time allowing two children to communicate with each other within a simple word processor.

Discover: Board (Don Johnston)
Alternate keyboard with bright colors and pictures so young children enjoy it. It works on the computer the same way the standard keyboard works. It has keys for entering text, talking phrases, moving the mouse and more. Includes software for customizing and printing your own overlays to work with any software.

Discover: Ke:nx (Don Johnston)
A keyboard and mouse alternative for student with disabilities. The hardware interface provides the connection for switches, keyboards, and other devices that match the physical needs of the students. Its on-screen or alternate keyboard layouts have keys for typing text, moving the mouse, clicking hot spots on programs, opening files, and pulling down menus.

Discover: Screen (Don Johnston)
Talking on-screen keyboard that supports writing and communicating.
Provides point and click access to standard keyboard letters, whole words,
and communication phases.

Discover: Switch (Don Johnston)
Talking computer switch that offers choices for writing or using the mouse.
Choices are automatically highlighted, and users press the Discover: Switch
to activate.

IntelliKeys (IntelliTools)
Oversized membrane keyboard that can be set up in different layouts/
overlays. Each standard overlay has a bar code that is instantly recognized by
IntelliKeys. Comes with two built-in switch connectors.

Key Largo (Don Johnston)
Expanded standard membrane keyboard that is ergonomically designed. The
keyboard includes 128 cells and can be used with paper overlays.

King Plug-In Keyboard (TASH)
Giant size alternative keyboard that plugs directly into a computer. Keys are
slightly recessed and provide both tactile and auditory feedback. Both
keyboard and mouse functions can be controlled by this keyboard, with
simple movement from mouse to keyboard mode.

MacMini and WinMini Plug-in Keyboard (TASH)
Small size alternative keyboard that plugs directly into a PC or Macintosh
computer. Membrane keys are less than .5" square and are closely-spaced for
easy access. The keyboard surface is very touch sensitive.

MouseMover (TASH)
Allows individual to control all mouse functions on both PC and Macintosh
computers using a combination of five single switches or any multiple
switch. Pressing on each switch then delivers a specific mouse function.

Say it Rocker Switch (Enabling Devices)
This is a device that combines a Talking Switch Plate that activates a 20
second message, in a Rocking plate that allows a child to use two switch
plates side by side (for example for yes/no responses).

Touch Window (Don Johnston, Edmark)
The Touch Window can be placed directly over the computer screen and
used like a mouse to access the computer. The mouse functions of clicking
and double-clicking can be carried out by simply pointing and touching on
the Touch Window surface.

APPENDIX D

Selected Books

The Alliance for Technology Access. (1996) *Computer resources for people with disabilities.* Alameda, CA: Hunter House.

Burkhart, L. (1980). *Homemade battery-powered toys and educational devices for severely handicapped children.* Eldersburg, MD: Author. Order from Linda Burkhart, 6201 Candle Court, Eldersburg, MD 21784.

Burkhart, L. (1985). *More homemade battery devices for severely handicapped children, with suggested activities.* Eldersburg, MD: Author. Order from same as above.

Burkhart, L. (1987). *Using computers and speech synthesis to facilitate communicative interaction with young and/or severely handicapped children.* College Park, MD: Author. Order from same as above.

Burkhart, L. (1993). *Total augmentative communication in the early childhood classroom.* Eldersburg. MD: Author. Order from same as above.

Goossens', C. & Crain, S. S. (1992). *Utilizing switch interfaces with children who are severely physically challenged.* Austin, TX: Pro-Ed.

Goossens', C., Crain, S., & Elder, P. (1992). *Engineering the preschool environment for interactive symbolic communication: An emphasis on the developmental period, 18 months to five years.* Birmingham, AL: Southeast Augmentative Communication Conference Publications. Order from : Southeast Augmentative Communication Conference, 2430 11th Ave. North, Birmingham, AL 35234.

Goossens', C., Crain, S., & Elder, P. *Communication display books for engineered environments: Preschool environments Books I and II.* Birmingham, AL: Southeast Augmentative Communication Publications. Order from same as above.

Hohman, C., Carmody, B., & McCabe-Branz, C. (1995). *High/Scope buyer's guide to children's software.* Ypsilanti, MI: High/Scope Press.

King-DeBaun, P. *STORYTIME: Stories, symbols and emergent literacy activities for young special needs children.* Park City, UT: Creative Communicating. Order from: Creative Communicating, P.O. Box 3358, Park City, UT 84060.

Levin, J. & Scherfenberg, L. (1987). *Selection and use of simple technology: In home, work and community settings.* Minneapolis: AbleNet.

Musselwhite, C. (1986). *Adaptive play for special needs children.* San Diego, CA: College Hill Press/Little Brown & Co. Order from: Pro-Ed, 5341 Industrial Oaks Blvd., Austin, TX 78735.

Musselwhite, C., & King-DeBaun, P. (1997). *Emergent literacy success: Merging technology and whole language for students with disabilities.* Park City, UT: Creative Communicating. Order from: Creative Communicating, P.O. Box 3358, Park City, UT 84060.

Wright, C., & Nomura, M. (1990). *From toys to computers.* San Jose, CA: Order from: Christine Wright, P.O. Box 700242, San Jose, CA 95170.

APPENDIX E

Assistive Technology Conferences

Annual Closing the Gap Conference (Fall)

Contact: Closing the Gap, Inc.
P.O. Box 68
526 Main Street
Henderson, MN 56044
(507) 248-3294
email: info@closingthegap.com
http://www.closingthegap.com

Technology and Persons with Disabilities Conference (Spring)

Contact: Center on Disabilities
California State University, Northridge
18111 Nordhoff St.
Northridge, CA 91330
(818) 677-2578
email: LTM@SCUN.EDU
http://www.csun.edu/cod/

ConnSENSE (Summer)

Contact: Chauncy N. Rucker, Director
A. J. Pappanikou Center Technology Lab
U-64, 249 Glenbrook Road
Storrs, CT 06269
(203) 486-0165

RESNA Annual Conference (Summer)

Contact: RESNA
1700 North Moore Street, Suite 1540
Arlington, VA 22209-1903
email: natloffice@resna.org
http://www.resna.org/resna/resdir.htm

Annual Southeast Augmentative Communication Conference (Fall)

Contact: Southeast Augmentative Communication
Publications
2430 11th Ave. N.
Birmingham, AL 35234
(202) 251-0165

CEC Technology and Media (TAM) Division
Annual Conference (Winter)

Contact: John Langone, Program Chairperson
Dept. of Special Education
573 Aderhold Hall
The University of Georgia
Athens, GA 30602
(707) 542-4588
email: jlangone@coe.uga.edu
http://www.ucc.ucon.edu/~tam/

TASH Conference (Fall)

Contact: TASH
29 W. Susquehanna Avenue, Suite 210
Baltimore, MD 21204 (800) 482-TASH
email: dmarsh@tash.org

Florida Assistive Technology Impact Conference (Fall)

Contact: Mary Stoltz
2845 Cinnamon Bear Trail
Palm Harbor, FL 34684 (813) 781-1239
email: stoltzm@mail.firn.edu

APPENDIX F

Legislative Context for Assistive Technology

Legislative policies to encourage assistive technology use for young children with disabilities have emerged only in the last 10 years. The recent federal legislation has done much to encourage the continued development and use of assistive technology and, more important, to encourage the innovative approaches to apply these technologies. Other major legislative initiatives that specifically address the technology-related needs of young children with disabilities will be discussed with respect to how they affect technology service delivery to young children with disabilities and their families.

Education of the Handicapped Act Amendments of 1986

The passage of P.L. 99-457, now consolidated in the *Individuals with Disabilities Education Act* (IDEA) *of 1990*, established a program to provide early intervention services to infants and toddlers with disabilities and their families, and to provide funds for technology-related research and development in special education. With the enactment of P.L. 99-457, Congress mandated that services for young children with disabilities be based on a family-focused approach. The law requires that early intervention programs develop Individualized Family Service Plans (IFSPs) to identify both child and family goals for all service recipients (Hauser-Cram, Upshur, Krauss, & Shonkoff, 1988). Similarly, the legislation requires that a multidisciplinary team of professionals and family members participate in the development of the IFSP, which may identify a range of early intervention services, including assistive technology, for a child with a disability. Implicit in this approach is an emphasis on parent input into the availability of effective and appropriate resources and support that are provided to them.

The use of assistive, orthotic, and other related devices and services are specifically mentioned in the regulations as types of early intervention services that could be provided. These services include:

- Auditory training, aural rehabilitation, speech reading and listening device orientation and training, and other services.
- Hearing loss prevention services.
- Determining the child's needs for individual amplification, including selecting, fitting, and dispensing appropriate listening and vibrotactile devices and evaluation of those devices.
- Selecting, designing, and fabricating assistive and orthotic devices to promote the acquisition of functional skills.
- Designing and adapting learning environments and activities that promote the child's acquisition of skills in a variety of developmental areas, including cognitive processes and social interaction.
- Orthotic or related services that prevent or alleviate movement dysfunction and related functional problems (Parette, Hofmann, & VanBiervliet, 1994).

Technology-Related Assistance for Individuals with Disabilities Act of 1988

The impetus for the use of assistive technology evolves from the passage of the *Technology-Related Assistance for Individuals with Disabilities Act of 1988* (Tech Act—P.L. 100-407), which expands the availability of assistive technology services and devices for persons of all ages with disabilities. The enactment of the Tech Act was unique in many ways. First, it recognized the importance of assistive technology in the lives of individuals with disabilities. The Tech Act recognized a federal role in removing federal barriers to finance technology and provide technical assistance and other capacity-building support to the states. The intent of the Tech Act was to promote a systems change or service delivery model that will ultimately result in full access to appropriate assistive technology devices and services for individuals with disabilities. Second, it defined assistive technology in a broad sense that has now become universal for most federal, state, and local institutions. This "flagship" definition of assistive technology now appears in the *IDEA*, the *Vocational Rehabilitation Act*, and the *Developmental Disabilities Act*. Third, it established discretionary funds to states on a competitive basis to help them develop and implement consumer-responsive, statewide programs of technology-related assistance for all persons with disabilities. The purpose of the state grants was to provide assistive technology devices and services, train personnel to assist with service delivery, develop an information dissemination system, fund resources to pay for assistive technology devices and services, design public awareness projects, and coordinate existing technology services among state agencies (Wallace, Flippo, Barcus, & Behrmann, 1995).

Technology-Related Assistance for Individuals with Disabilities Act Amendments of 1994

The reauthorization of the Tech Act in 1994 (P.L. 103-218) extends congressional support of the original Tech Act to support state efforts to continue developing plans and working toward incorporating assistive technology into state systems in anticipation of the end of federal funding (which is projected to occur 10 years after a program begins or March 1999). The primary purpose of the Tech Act is to support state systems change activities. Under Title I, Congress directed states to perform specific activities leading to systems change and increased advocacy that include (a) development and implementation of strategies to overcome barriers regarding access to, provision of, and funding for devices and services; (b) technology advocacy for family members in the selection and procurement of assistive technology; (c) outreach and advocacy for underrepresented and rural populations; and (d) development and implementation of strategies to ensure the timely acquisition of technology. The focus is on improving access for individuals in rural areas and minority populations since assistive technology service delivery with these underserved and underrepresented populations is an ongoing issue for service providers (Krajicek & Tompkins, 1993; Parette, 1994; Parette, Bartlett, & Holder-Brown, 1994).

The Tech Act of 1994 also includes key definitions to strengthen implementation of state activities and clarify federal expectations. Terms defined in the Act include consumer-responsive activities, advocacy services, and systems change and advocacy activities. These new definitions underscore the critical part consumers have in planning and implementing state and local assistive technology systems. Consumer responsive indicates that activities or programs are to be easily accessible and usable to individuals with disabilities and, when appropriate, their families. Activities are to be conducted in a timely, appropriate manner that facilitates the full, meaningful participation of individuals with disabilities, as well as their families, in decisions related to the provision of assistive technology devices and services (P.L. 103-218, §4[5]).

Advocacy services are to assist individuals with disabilities and their families gain access to assistive technology devices and services. Advocacy services can include dissemination of information and individual case management, representation of individuals with disabilities, and training of individuals with disabilities and their families to successfully conduct advocacy for themselves (P.L. 103-218, §4[1]).

Systems change and advocacy activities are designed to help facilitate and increase access to, provision of, and funding for assistive technology devices and services on a permanent basis. These advocacy and system change efforts are meant to result in laws, regulations, policies, and practices or organizational structures to empower individuals with disabilities and family members in selecting and obtaining assistive technology (P.L. 103-218, §4[12]; Wallace et al., 1995).

REFERENCES

Abidin, R.R. (1986). *Parenting stress index: Manual* (PSI) (2nd ed.). Charlottesville, VA: Pediatric Psychology Press.

Ainlay, S.C., Becker, G., & Coleman, L. (1986). *The dilemma of difference: A multidisciplinary view of stigma*. New York: Plenum Press.

Ainsa, P. A., Murphy, D., Thouvenelle, S., & Wright, J. L. (1994). Family choice at home and school. In J. L. Wright & D. D. Shade (Eds.), *Young children: Active learners in a technological age* (pp. 121-131). Washington, DC: National Association for the Education of Young Children.

Allaire, J.H., Gressard, R.P., Blackman, J.A., & Hostler, S.L. (1991). Children with severe speech impairments: Caregiver survey of AAC use. *Augmentative and Alternative Communication, 7*, 248-255.

Almy, M., Monighan, P., Scales, B., & Van Hoorn, J. (1984). Recent research on play: The teacher's perspective. In L.G. Katz (Ed.), *Current topics in early childhood education*, (Vol. 5) (pp. 1-25). Norwood, NJ: Ablex.

Alper, S.K., Schloss, P.J., & Schloss, C.N. (1994). *Families of students with disabilities. Consultation and advocacy*. Boston: Allyn & Bacon.

Althen, G. (1988). *American ways: A guide for foreigners in the United States*. Yarmouth, ME: Intercultural Press.

American Nurses Association (1990). *National standards of nursing practice for early intervention services*. Rockville, MD: Author.

American Speech-Language-Hearing Association. (1995). *ASHA's building bridges: Multicultural preschool project. Assistive technology*. Rockville, MD: Author.

Anderson, M., & Goldberg, P.F. (1991). *Cultural competence in screening and assessment. Implications for services to young children with special needs ages birth through five*. Minneapolis, MN: PACER Center.

Anderson, N.B., & Battle, D.E. (1993). Cultural diversity in the development of language. In D.E. Battle (Ed.), *Communication disorders in multicultural populations* (pp. 158-182). Boston: Andover Medical Publishers.

Angelo, D.H. (1997). AAC in the family and home. In S. Glennen & D. DeCoste (Eds.), *The handbook of augmentative communication* (pp. 523-541). San Diego, CA: Singular Publishing.

Angelo, D.H., Jones, S.D., & Kokoska, S.M. (1995). A family perspective on augmentative and alternative communication: Families of young children. *Augmentative and Alternative Communication, 11*, 193-201.

Angelo, D.H., Kokoska, S.M., & Jones, S.D. (1996). A family perspective on augmentative and alternative communication: Families of adolescents and young adults. *Augmentative and Alternative Communication, 12*, 13-20.

Asbury, C., Walker, S., Maholmes, V., Rackley, R., & White, S. (1991). *Disability prevalence and demographic association among race/ethnic minorities in the United States: Implications for the 21st century.* Washington, DC: The Howard University Research and Training Center for Access to Rehabilitation and Economic Opportunity. NARIC Accession Number: XO10122.

Augusto, C.R., & Schroeder, P.W. (1995). Ensuring equal access to information for people who are blind or visually impaired. *Journal of Visual Impairment and Blindness, 89*(4), 9-11.

Bailey, D.B., Jr. (1989). Issues and directions in preparing professionals to work with young handicapped children and their families. In J. Gallagher, P. Trohanis, & R. Clifford (Eds.), *Policy implementation and P.L. 99-457: Planning for young children with special needs* (pp. 97-132). Baltimore: Brookes.

Bailey, D.B., Jr. (1996). An overview of interdisciplinary training. In D. Bricker & A. Widerstrom (Eds.), *Preparing personnel to work with infants and young children and their families: A team approach* (pp. 3-21). Baltimore: Brookes.

Bailey, D.B., Jr., McWilliam, P.J., & Winton, P.J. (1992). Building family-centered practices in early intervention: A team-based model for change. *Infants and Young Children, 5*(1), 73-82.

Bailey, D.B., Palsha, S., & Simeonsson, R. (1991). Professional skills, concerns and perceived importance of work with families in early intervention. *Exceptional Children, 58*, 156-165.

Bailey, D.B., Jr., Simeonsson, R.J., Yoder, D.E., & Huntington, G.S. (1990). Preparing professionals to serve infants and toddlers with handicaps and their families: An integrative analysis across eight disciplines. *Exceptional Children, 57*, 26-34.

Barcus, M.J., Everson, J.M., & Hall, S. (1987). Inservice training in human service agencies and organizations. In J.M. Everson, M.J. Barcus, J.S. Moon, & M.V. Morton (Eds.), *Achieving outcomes: A guide to interagency training in transition and supported employment* (pp. 1-58). Richmond: Virginia Commonwealth University/Rehabilitation Research Training Center.

Baroni, M.A., Tuthill, P., Feenan, L., & Schroeder, M. (1994). Technology-dependent infants and young children: A retrospective case analysis of service coordination across state lines. *Infants and Young Children, 7*(1), 69-78.

Barrera, I. (1993). Effective and appropriate instruction for all children: The challenge of cultural/linguistic diversity and young children with special needs. *Topics in Early Childhood Special Education, 13*(4), 461-487.

Baruth, L.G., & Manning, M.L. (1992). *Multicultural education of children and adolescents.* Boston: Allyn & Bacon.

Batavia, A.I., & Hammer, G. (1990). Toward the development of consumer-based criteria for the evaluation of assistive devices. *Journal of*

Rehabilitation Research and Development, 27, 425-436.

Battle, D.E. (1993). *Communication disorders in multicultural populations.* Boston: Andover Medical Publishers.

Baumgart, D., Brown, L., Pumpian, I., Nisbet, J., Ford, A., Sweet, M., Messina, R., & Schroeder, J. (1982). Principle of partial participation and individualize adaptations in education programs for severely handicapped students. *The Journal of The Association for Persons with Severe Handicaps, 7*(2), 17-27.

Becker, G., & Kaufman, S. (1988). Old age, rehabilitation, and research: A review of the issues. *The Gerontologist, 28*(4), 459-468.

Becker, H. (1990). How computers are used in United States' schools: Basic data from the 1989 I.E.A. Computers in Education Survey. *Journal of Educational Computing Research, 7,* 385-406.

Beckman, P.J. (1991). Comparison of mothers' and fathers' perceptions of the effect of young children with and without disabilities. *American Journal of Mental Retardation, 95,* 585-595.

Beckman, P.J., Robinson, C.C., Rosenberg, S., & Filer, J. (1994). Family involvement in early intervention. The evolution of family-centered services. In L.J. Johnson, R.J. Gallagher, M.J. LaMontagne, J.B. Jordan, J.J. Gallagher, P.L. Hutinger, & M.B. Karnes (Eds.), *Meeting early intervention challenges. Issues from birth to three* (2nd ed.) (pp. 13-31). Baltimore: Brookes.

Behrmann, M.M. (1994). Assistive technology for students with mild disabilities. *Intervention in School and Clinic, 30,* 70-83.

Behrmann, M.M. (1995). Assistive technology training. In K.F. Flippo, K.J. Inge, & J.M. Barcus (Eds.), *Assistive technology: A resource for school, work, and community* (pp. 211-222). Baltimore: Brookes.

Behrmann, M.M., Jones, J.K., & Wilds, M.L. (1989). Technology intervention for very young children with disabilities. *Infants and Young Children, 1*(4), 66-77.

Behrmann, M., & Lahm, L. (1983). Multiple handicapped babies using computers. *Closing the Gap, 14,* 6-8.

Behrmann, M.M., & Schepis, M. (1994). Assistive technology assessment: A multiple case study review of three approaches with students with physical disabilities during the transition from school to work. *Journal of Vocational Rehabilitation, 4*(3), 202-210.

Beukelman, D.R., & Mirenda, P. (1992). Augmentative and alternative communication: Management of severe communication disorders in children and adults. Baltimore: Brookes.

Bennett, A.T. (1988). Gateways to powerlessness: Incorporating Hispanic deaf children and families into formal schooling. *Disability, Handicap and Society, 3*(2), 119-151.

Bennett, T., & Watson, A.L. (1993). A new perspective on training: Competence-building. *Journal of Early Intervention, 17,* 309-321.

Bennett, C.I. (1990). *Comprehensive multicultural education.* Needham Heights, MA: Allyn and Bacon.

Bernstein, G.S., & Zarnick, J.P. (1982). Proactive identification of staff development needs: A model and methodology. *The Journal of the*

Association for the Severely Handicapped, 7, 97-104.

Berry, J.O. (1987). Strategies for involving parents in programs for young children using augmentative and alternative communication. *Augmentative and Alternative Communication, 3*, 90-93.

Blackstone, S. (1993). For consumers. Culture in the community. *Augmentative Communication News, 6*(2), 1-3.

Blackstone, S.W. (Ed.). (1994). *Augmentative Communication News, 7*(6).

Bowe, F.G. (1995). *Birth to five: Early childhood special education.* New York: Delmar.

Bowman, B. T., & Beyer, E. R. (1994). Thoughts on technology and early childhood education. In J. L. Wright & D. D. Shade (Eds.), *Young children: Active learners in a technological age* (pp. 19-30). Washington, DC: National Association for the Education of Young Children.

Brady, E., & Hill, S. (1984). Young children and microcomputers: Research issues and directions. *Young Children, 39*(3), 49-61.

Bradley, R.H., Parette, H.P., & VanBiervliet, A. (1995). Families of young technology-dependent children and the social worker. *Social Work in Health Care, 21*(1), 23-37.

Bredekamp, S. (1992). *Developmentally appropriate practice in early childhood programs serving children birth through age 8.* Washington, DC: National Association for the Education of Young Children.

Bricker, D., & Cripe, J.J. (1992). *An activity-based approach to early intervention.* Baltimore: Brookes.

Briggs, M.H. (1996). Creating change

on early intervention teams: A systems view. *Infant-Toddler Intervention, 6*, 333-347.

Brinker, R., & Lewis, M. (1982). Making the world work with microcomputers: A learning prosthesis for handicapped infants. *Exceptional Children, 49*, 163-170.

Brinker, R.P., & Lewis, M.L. (1982). Contingency intervention. In J.D. Anderson (Ed.), *Curricula for high-risk and handicapped infants* (pp. 37-44). University of North Carolina, Chapel Hill: Technical Assistance Development Systems.

Brody, S.J., & Ruff, G. (1986). *Aging and rehabilitation: Advances in the state of the art.* New York: Springer.

Bronfenbrenner, U. (1979). *The ecology of human development.* Cambridge, MA: Harvard University Press.

Brotherson, M.J., Cook, C.C., & Parette, H.P. (1996). A home-centered approach to assistive technology provision for young children with disabilities. *Focus on Autism and Other Developmental Disabilities, 11*(2), 86-95.

Brotherson, M.J., & Goldstein, B. (1992). Time as a resource and constraint for parents of young children with disabilities: Implication for early intervention services. *Topics in Early Childhood Special Education, 12*, 508-527.

Brotherson, M.J., Oakland, M.J., Secrist-Mertz, C., Litchfield, R., & Larson, K. (1995). Quality of life issues for families who make the decision to use a feeding tube for their child. *Journal of the Association for Persons with Severe Handicaps, 20*, 202-212.

Brown, D. (1990). Facing the future: Readying rehabilitation in the year

2000. *Journal of Rehabilitation*, *56*(1), 17-20.

Bruder, M.B. (1996). An inservice model to build state personnel capacities on collaborations with families, staff, and agencies for early intervention. Unpublished Final Report submitted to the U.S. Department of Education.

Bruder, M.B., & Bologna, T.M. (1993). Collaboration and service coordination for effective early intervention. In W. Brown, S.K. Thurman, & L.F. Pearl (Eds.), *Family-centered early intervention with infants and toddlers: Innovative cross-disciplinary approaches* (pp. 103-127). Baltimore: Paul H. Brookes.

Bruder, M.B., Brinckerhoff, J., & Spence, K. (1991). Meeting the personnel needs of P.L. 99-457: A model interdisciplinary institute for infant specialists. *Teacher Education and Special Education, 14*, 77-87.

Bruder, M.B., Lippman, C., & Bologna, T.M. (1994). Personnel preparation in early intervention: Building capacity for program expansion within institutions of higher education. *Journal of Early Intervention, 18*, 103-110.

Bruder, M.B., & Nikitas, T. (1992). Changing the professional practice of early interventionists: An inservice model to meet the needs of Public Law 99-457. *Journal of Early Intervention, 16*, 173-180.

Buckleitner, W. (1996). The case for computers. *Early Childhood Today, 10*(5), 25-27.

Burkhart, L.J. (1980). *Homemade battery powered toys and educational devices for severely handicapped children*. Santa Barbara, CA: Special Needs Project.

Burkhart, L.J. (1985). *More homemade battery powered toys and educational devices for severely handicapped children*. Santa Barbara, CA: Special Needs Project.

Burkhart, L.J. (1993). *Total augmentative communication in the early childhood classroom*. Santa Barbara, CA: Special Needs Project.

Butler, C. (1988). High tech tots: Technology for mobility, manipulation, communication, and learning in early childhood. *Infants and Young Children, 1*, 66-73.

Butler, C. (1989). High tech tots: Technology for mobility, manipulation, communication, and learning in early childhood. *Infants and Young Children, 1*, 66-73.

Butler, C., Okamoto, G.A., McKay, T.M. (1983). Powered mobility for very young disabled children. *Developmental Medicine and Child Neurology, 25*, 472-474.

Buzolich, M, Harris, O., Lloyd, L.L., Soto, G., & Taylor, O.L. (1994, November). *Multicultural issues in augmentative and alternative communication*. Miniseminar presented at the American Speech-Language-Hearing Association Annual Convention, New Orleans, LA.

Campbell, P.H., Bricker, W.A., & Esposito, L. (1980). Technology in the education of the severely handicapped. In B. Wilcox & B. York (Eds.), *Quality education for the severely handicapped* (pp. 223-246). Washington, DC: U.S. Department of Education.

Campbell, P., & Fein, G. (Eds.). (1986). *Young children and microcomputers*. Englewood Cliffs, NJ: Prentice-Hall.

Campbell, P.H., McGregor, G., &

Nasik, E. (1994). Promoting the development of young children through use of technology. In P.L. Safford, B. Spodek, & O.N. Saracho (Eds.), *Early Childhood Special Education, Vol. 5.* (pp. 192-217). New York: Teachers College Press.

Capone, A., Hull, K., & DiVenere, N. (1997). Parent professional partnerships in preservice and inservice instruction. In P.J. Winton, J.A. McCollum, & C. Catlett (Eds.), *Reforming personnel preparation in early intervention: Issues, models, and practical strategies* (pp. 435-451). Baltimore: Brookes.

Carey, D.M., & Sale, P. (1994). Practical considerations in the use of technology to facilitate the inclusion of students with severe disabilities. *Technology and Disability, 3,* 77-86.

Catlett, C., & Winton, P.J. (1997). Putting it all together: The nuts and bolts of personnel preparation. In P.J. Winton, J.A. McCollum, & C. Catlett (Eds.), *Reforming personnel preparation in early intervention: Issues, models, and practical strategies* (pp. 527-544). Baltimore: Brookes.

Cavalier, A.R., & Mineo, B. (1987). The application of technology in the classroom and workplace: Unvoiced premises and ethical issues. In A. Gartner & T. Joe (Eds.), *Images of the disabled/disabling images* (pp. 129-141). New York: Praeger.

Center for Special Education Technology. (1991). *NASA-developed technology for students with disabilities.* Reston, VA: Council for Exceptional Children. (ERIC Product Reproduction Service No. ED 338 005)

Chan, S. (1986). Parents of exceptional Asian children. In M.K. Kitano & P.C. Chinn (Eds.), *Exceptional Asian children and youth* (pp. 12-28). Reston, VA: Council for Exceptional Children.

Chan, S. (1990). Early intervention with culturally diverse families of infants and toddlers with disabilities. *Infants and Young Children, 3*(2), 78-87.

Chin, J.L. (1983). Diagnostic considerations in working with Asian Americans. *American Journal of Orthopsychiatry, 53*(1), 100-109.

Church, G. (1992). Adaptive access for microcomputers. In G. Church & S. Glennen (Eds.), *The handbook of assistive technology* (pp. 123-172). San Diego, CA: Singular.

Church, G., & Glennen, S. (1992). *The handbook of assistive technology.* San Diego, CA: Singular.

Church, G., & Glennen, S. (1992). Assistive technology program development. In G. Church & S. Glennen (Eds.), *The handbook of assistive technology* (pp. 1-26). San Diego, CA: Singular Publishing Group.

Clay, J. (1993). Prevention of primary and secondary disabilities. In T.J. Wright & P. Leung (Eds.), *The unique needs of minorities with disabilities: Setting an agenda for the future* (pp. 113-117). Washington, DC: National Council on Disability.

Clements, D. H. (1987). Computers and young children: A review of the research. *Young Children, 43*(1), 34-44.

Clements, D. H., & Nastasi, B. K. (1992). Computers and early childhood education. In M. Gettinger, S. N. Elliot, & T. R. Kratochwill (Eds.), *Advances in school psychology: Preschool and early childhood treatment directions* (pp. 187-246).

Hillsdale, NJ: Erlbaum.

Clements, D. H., Nastasi, B. K., & Swaminathan, S. (1993). Young children and computers: Crossroads and directions from research. *Young Children, 48*(2), 56-64.

Clements, D. H., & Swaminathan, S. (1995). Technology and school change: New lamps for old? *Childhood Education, 71*(5), 275-281.

Collins, B.C., Hemmeter, M.L., Schuster, J.W., & Stevens, K.B. (1996). Using team teaching to deliver coursework via distance learning technology. *Teacher Education and Special Education, 19*, 49-58.

Condry, S. (1989). *A literature review of topics concerning children who are technology-supported and their families.* Lawrence, KS: Beach Center on Families and Disability.

CO-NET (Cooperative Assistive Technology Database Dissemination Network). (1991). *Hyper-ABLEDATA database, CO-NET CD-ROM version* (3rd ed.). Madison, WI: Trace Research and Development Center.

Cook, R.E., Tessier, A., & Klein, M.D. (1992). *Adapting early childhood curricula for children with special needs.* New York: Macmillan.

Cook, R.E., Tessier, A., & Klein, M.D. (1996). *Adapting early childhood curricula for children in inclusive settings* (4th ed.). Englewood Cliffs, NJ: Merrill.

Cooper, C.S., & Allred, K.W. (1992). A comparison of mothers' versus fathers' needs for support in caring for a young child with special needs. *Infant-Toddler Intervention, 2*, 205-221.

Correa, V. (1987). Involving culturally diverse families in the educational process. In S.H. Fradd & M.J. Weismantel (Eds.), *Meeting the needs of culturally and linguistically different students: A handbook for educators* (pp. 130-144). Boston: College Hill.

Council of Exceptional Children (CEC) IDEA Testimony: Call for Action. (1994). *CEC Today, September,* 1, 6.

Courtnage, L., & Smith-Davis, J. (1987). Interdisciplinary team training: A national survey of special education teacher training programs. *Exceptional Children, 53*, 451-458.

Cox, A. (1996). Disciplinary perspectives on training: Preparing nurses. In D. Bricker & A. Widerstrom (Eds.), *Preparing personnel to work with infants and young children and their families* (pp. 161-179). Baltimore: Brookes.

Crais, E.R. (1991). Moving from "parent involvement" to family-centered services. *American Journal of Speech-Language Pathology, 1*, 5-8.

Crais, E.R. (1991). *A practical guide to embedding family-centered content into existing speech-language pathology coursework.* Chapel Hill, NC: Carolina Institute for Research on Infant Personnel Preparation. Frank Porter Graham Child Development Center.

Cramer, S.F. (1992). Assistive technology training for special educators. *Technology and Disability (3)*, 1-5.

Croft, D.J., & Hess, R.D. (1980). *An activities handbook for teachers of young children* (3rd ed.). Boston: Houghton Mifflin.

Cross, T.L., Bazron, B.J., Dennis, K.W., & Isaacs, M.R. (1989). *Towards a culturally competent system of care.* Washington, DC: CASSP Technical Assistance Center.

Culp, D.M. (1987). Outcome measurement: The impact of communication augmentation. *Seminars in Speech and Language, 9,* 169-184.

Culp, D.M., Ambrosi, D.M., Berniger, T.M., & Mitchell, J.O. (1986). Augmentative and alternative communication aid use—A follow-up study. *Augmentative and Alternative Communication, 2,* 19-24.

Damen, L. (1987). *Culture learning: The fifth dimension in the language classroom.* Reading, MA: Addison-Wesley.

Daniels, L.E., Sparling, J.W., Reilly, M., & Humphry, R. (1995). Use of assistive technology with young children with severe and profound disabilities. *Infant-Toddler Intervention, 5,* 91-112.

Darling, R.B., & Baxter, C. (1996). *Families in focus: Sociological methods in early intervention.* Austin, TX: PRO-ED.

Davidson, J.I. (1996). *Emergent literacy and dramatic play in early education.* Albany, NY: Delmar.

Dederer, T., Ellis, T., Thompson, R., Cunningham, J., Lam, C., & Chan, F. (1991). Utilization of assistive technology in state vocational rehabilitation: A needs assessment. *Rehabilitation Education, 5,* 265-272.

Derer, K., Polsgrove, L., & Rieth, H. (1996). A survey of assistive technology applications in schools and recommendations for practice. *Journal of Special education Technology, 8,* 62-80.

Dillard, D. (1989). *National study on abandonment of technology. 1989 Annual Report on the National Rehabilitation Hospital's Rehabilitation Engineering Center's Evaluation of Assistive Technology* (Cooperative Agreement No. H133E0016).

Washington, DC: National Institute on Disability and Rehabilitation Research.

Doernberg, N.L. (1978). Some negative effects on family integration of health and educational services for young handicapped children. *Rehabilitation Literature, 39,* 107-110.

Donahue-Kilburg, G. (1992). *Family-centered early intervention for communication disorders. Prevention and treatment.* Gaithersburg, MD: Aspen.

Drotar, D., & Sturn, L. (1989). Training of psychologists as infant specialists. *Infants and Young Children, 2*(2), 58-66.

Dunst, C.J., Cushing, P., & Vance, S.D. (1985). Response contingent learning in profoundly handicapped infants: A social systems perspective. *Analysis and Intervention in Developmental Disabilities, 5,* 33-47.

Dunst, C., Trivette, C., & Deal, A. (Eds.). (1988). *Enabling and empowering families.* Cambridge, MA: Brookline Books.

Dunst, C.J., & Paget, K.D. (1991). Parent-professional partnerships and family empowerment. In M. Fine (Ed.), *Collaborative involvement with parents of exceptional children* (pp. 25-44). Brandon, VT: Clinical Psychology Publishing Co.

Dunst, C.J., Trivette, C.M., & Deal, A.G. (1994) *Supporting and strengthening families.* Cambridge, MA: Brookline Books.

Erickson, K. & Koppenhaver, D. (1995). Developing a literacy program for children with severe disabilities. *The Reading Teacher, 48,* 676-684.

Everix, N. (1991). *Ethnic celebrations around the world: Festivals, holi-*

days and celebrations. Carthage, IL: Good Apple.

Fallon, M.A. (1996). Case-study teaching: A tool for training early interventionists. *Infants and Young Children, 8*(4), 59-62.

Fell, H.J., & Ferrier, L.J. (1994). The Baby Babble Blanket. *Technology for Early Intervention.*

Fenichel, E. (1992). *Learning through supervision and mentorship to support the development of infants, toddlers and their families: A source book.* Arlington, VA: Zero to Three/National Center for Clinical Infant Programs.

Fenichel, E., & Eggbeer, L. (1990). Educating allies: Issues and recommendations in the training of practitioners to work with infants, toddlers, and their families. *Zero to Three, 10*(1), 1-7.

Ferguson, D.L., & Baumgart, D. (1991). Partial participation revisited. *The Journal of The Association for Persons with Severe Handicaps, 16,* 218-227.

Flemming, B.M., Hamilton, D.S., & Hicks, J.D. (1977). *Resources for creative teaching in early childhood education.* New York: Harcourt Brace.

Gallagher, J.J., Harbin, G., Eckland, J., & Clifford, R. (1994). State diversity and policy implementation. In L.J. Johnson, R.J. Gallagher, M.. . LaMontagne, J.B. Jordan, J.J. Gallagher, P.L. Hutinger, & M.B. Karnes (Eds.), *Meeting early intervention challenges: Issues from birth to three* (2nd ed.) (pp. 235-250). Baltimore: Brookes.

Galvin, J.C. (1990, March). *Perspectives on private insurance: The who and how of decisions of coverage.* Paper presented to the RESNA Technical Assistance Project Workshop, Funding Assistive Technology for Individuals with Disabilities: A Blueprint for Change, Washington, DC.

Gardner, H. (1983). *Frames of mind.* New York: Basic Books.

Gardner, H. (1993). *Multiple intelligences.* New York: Basic Books.

Garshelis, J.A., & McConnell, S.R. (1993). Comparison of family needs assessed by mothers, individual professionals, and interdisciplinary teams. *Journal of Early Intervention, 17*(1), 36-49.

Gilson, B.B., & Huss, D.S. (1995). Mobility: Getting to where you want to go. In K.F. Flippo, K.J. Inge, & J.M. Barcus (Eds.), *Assistive technology: A resource for school, work, and community* (pp. 87-103). Baltimore: Brookes.

Glennen, S. (1992). Augmentative and alternative communication. In G. Church & S. Glennen (Eds.), *The handbook of assistive technology* (pp. 93-122). San Diego, CA: Singular.

Goossens', C., & Crain, S.S. (1992). *Utilizing switch interfaces with children who are severely physically challenged.* Austin, TX: PROED.

Goossens', C., Crain, S., & Elder, P. (1994). *Communication display books for engineered environments: Preschool environments Books I and II.* Birmingham, AL: Southeast Augmentative Communication Publications.

Haddad, A. (1992). The long-term implications of caring for a ventilator-dependent child at home. *Home Healthcare Nurse, 10,* 10-11, 57.

Hall, E.T. (1974). *Beyond culture.* Garden City, NY: Anchor Books.

Hanft, B., Burke, J.P., & Swenson-Miller, K. (1996). Disciplinary perspectives on training: Preparing occupational therapists. In D. Bricker & A. Widerstrom (Eds.), *Preparing personnel to work with infants and young children and their families* (pp. 115-134). Baltimore: Brookes.

Hanft, B., & Humphry, R. (1989). Training occupational therapists in early intervention. *Infants and Young Children, 1,*(4)54-65.

Hanline, M.F., & Daley, S.E. (1992). Family coping strategies and strengths in Hispanic, African-American, and Caucasian families of young children. *Topics in Early Childhood Special Education, 12*(3), 351-366.

Hanson, M.J. (1992). Families with Anglo-European roots. In E.W. Lynch & M.J. Hanson, *Developing cross-cultural competence: A guide for working with young children and their families* (pp. 65-87). Baltimore: Brookes.

Hanson, M.J., & Hanline, M.F. (1990). Parenting a child with a disability: A longitudinal study of parental stress and adaptation. *Journal of Early Intervention, 14*, 234-248.

Hanson, M.J., & Lynch, E.W. (1995). *Early intervention. Implementing child and family services for infants and toddlers who are at risk or disabled* (2nd ed.). Austin, TX: PRO-ED.

Hanson, M.J., Lynch, E.W., & Wayman, K.I. (1990). Honoring the cultural diversity of families when gathering data. *Topics in Early Childhood Special Education, 10*, 112-131.

Harbin, G.L., & McNulty, B.A. (1990). Policy implementation: Perspectives on service coordination and inter-agency cooperation. In S.L. Meisels & J.B. Shonkoff (Eds.), *Handbook of early intervention* (pp. 700-722). Cambridge, England: Cambridge University Press.

Harris, D. (1982). Communication interaction process involving nonvocal physically handicapped children. *Topics in Language Disorders, 2*, 21-37.

Harris, P. (1988). Sometimes pediatric home care doesn't work. *American Journal of Nursing, 88*, 851-854.

Harry, B. (1992). *Cultural diversity, families, and the special education system.* New York: Teachers College Press.

Harry, B. (1995, November). *Leaning forward or bending over backwards: Cultural reciprocity in working with families.* Presentation to the 11th Annual International Early Childhood Conference on Children with Special Needs, Orlando, FL.

Harry, B., Allen, N., & McLaughlin, M. (1992, April). *Communication versus compliance: Working with African American parents in special education.* Paper presented at the Annual Meeting of the American Educational Research Association, San Francisco.

Harry, B., Grenot-Scheyer, M., Smith-Lewis, M., Park, H.S., Xin, F., & Schwartz, I. (1995). Developing culturally inclusive services for persons with severe disabilities. *Journal of the Association for the Severely Handicapped, 20*, 99-109.

Haugland, S. W. (1992). The effect of computer software on preschool children's developmental gains. *Journal of Computing in Childhood Education, 3*(1), 14-30.

Haugland, S.W., & Shade, D.D. (1990).

Developmental evaluations of software for young children, 1990 Edition. Albany, NY: Delmar Publishers.

Hayward, B.J., & Elliott, B.G. (1992). *National evaluation of state grants for technology-related assistance for individuals with disabilities programs. Final report. Perspectives of consumers: Findings from focus groups* (Vol. II). Research Triangle Park: Research Triangle Institute.

Hayward, B., Tashjian, M.D., & Wehman, P. (1995). Development of assistive technology systems. In K.F. Flippo, K.J. Inge, & J.M. Barcus (Eds.), *Assistive technology: A resource for school, work, and community* (pp. 23-53). Baltimore: Brookes.

Hearthsong Catalog (1996). California locations: (800) 325-2502.

Hecht, M.L., Andersen, P.A., & Ribeau, S.A. (1989). The cultural dimensions of nonverbal communication. In M.K. Asante & W.B. Gudykunst (Eds.), *Handbook of international and intercultural communication* (pp. 163-185). Newbury Park, CA: Sage.

Henniger, M.L. (1994). Computers and preschool children's play: Are they compatible? *Journal of Computing in Childhood Education, 5* (3/4), 231-239.

Hetzroni, O.E., & Harris, O.L. (1996). Cultural aspects in the development of AAC users. *Augmentative and Alternative Communication, 12,* 52-58.

Hofmann, A. (1988). Funding: How you can make it work. In C.A. Costor (Ed.), *Planning and implementing augmentative communication services delivery* (pp. 80-93). Washington, DC: RESNA Press.

Holder-Brown, L., & Parette, H.P. (1992). Children with disabilities who use assistive technology: Ethical considerations. *Young Children, 47,* 73-77.

Howard, J., Greyrose, E., & Beckwith, L. (Spring, 1996). Teacher-facilitated microcomputer activities: Enhancing social play and affect in young children with disabilities. *Journal of Special Education Technology, 13*(1), 36-46.

Huer, M.B. (1994). *A master's program in speech-language pathology with special emphasis in augmentative and alternative communication and multi-culturalism.* Grant funded by the U.S. Department of Education, Training Personnel for the Education of the Handicapped (No. H029B40232).

Huer, M.B., & Lloyd, L.L. (1990). AAC users' perspectives on augmentative and alternative communication. *Augmentative and Alternative Communication, 6,* 242-249.

Hutinger, P. (1987). Computer-based learning for young children. In J.L. Roopnarine & J.E. Johnson (Eds.), *Approaches to early childhood education* (pp. 213-234). Columbus, OH: Charles E. Merrill.

Hutinger, P.L. (1994). *State of practice: How assistive technologies are used in educational programs of children with multiple disabilities.* Final report for the project *Effective use of technology to meet educational goals of children with disabilities* (PR#180R10020). Macomb, IL: Western Illinois University.

Hutinger, P.L. (1995). *Technology Inservice Project (TIP) Final Report.* Macomb, IL: Western Illinois University. (ERIC Document Reproduction Service No. 385991)

Hutinger, P.L. (1996). Computer applications in programs for young children with disabilities: Recurring themes. *Focus on Autism and Other Developmental Disabilities, 11*, 105-114.

Hutinger, P.L. (1987). Computer-based learning for young children. In J.L. Roopnarine & J.E. Johnson (Eds.), *Approaches to early childhood education* (pp. 213-234). Columbus, OH: Merrill.

Hutinger, P. (1987, May). *The effects of LOGO on preschool handicapped children.* Invitational Research Symposium on Special Education Technology, Center for Special Education Technology, Council for Exceptional Children, Washington, DC.

Hutinger, P., & Bell, D. (1997, February). *The effects of technology on emergent literacy in children with mild to moderate disabilities.* Presented at the Technology and Media Division of the Council for Exceptional Children 1997 Conference, San Jose, CA.

Hutinger, P., & Gentry, D. (1986). Microcomputer applications for young handicapped children: Report from the ACTT symposium. *Journal of the Division for Early Childhood, 10*, 240-246

Hutinger, P., Hall, S., Johanson, J., Robinson, L., Stoneburner, R., & Wisslead, K. (1994). *State of the practice: How assistive technologies are used in educational programs of children with multiple disabilities* (Final report). Macomb, IL: Western Illinois University.

Hutinger, P., Johanson, J., & Stoneburner, R. (1996). Assistive technol-ogy applications in educational programs of children with multiple disabilities: A case study report on the state of the practice. *Journal of Special Education Technology, 13*, 16-35.

Hutinger, P.L., Robinson, L., & Clark, L. (1990). *Technology applications to meet training challenges.* Macomb, IL: Macomb Projects, Western Illinois University.

Hutinger, P., Robinson, L., & Johanson, J. (1990). Adapting a computer curriculum to Head Start. *Children Today, 19*, 31-33.

Hutinger, P., & Ward, E. (1988, December). *Technology for the preschool handicapped classroom: New learning tools to assist the teacher.* Paper presented at CEC/TAM Conference on Special Education and Technology, Reno, NV.

HyperStudio 3.0 [Computer software]. (1993). El Cajon, CA: Roger Wagner Publishing.

Individuals with Disabilities Education Act (IDEA) of 1990, P.L. 101-476. (October 30, 1990). 20 U.S.C. 1400 et seq: *U.S. Statutes at Large, 104*, 1103-1151.

Individuals with Disabilities Education Act Amendments of 1991, P.L. 102-119 (October 7, 1991). 20 U.S.C. §1400 *et seq*: *U.S. Statutes at Large, 105*, 587-608.

Inge, K.J., Flippo, K.F., & Barcus, J.M. (1995). Staff development for assistive technology personnel. In K.F. Flippo, K.J. Inge, & J.M. Barcus (Eds.), *Assistive technology: A resource for school, work, and community* (pp. 223-243). Baltimore: Brookes.

Inge, K.J., & Shepherd, J. (1995). Assistive technology applications and strategies for school system personnel. In K.F. Flippo, K.J. Inge, & J.M. Barcus (Eds.), *Assistive technology: A resource for school, work, and community* (pp. 133-166). Baltimore: Brookes.

Jones, S.D., Angelo, D.H., & Kokoska, S.M. (1996). *Stressors and family supports: Families with children using augmentative and alternative technology.* Manuscript submitted for publication.

Joyce, B., & Showers, B. (1980). Improving inservice training: The message of research. *Educational Leadership, 37,* 379-385.

Kafai, Y., & Soloway, E. (1994). Computational gifts for the Barney generation. *Communications of the ACM, 37*(9), 19-22.

Kaufert, J., & Locker, D. (1990). Rehabilitation ideology and respiratory support technology. *Social Science and Medicine, 6*(19), 609-618.

Kaufman, M. (1989). Are dietitians prepared to work with handicapped infants? P.L. 99-457 offers new opportunities. *Journal of the American Dietetic Association, 89*(11), 1602-1605.

King-DeBaun, P. (1990). *Storytime: Stories, symbols, and emergent literacy activities for young, special needs children.* Park City, UT: Creative Communicating.

King-DeBaun, P. (1993). *Storytime! Just for fun.* Park City, UT: Creative Communicating.

King-DeBaun, P. (1994). *Storytime! Holiday Fun.* Park City, UT: Creative Communicating.

Kinney, P.G., & Blackhurst, A.E. (1987). Technology competencies for teachers of young children with severe handicaps. *Topics in Early Childhood Special Education, 7,* 105-115.

Kinsley, T.C., & Langone, J. (1995). Applications of technology for infants, toddlers, and preschoolers with disabilities. *Journal of Special Education Technology, 12,* 312-324.

Klein, C.E., Walker, D.W., & Foster, I.R. (1994/95). Accessing alternative assistive technology funding sources. *Case in Point, 9*(1), 33-40.

Klein, N.K., & Campbell, P. (1990). Preparing personnel to serve at-risk and disabled infants, toddlers, and preschoolers. In S.J. Meisels & M.P. Shonkoff (Eds.), *Handbook of early childhood intervention* (pp. 679-699). New York: Cambridge University Press.

Knowles, M. (1978). *The adult learner: A neglected species.* Houston: Gulf Publishing.

Knowles, M. (1980). *The modern practice of adult education: From pedagogy to androgogy.* Chicago: Association Press Follett Publishing Company.

Kontos, S., & File, N. (1992). Conditions of employment, job satisfaction, and job commitment among early intervention personnel. *Journal of Early Intervention, 16,* 155-165.

Kristeller, J. (1996). The age of multimedia. *Early Childhood Today, 10*(5), 2.

Kroeber, A., & Kluckhoehn, C. (1952). *Culture: A critical review of concepts and definitions.* New York: Random House.

Kumabe, K.T., Nishida, C., & Hepworth, D.H. (Eds.). (1985). *Bridging the ethnocultural diversities in social work and health.* Honolulu: University of Hawaii School of Social Work.

Kundu, M.M., & Dutta, A. (1995). *Implementation of counselor training programs at historically black colleges and universities in disability and diversity: New leadership for a new era.* Washington, DC: President's Committee on Employment of People with Disabilities in collaboration with Howard University Research and Training Center.

Kunkel, M.A. (1990). Expectations about counseling in relation to acculturation in Mexican-American and Anglo-American student samples. *Journal of Counseling Psychology, 37*, 286-292.

Lahm, E.A. (1996a). Filling the role of assistive technology specialist. *CEC Today, 3*(2), 14.

Lahm, E.A. (1996b). Software that engages young children with disabilities: A study of design features. *Focus on Autism and Other Developmental Disabilities, 11*(2), 115-124.

Laird, D. (1985). *Approaches to training and development* (2nd ed.). Reading, MA: Addison-Wesley.

LaPlante, M.P., Hendershot, G.E., & Moss, A.J. (1992, September 16). Assistive technology devices and home accessibility features: Prevalence, payment, need, and trends. *Advance Data* (National Center for Health Statistics), No. 217.

Leisk, D.J. (1957). *Harold's trip to the sky.* New York: Harper.

Lesar, S. (1998). Use of assistive technology with young children with disabilites: Current status and training needs. *Journal of Early Intervention, 21*, 146-159.

Lesar, S., Lowe, L.W., & Bartholomew, P.C. (1994, October). *Expanding the vision of assistive technology with young children and families.* Paper presented at the 10th Annual International Early Childhood Conference on Children with Special Needs, St. Louis, MO.

Levin, J., & Enselein, K. (1990). *Fun for everyone: A guide to adapted leisure activities for children with disabilities.* Minneapolis: Ablenet.

Levy, S.E., & Pilmer, S.L. (1992). The technology-assisted child. In M.C. Batshaw & Y.M. Perret (Eds.), *Children with disabilities: A medical primer* (pp. 137-157). Baltimore: Brookes.

Lian, M.J., & Aloia, G.F. (1994). Parental responses, roles, and responsibilities. In S.K. Alper, P.J. Schloss, & C.N. Schloss (Eds.), *Families of students with disabilities: Consultation and advocacy* (pp. 51-93). Boston: Allyn & Bacon.

Library of Congress, United States Copyright Office (1978). *General Guide to the Copyright Act of 1996.* Washington, DC: U.S. Government Printing Office.

Light, J., Collier, B., & Parnes, P. (1985). Communicative interaction between young nonspeaking physically disabled children and their primary caregivers: Part III-Modes of Communication. *Augmentative and Alternative Communication, 1*, 125-133.

Linder, T.W. (1993). *Transdisciplinary play-based assessment.* Baltimore: Brookes.

Losardo, A. (1996). Disciplinary perspectives on training: Preparing communication specialists. In D. Bricker & A. Widerstrom (Eds.), *Preparing personnel to work with infants and young children and their families: A team approach* (pp. 91-113). Baltimore: Brookes.

Lowenthal, B. (1996). Emerging trends in the training of early interventionists. *Infant-Toddler Intervention, 6*, 325-331.

Luborsky, M. (1991). The cultural context of polio biographies. *Orthopedics, 11*(14), 1173-1181.

Luborsky, M.R. (1993). Sociocultural factors shaping technology usage: Fulfilling the promise. *Technology and Disability, 2*(1) 71-78.

Ludlow, B.L. (1994). Using distance education to prepare early intervention personnel. *Infants and Young Children, 7*(1), 51-59.

Lynch, E.W. (1992). From culture shock to culture learning. In E.W. Lynch & M. Hanson (Eds.), *Developing cross-cultural competence: A guide for working with young children and their families* (pp. 19-59). Baltimore: Brookes.

Lynch, E.W., & Hanson, M.J. (Eds.) (1992a). *Developing cross-cultural competence. A guide for working with young children and their families.* Baltimore: Brookes.

Lynch, E.W., & Hanson, M.J. (1992b). Steps in the right direction. Implications for interventionists. In E.W. Lynch & M.J. Hanson (Eds.), *Developing cross-cultural competence. A guide for working with young children and their families* (pp. 355-370). Baltimore: Brookes.

Male, M. (1994). *Technology for inclusion* (2nd ed.). Boston: Allyn & Bacon.

Male, M. (1997). *Technology for inclusion.* Boston: Allyn & Bacon.

Mann, W.C., & Lane, J.P. (1991). *Assistive technology for persons with disabilities: The role of occupational therapy.* Rockville, MD: American Occupational Therapy Association.

Mann, W.C., & Lane, J.P. (1995). *Assistive technology for persons with disabilities. The role of occupational therapy* (2nd ed.). Rockville, MD: American Occupational Therapy Association.

Margalit, M. (1990). *Effective technology integration for disabled children: The family perspective.* New York: Springer-Verlag.

Marin, G., & Marin, B. (1991). Hispanics: Who are they? In G. Marin & B. Marin (Eds.), *Research with Hispanic populations* (pp. 1-7). Beverly Hills, CA: Sage.

Markowicz, A., & Reeb, K.G., Jr. (1989). Medicaid payment for rehabilitation equipment: Overview. *Assistive Technology, 1*, 11-17.

Martinez, C. (1977). Psychiatric consultation in a rural Mexican-American clinic. *Psychiatric Annals, 7*, 325-333.

Mayer, M. (1981). *Just Grandma and me.* Racine, WI: Western Publishing.

McBride, S.L., Brotherson, M.J., Joanning, H., Whiddon, D., & Demmitt, A. (1993). Implementation of family-centered services: Perceptions of families and professionals. *Journal of Early Intervention, 17*, 414-430.

McBride, S.L., Sharp, L., Hains, A.H., & Whitehead, A. (1995). Parents as co-instructors in preservice training: A pathway to family-centered practice. *Journal of Early Intervention, 19*, 343-389.

McCollum, J.A., & Bailey, D.B. (1991). Developing comprehensive personnel systems: Issues and alternatives. *Journal of Early Intervention, 15*, 57-65.

McCollum, J.A., & Stayton, V.D. (1996). Interdisciplinary training of early childhood special educators. In A. Widerstrom & D. Bricker (Eds.), *Preparing personnel to work with infants and young children and their families: A team approach* (pp. 67-90). Baltimore: Brookes.

McCollum, J.A., & Yates, T.J. (1994). Technical assistance for meeting early intervention personnel standards: Statewide processes based on peer review. *Topics in Early Childhood Special Education, 14*, 295-310.

McCord, S. (1995). *The storybook journey: Pathways to literacy through story and play*. Englewood Cliffs, NJ: Prentice-Hall.

McCormick, L. (1987). Comparison of the effects of a microcomputer activity and toy play on social and communication behaviors of young children. *Journal of the Division for Early Childhood, 11*, 195-205.

McEwen, I.R., & Shelden, M.L. (1996). Disciplinary perspectives on training: Preparing physical therapists. In D. Bricker & A. Widerstrom (Eds.), *Preparing personnel to work with infants and young children and their families* (pp. 135-159). Baltimore: Brookes.

McGonigel, M., & Garland, C. (1988). The individualized family service plan and the early intervention team: Team and family issues and recommended practices. *Infants and Young Children, 1*(1), 10-21.

McGuiness, K. (1982). *Stalking the elusive buck*. Boston: Environments Center, Massachusetts College of Art.

McNaughton, S. (1990). Gaining the most from AAC's growing years. *Augmentative and Alternative Communication, 6*(1), 2-14.

McNutty, B. (1988, May). *Assistive technology: The Colorado effort* (Senate Report 100-438). Paper and testimony presented to the Senate Subcommittee on the Handicapped, Senator Thomas Harkin (Chairperson), Washington, DC.

Mendelsohn, S. (1989, March). *Payment issues and options in the utilization of assistive technology*. Paper presented to the National Workshop on Implementing Technology Utilization, Washington, DC.

Meyers, L., & Beckwith, L. (November, 1988). *Motivation and language learning in Down syndrome children*. Final report for NICHD Grant No. HD16764-02.

Miller, D.L. (1979). *Mother's perception of Indian child development*. Unpublished research report, Institute for Scientific Analysis, San Francisco.

Miller, P.S. (1992). State interagency coordination for personnel development under Public Law 99-457: Building teams for effective planning. *Journal of Early Intervention, 16*, 146-154.

Mills, J. (January/February, 1995). Computers in preschool. *Family PC*, 161-166.

Minelli, T.M. (1994). *Chanukah fun*. New York: Tupelo Books.

Minuchin, S. (1974). *Families and family therapy*. Cambridge, MA: Harvard University Press.

Misra, A. (1994). Partnership with multicultural families. In S.K. Alper, P.J. Schloss, & C.N. Schloss (Eds.), *Families of students with disabilities* (pp. 143-179). Boston: Allyn & Bacon.

Mistrett, S.G., Raimondi, S.L., & Barnett, M.P. (1990). *The use of technology with preschoolers with handicaps*. Buffalo, NY: Preschool

Integration Through Technology Systems.

Moratinos, G.S. (1995). Teachers' attitudes toward the provision and use of augmentative and alternative communication systems by students with severe communication impairments: A structural equation model. *Dissertation Abstracts International, 56*(2), 515-A.

Mowder, B.A. (1996). Disciplinary perspectives on training: Preparing school psychologists. In D. Bricker & A. Widerstrom (Eds.), *Preparing personnel to work with infants and young children and their families: A team approach* (pp. 217-230). Baltimore: Brookes.

Morris, M.W. (1990). *Assistive technology funding. A user friendly workbook.* Washington, DC: RESNA Technical Assistance Project.

Murphy, K.E. (1988). *Thinking about setting up the home environment.* Chicago: Division of Services for Crippled Children, University of Illinois at Chicago.

Murphy, R. (1987). *The body silent.* New York: Columbia University Press.

Naisbitt, J. (1984). *Megatrends.* New York: Warner.

Nastasi, B.K., Clements, D.H., & Battista, M.T. (1990). Social-cognitive interactions, motivation, and cognitive growth in Logo programming and CAI problem-solving environments. *Journal of Educational Psychology, 82,* 150-158.

Nespor, J. (1987). The role of beliefs in the practice of teaching, *Journal of Curriculum Studies, 19,* 317-328.

Nieto, S. (1992). *Affirming diversity: The sociopolitical context of multicultural education.* White Plains,

NY: Longman.

Nover, A., & Timberlake, E. (1989). Meeting the challenge: The educational preparation of social workers for practice with at risk children (0-3) and their families. *Infants and Young Children, 2*(1), 59-65.

O'Connor, L., & Schery, T. (1986). A comparison of microcomputer-aided and traditional language therapy for developing communication skills in non-oral toddlers. *Journal of Speech and Hearing Disorders, 51,* 356-61.

Odom, S., & Warren, S. (1988). Early childhood special education in the year 2000. *Journal of the Division of Early Childhood, 12,* 263-273.

Office of Technology Assessment (1982). *Technology and handicapped people.* New York: Springer.

Ory, M., & Williams, T.F. (1990). Rehabilitation: Small goals, sustained interventions. *Annals of the American Academy of Political and Social Science, 503,* 61-76.

Owens, R.E. (1988). *Language development: An introduction.* Columbus, OH: Merrill.

Palfrey, J.S., Walker, D.K., Haynie, M., Singer, J.D., Porter, S., Bushey, B., & Cooperman, P. (1991). Technology's children: Report of a statewide consensus of children dependent on medical supports. *Pediatrics, 87,* 611-618.

Parette, H.P. (1991). The importance of technology in the education and training of persons with mental retardation. *Education and Training in Mental Retardation, 26*(3), 165-178.

Parette, H.P. (1991). *Professionals working with people with disabilities: Technology training implica-*

tions for teacher educators. (ERIC Document Reproduction Service No. ED 333 679)

Parette, H.P. (1993). Selection of appropriate technology for children with disabilities. *Teaching Exceptional Children, 25*, 18-22.

Parette, H.P. (1994). Need for assessing the influence of augmentative and alternative communication (AAC) devices on families of young children with disabilities. *Perceptual and Motor Skills, 78*, 1361-1362.

Parette, H.P. (1994, October). Family functioning and alternative communication (AAC) device prescriptive practices. Paper presented at the DEC Early Childhood Conference on Children with Special Needs, St. Louis.

Parette, H.P. (1995). Augmentative and alternative communication (AAC) assessment and prescriptive practices for young children with disabilities: Preliminary examination of state practices. *Technology and Disability, 4*, 215-231.

Parette, H.P. (1996). Introduction to the special series. *Focus on Autism and Other Developmental Disabilities, 11*(2), 66-68.

Parette, H.P. (1996, October). *Students who use augmentative and alternative communication (AAC) devices: Implications for working with families across cultures.* Paper presented to the Fifth International Conference on Mental Retardation and Developmental Disabilities, Austin, TX.

Parette, H.P. (1998). Assistive technology effective practices for students with mental retardation and developmental disabilities. In A. Hilton & R. Ringlaben (Eds.), *Best and promising practices in developmental*

disabilities (pp. 205-224). Austin, TX: PRO-ED.

Parette, H.P. (in press). Effective and promising assistive technology practices for students with mental retardation and developmental disabilities. In A. Hilton & R. Ringlaben (Eds.), *Effective and promising practices in developmental disabilities.* Austin, TX: PRO-ED.

Parette, H.P. (in press). Assistive technology devices and services. *Education and Training in Mental Retardation and Developmental Disabilities.*

Parette, H.P., & Angelo, D.H. (1996). Augmentative and alternative communication impact on families: Trends and future directions. *The Journal of Special Education, 30*(1), 77-98.

Parette, H.P., & Brotherson, M.J. (1996). Family participation in assistive technology assessment for young children with disabilities. *Education and Training in Mental Retardation and Developmental Disabilities, 31*(1), 29-43.

Parette, H.P., Brotherson, M.J., Hoge, D.R., & Hostetler, S.A. (1996, December). *Family-centered augmentative and alternative communication issues: Implications across cultures.* Paper presented to the International Early Childhood Conference on Children with Special Needs, Phoenix, AZ.

Parette, H.P., Brotherson, M.J., Hourcade, J.J., & Bradley, R.H. (1996). Family-centered assistive technology assessment. *Intervention in School and Clinic, 32*(2), 104-112.

Parette, H.P., Hofmann, A., & VanBiervliet, A. (1994). The professional's role in obtaining funding for assistive technology for infants and toddlers with disabilities. *Teaching Exceptional Children, 26,* 22-28.

Parette, H.P., & Hourcade, J.J. (1996, April). *Best practices in identifying assistive technology from a cultural perspective.* Paper presented to the 1996 Meeting of the Council for Exceptional Children, Orlando, FL.

Parette, H.P., Hourcade, J.J., & VanBiervliet, A. (1993). Selection of appropriate technology for children with disabilities. *Teaching Exceptional Children, 25*(3), 18-22.

Parette, H.P., & VanBiervliet, A. (1990a). *Assistive technology and disabilities: A guide for parents and students.* Little Rock: UALR Press. (ERIC Document Reproduction Service, ED 364 026)

Parette, H.P., & VanBiervliet, A. (1990b). *Assistive technology guide for young children with disabilities.* Little Rock, AR: University of Arkansas at Little Rock. (ERIC Document Reproduction Service, ED 324 888)

Parette, H.P., & VanBiervliet, A. (1990a). A prospective inquiry into technology needs and practices of school-age children with disabilities. *Journal of Special Education Technology, 10,* 198-206.

Parette, H.P., & VanBiervliet, A. (1990b). *Consumer and professional technology needs: An exploratory investigation of Arkansans with disabilities.* Little Rock, AR: Center for Research on Teaching and Learning.

Parette, H.P., & VanBiervliet, A. (1991). Rehabilitation assistive technology issues for infants and young children with disabilities: A preliminary examination. *Journal of Rehabilitation, 57,* 27-36.

Parette, H.P., & VanBiervliet, A. (1991). *Assistive technology curriculum: A module for inservice [and] instructor's supplment.* Little Rock, AR: University of Arkansas. (ERIC Document Reproduction Service No. ED 324 887)

Parette, H.P., & VanBiervliet, A. (1995). *Culture, families, and augmentative and alternative communication (AAC) impact: A multimedia instructional program for related services personnel and family members.* Grant funded by the U.S. Department of Education, Office of Special Education and Rehabilitative Services (No. H029K50072).

Parette, H.P., VanBiervliet, A., & Bradley, R.H. (1994, June). *Impact of augmenative and alternative communication (AAC) devices on family functioning: An examination of current state assessment and prescription practices.* Paper presented to the 118th Annual Meeting of the American Association on Mental Retardation, Boston, MA.

Paulson, K., & Christofferson, M. (1984). Psychosocial aspects of technical aids: How does independent mobility affect the psychosocial and intellectual development of children with physical disabilities. *Proceedings from the Second International Conferences on Rehabilitation Engineering* (pp. 282-286). Ottawa, Canada: RESNA.

Peterson, N.L. (1987). *Early intervention for handicapped and at-risk children.* Denver: Love.

Peterson, R.L., & Ishii-Jordan, S. (1994). *Multicultural issues in the education of students with behavioral disorders.* Cambridge, MA: Brookline Books.

Petty, L. (1994). Powered mobility for

your child? *Exceptional Parent, 24*, 33-35.

Phillips, B., & Zhao, H. (1993). Predictors of assistive technology abandonment. *Assistive Technology, 5*, 36-45.

Piaget, J. (1962). *Play, dreams and imitation in childhood.* (G. Gattegno & F.M. Hodgsom, Trans.). New York: W.W. Norton & Company.

Pierce, P. L. (1994). *Technology integration into early childhood curricula: Where we've been, where we are, where we should go.* University of North Carolina at Chapel Hill: Center for Literacy and Disability Studies. (ERIC Document Reproduction Service No. ED 386 901).

Pomales, J., & Williams, V. (1989). Effects of level of acculturation and counseling style on Hispanic students' perceptions of counselors. *Journal of Counseling Psychology, 36*, 79-83.

Pracek, E., & Atwood, B. (1993). *An exploration in matching software to Gardner's seven types of intelligences.* Handout from The Magic of the Music Mat presentation, TAM Conference. Cromwell, CT.

Ray, J., & Warden, M.K. (1995). *Technology, computers, and the special needs learner.* Albany, NY: Delmar.

Reeb, K.G. (1987). *Final report of the National Task Force on Third Party Payment for Rehabilitation Equipment.* Washington, DC: Electronic Industries Foundation.

Reed, P., & Bowser, G. (1991). *The role of occupational and physical therapy in assistive technology.* Reston, VA: Center for Special Education Technology.

Reinhartsen, D. (Ed.). (1995). *Technol-ogy for infants and toddlers made easy.* Raleigh: North Carolina Department of Human Resources, Division of Developmental Disabilities/Mental Retardation/Substance Abuse and the North Carolina Department of Environment, Health, and Natural Resources, Division of Maternal and Child Health.

Research Triangle Institute. (1992). *National evaluation of state grants for technology-related assistance for individuals with disabilities program, final report, Volume I: Evaluation findings and recommendations.* Research Triangle Park, NC: Author.

RESNA. (1989). *Technology related assistance for individuals with disabilities. Summaries of 1989 successful grant applications awarded under P.L. 100-407.* Washington, DC: RESNA Press.

Roberts, R.N. (1990). *Developing culturally competent programs for families of children with special needs* (2nd ed.). Washington, DC: Georgetown University Child Development Center.

Robinson, L. (1995) Integrating technology into birth to three programs. *Keyhole Communiqué, Assistive Technology Educational Network of Florida, 8*(2).

Roos, P. (1985). Parents of mentally retarded children: Misunderstood and mistreated. In H.R. Turnbull & A.P. Turnbull (Eds.), *Parents speak out: Then and now* (pp. 245-257). Columbus, OH: Merrill.

Rose, D., & Smith, B.J. (1994). Providing public education services to preschoolers with disabilities in community-based programs: Who's responsible for what? *Young Chil-*

dren, 49(6), 64-68.

Rowland, C., Rule, S., & Decker, D. (1996). The promise and practical application of technology to prepare early intervention personnel. *Infants and Young Children*, 9(1), 63-74.

Rozakis, L., & Armstrong, B. (1993). *Celebrate! Holidays around the world, Facts and fun for ages 5-9*. Santa Barbara, CA: The Learning Works.

Ruiz, R.A. (1981). Cultural and historical perspectives in counseling Hispanics. In D.W. Sue (Ed.), *Counseling the culturally different* (pp. 186-215). New York: Wiley and Sons.

Rutman, S.G. (1992). *Let's celebrate! A year's worth of holiday projects*. Troll Associates.

Scherer, M. (1991). Assistive technology use, avoidance and abandonment: What we know so far. *Proceedings of the 6th annual technology and persons with disabilities conference* (pp. 815-826). Washington, DC: Rehabilitation Engineering Center, National Rehabilitation Hospital.

Scherer, M.J. (1996). *Living in the state of stuck: How technology impacts the lives of people with disabilities* (2nd ed.). Cambridge, MA: Brookline Books.

Schwartz, S., & Miller, J.E.H. (1988) *The language of toys: Teaching communication skills to special-needs children*. Kensington, MD: Woodbine House.

Seligman, M.E. (1975). *Helplessness: On depression, death and development*. San Francisco: Freeman.

Sexton, D., Snyder, P., Wolfe, B., Lobman, M., Stricklin, S., & Akers, P. (1996). Early intervention inservice training strategies: Perceptions and suggestions from the field. *Excep-*

tional Children, 62, 485-496.

Shade, D., & Watson, J. A. (1990). Computers in early childhood: Issues put to rest, theoretical links to sound practice, and the potential contribution of microworlds. *Journal of Education Computing Research, 6,* 375-392.

Shaperman, J., Howard, J., & Kehr, K. (1989, October). *Beyond fun and games: The computer's role in a child's development*. Presentation presented at the meeting of the Closing the Gap Conference, Bloomington, MN.

Sheiman, D.L. (1986). Infant play. In H. Nuba-Scheffler, D.L. Sheiman, & K.P. Watkins (Eds.), *Infancy: A guide to research and resources* (pp. 113-127). New York: Teachers College Press.

Silverman, F.H. (1989). *Communication for the speechless*. Engelwood Cliffs, NJ: Prentice-Hall.

Sivin-Kachala, J. & Bialo, E. (1996). *Report on the effectiveness of technology in schools, 95-96*. Washington, DC: Software Publishers Association.

Smart, J.F., & Smart, D.W. (1992). Cultural changes in multicultural rehabilitation. *Rehabilitation Education, 6*(2), 105-122.

Smedley, C.E., Heiple, V.S., Baker, S., Dunn, N., Parette, H.P., & Hendricks, M. (1997). *Keyboard Kids: Using computers to teach young children*. Little Rock, AR: Arkansas Easter Seal Society.

Smilansky, S., & Shefatya, L. (1990). *Facilitating play: A medium for providing cognitive, socioemotional, and academic development in young children*. Gaithersburg, MD: Psychosocial and Educational Publications.

Smith, R., Benge, M., & Hall, M. (1994). Technology for self-care. In C. Christiansen (Ed.), *Ways of living: Self-care strategies for special needs* (pp. 379-422). Rockville, MD: American Occupational Therapy Association.

Smith, R.O., Vanderheiden, G.C., Berliss, J, & Angelo, J. (1989). Creating and testing an effective design for a desktop version of ABLEDATA. In J.J. Presperin (Ed.), *RESNA '89. Technology for the Next Decade.* New Orleans: RESNA Press.

Smith, R.W., Osborne, L.T., Crim, D., & Rhu, A.H. (1986). Labeling theory as applied to learning disabilities: Findings and policy suggestions. *Journal of Learning Disabilities, 19*(4), 195-202.

Smith-Lewis, M. (1992). *What is mental retardation? Perceptions from the African American community.* Unpublished manuscript. Hunter College, New York.

Smith-Lewis, M.R., & Ford, A. (1987). A user's perspective on augmentative communication. *Augmentative and Alternative Communication, 3*, 12-17.

Software for special education needn't be boring. (1996, August/September). *Children's Software Revue, 4*(4), 19.

Somerville, N.J., Wilson, D.J., Shanfield, K.J., & Mack, W. (1990). A survey of the assistive technology training needs of occupational therapists. *Assistive Technology, 2*, 41-49.

Soto, G. (1995). A cultural perspective on augmentative and alternative communication. *ASHA Special Interest Divisions* (Division 12), *3*(3), 6-7.

Soto, G., Huer, M.B., & Taylor, O. (1997). Multicultural issues. In L.L. Lloyd, D.H. Fuller, & H.H. Arvidson (Eds.), *Augmentative and alternative communication* (pp. 406-413). Boston: Allyn and Bacon.

Sparks, G.M. (1986). The effectiveness of alternative training activities in changing practices. *American Educational Research Journal, 23*, 217-225.

Spiegel-McGill, P., Zippiroli, S.M., & Mistrett, S.G. (1989). Microcomputers as social facilitators in integrated preschools. *Journal of Early Intervention, 13*, 249-260.

STARNet. (1996, December). *Once upon a time...: Computers and early literacy development* [videotape]. Available from Macomb Projects, 27 Horrabin Hall, Western Illinois University, Macomb, IL 61455.

Strickland, D.S. (1990). Emergent literacy: How young children learn to read and write. *Educational Leadership, 47*(6), 18-23.

Sullivan, M.W., & Lewis, M. (1990). Contingency intervention: A program portrait. *Journal of Early Intervention, 14*, 367-375.

Sullivan, M.W., & Lewis, M. (1993). Contingency, means-end skills, and the use of technology in infant intervention. *Infants and Young Children, 5*(4), 58-77.

Summers, J.A., Dell'Oliver, C., Turnbull, A., Benson, H.A., Santelli, E., Campbell, M., & Siegel-Causey, E. (1990). Examining the individualized family service plan process: What are family and practitioner preferences? *Topics in Early Childhood Special Education, 10*, 78-99.

Swartz, A. (1994). Computer or related technology use at home by children and youth with disabilities: A survey of parents. *Dissertation Abstracts International, 54*(12), 4408-A.

Tanchak, T.L., & Sawyer, C. (1995). Augmentative communication. In K.F. Flippo, K.J. Inge, & J.M. Barcus (Eds.), *Assistive technology: A resource for school, work, and community* (pp. 57-79). Baltimore: Brookes.

Taylor, O.L., & Clarke, M.G. (1994). Culture and communication disorders: A theoretical framework. *Seminars in Speech and Language, 15*, 103-113.

Taylor, R.P. (1980). *The computer in the school: Tutor, tool, tutee.* New York: NY: Teacher's College Press.

Technology-Related Assistance for Individuals with Disabilities Act of 1988, P.L 100-407. (August 19, 1988). Title 29, U.S.C. 2201 *et seq: U.S. Statutes at Large, 102*, 1044-1065.

Technology-Related Assistance for Individuals with Disabilities Act of 1994, PL 103-218. (March 9, 1994). Title 29, U.S.C. 2201 et seq: *U.S. Statutes at Large, 108*, 50-97.

Thorkildsen, R. (1994). *Executive summary of research synthesis on quality and availability of assistive technology devices.* Technical Report No. 8. Eugene, OR: National Center to Improve the Tools of Educators, College of Education.

Thorp, E.K., & McCollum, J.A. (1994). Personnel in early intervention programs: Areas of needed competence. In L.J. Johnson, R.J. Gallagher, M.J. LaMontagne, J.B. Jordan, J.J. Gallagher, P.L. Hutinger, & M.B. Karnes (Eds.), *Meeting early intervention challenges* (pp. 167-184). Baltimore: Brookes.

Torres-Davis, A., & Trivelli, L.U.

(1994). *Project Reaching Out: Part II—Technology training for Hispanics with disabilities.* Arlington, VA: RESNA.

Trachtman, L.H., & Pierce, P.L. (1995). *North Carolina infant, toddler and preschooler assistive technology needs assessment: A report on the provision of assistive technology to children with disabilities from birth to age five in North Carolina.* Raleigh, NC: North Carolina Assistive Technology Project.

Trohanis, P.L. (1994). Planning for successful inservice education for local early childhood programs. *Topics in Early Childhood Special Education, 14*, 311-332.

Turnbull, A.P., Summers, J.A., & Brotherson, M.J. (1984). *Working with families with disabled members: A family systems approach.* Lawrence, KS: University of Kansas, Kansas University Affiliated Facility.

Turnbull, A.P., & Turnbull, H.R. (1990). *Families, professionals, and exceptionality: A special partnership* (2nd ed.). Columbus, OH: Merrill.

Turner, E., Barrett, C., Cutshall, A., Lacy, B.K., Keiningham, J., & Webster, M.K. (1995). The user's perspective of assistive technology. In K.F. Flippo, K.J. Inge, & J.M. Barcus (Eds.), *Assistive technology: A resource for school, work, and community* (pp. 283-290). Baltimore: Brookes.

Turner, R., & Noh, S. (1988). Physical disability and depression: A longitudinal analysis. *Journal of Health Behavior, 29*, 23-37.

U.S. Congress Office of Technology Assessment (1987). *Technology-dependent children: Hospital v. home care—A technical memorandum*

(OTS-TM-H-38). Washington, DC: U.S. Government Printing Office.

VanBiervliet, A., & Cox, G. (1991). An MS-DOS and screen reader compatible program for retrieving information from ABLEDATA. In J.J. Presperin (Ed.), *RESNA '91: Technology for the Nineties* (pp. 74-75). Kansas City, MO: RESNA Press.

Vanderheiden, G.C. (1990). Development of a public domain, user accessible, inter-state directory/database for assistive technology service delivery programs. In J.J. Presperin (Ed.), *RESNA '90. Capitalizing on technology for persons with disabilities* (pp. 222-223). Washington, DC: RESNA Press.

Van Dyck, M., Allaire, J., & Gressard, R. (1990). AAC decision-making. *Communication Outlook, 11*, 12-14.

Virginia Assistive Technology System. (1993). *National research of loan-financing practice*. Richmond, VA: Author.

Vygotsky, L.S. (1986). *Thought and language*. (A. Kozulin, Trans.) Cambridge, MA: MIT Press. (Original work published 1962.)

Wachtel, R.C., & Compart, P.J. (1996). Disciplinary perspectives on training: Preparing pediatricians. In D. Bricker & A. Widerstrom (Eds.), *Preparing personnel to work with infants and young children and their families* (pp. 181-198). Baltimore: Brookes.

Wallace, J.F. (1995). Creative financing of assistive technology. In K.F. Flippo, K.J. Inge, & J.M. Barcus (Eds.), *Assistive technology: A resource for school, work, and community* (pp. 245-268). Baltimore: Brookes.

Ward, C. (1989). *Subsidy programs for assistive devices*. Washington, DC: Electronic Industries Foundation.

Waters, K., & Slovenz-Low, M. (1990). *Lion dancer: Ernie Wan's Chinese new year*. New York: Scholastic.

Watson, A.J., Lange, G.J., Brinkley, V.M. (1992). Logo mastery and spatial problem-solving by young children: Effects of Logo language training, route-strategy training, and learning styles on immediate learning and transfer. *Journal of Educational Computing Research, 8* (4), 521-40.

Wells, G. (1986). *The meaning makers: Children learning language and using language to learn*. Portsmouth, NH: Heinemann.

Wershing, A. (April, 1990). Switch-ing toys, Part 1. *Exceptional Parent, 72*.

Wershing, A., & Symington, L. (1996). *High tech and small folks: Learning and growing with technology*. Sevierville, TN: International Network Publishers. (Available from Special Needs Project, (800) 333-6687).

Widerstrom, A., & Abelman, D. (1996). Team training issues. In D. Bricker & A. Widerstrom (Eds.), *Preparing personnel to work with infants and young children and their families* (pp. 23-41). Baltimore: Brookes.

Winton, P. (1990). A systematic approach for planning inservice training related to Public Law 99-457. *Infants and Young Children, 3*(1), 51-60.

Winton, P.J., & Bailey, D.B. (1990). Early intervention training related to family interviewing. *Topics in Early Childhood Special Education, 10*, 50-62.

Winton, P.J., McCollum, J.A., & Catlett, C. (Eds.). (1997). *Reforming person-*

nel preparation in early interven-tion: Issues, models, and practical strategies. Baltimore, MD: Brookes.

Wischnowski, M.W., Yates, T.J., & McCollum, J.A. (1996). Expanding training options for early intervention personnel: Developing a state-wide staff mentoring system. Infants and Young Children, 8(4), 49-58.

Wolery, M., Strain, P., & Bailey, D. (1992). Reaching potentials of children with special needs. In S. Bredekamp & T. Rosegrant (Eds.), Reaching potentials: Appropriate curriculum and assessment for young children (Vol. 1) (pp. 92-113). Washington, DC: National Association for the Education of Young Children.

Woodruff, G., & McGonigel, M. (1988). Early intervention team approaches: The transdisciplinay model. In J. Gordon, P. Hutinger, M. Karnes, & J. Gallagher (Eds.), Early childhood special education (pp. 163-181). Reston, VA: Council for Exceptional Children.

Wright, C., & Nomura, (1991). From toys to computers. Santa Barbara, CA: Special Needs Project.

Wright, J. L., & Shade, D. D. (1994). Young Children: Active Learners in a Technological Age. Washington, DC: NAEYC.

Yelland, N. (1992-1993). Introducing young children to Logo. Computing Teacher, 20(4), 12-14.

Yelland, N. (1995a). Encouraging young children's thinking skills with Logo. Childhood Education, 71(3), 152-155.

Yelland, N. (1995b). Experiences with young children: Describing performance, problem-solving, and social contexts of learning. Early Childhood Development and Care, 109, 61-74.

Yelland, N. (1995c). Experiences with young children: Describing performance, problem-solving, and social contexts of learning. Early Childhood Development and Care, 110, 33-46.

Zipper, I.N., Weil, M. & Rounds, K. (1991). Service coordination for early intervention: Parents and professionals. Chapel Hill, NC: Carolina Institute for Research on Infant Personnel Preparations, Frank Porter Graham Child Development Center, University of North Carolina.

Zippiroli, S., Bayer, D., & Mistrett, S. (1988). Use of the microcomputer as a social facilitator between physically handicapped and non-handicapped preschoolers. Final report for HCEEP. (Available through UCPA of Western New York, 4635 Union Rd., Cheektowaga, NY 14225).

INDEX

A

software *(Continued)*
  basic features, 118, 119
    compatibility and system requirements, 116-118
  children's interaction with, 105-106
  children's preferences in, 109
  classification, 93-94
    into curricular themes, 96
  design features, 120, 122-124
    characteristics of young children and, 121-122
    literacy and developmental concerns, 121
  evaluation, 124-125
  history, 90-93
  "housekeeping" and "management," 114-116
  licensing and consumer rights, 113-114
  open-ended, 89
  paired with computers, benefits to children of, 87-90
  resource use, wise, 111
  selected for adaptive devices, 84
  shareware and freeware, 111-112
  teaching switch keys, 86-87
software functions, 94-99
  interactivity and, 99-102
  levels of, 100, 101
software resources, 253-256
  internet, 256-258
software users
  responsibility and legal requirements, 112-113
  young children as, 78-79, 121-122
Soloway, E., 120, 122
Somerville, N.J., 237
Soto, G., 185, 186, 200, 241
Sparks, G.M., 216
Sparling, J.W., 17, 212
Speaking Dynamically, writing activity using, 72-74
special education and intervention. *See also* early intervention
  early childhood, 213-215
  guidelines for, 47-48
speech output of auditory devices, digitized *vs.* synthesized, 35-36

Spence, K., 214, 221
Spiegel-McGill, P., 2, 17, 39, 64, 211
staff. *See* personnel; professionals
Stayton, V.D., 214
Stevens, K.B., 221
stigma of using AT devices, 195, 198
  culture and, 195
Stoneburner, R., 8, 10
story time, 29-30
Strain, P., 19
Strickland, D.S., 59
Stricklin, S., 215, 221, 222
Sturn, L., 214
Sullivan, M.W., 17, 211, 212
Summers, J.A., 182
Swaminathan, S., 89, 90
Swartz, A., 137
Swenson-Miller, K., 214
switch-adapted toys, alternative input devices and, 49
switches, actions required for activating, 20-23
switch keys, teaching, 86-87
symbolic (pretend) play, 20, 23
  adults' roles in, 23-24
  technology in, 23-25
    software, 25
Symington, L., 53, 67, 70
systems perspective, 152. *See also* family, as system
  interaction within spheres of influence, 202-203

T

Tanchak, T.L., 34
Tashjian, M.D., 6, 10
Taylor, O., 185, 186, 241
Taylor, O.L., 201
Taylor, R.P., 94, 99
teachers, limited knowledge and usage of AT, 7
team collaboration, 127-128. *See also* assessment, team-based; family involvement; family-professional teaming
  family needs and, 160-161

About the Editors

Sharon Lesar Judge, Ph.D., is an assistant professor in the College of Education at the University of Tennessee in Knoxville. She received her doctorate in 1993 from the University of California, Santa Barbara. During her more than 20 years in early intervention, she has been involved in direct services and personnel preparation and has conducted numerous studies in the area of family-centered practices and assistive technology. Dr. Judge currently directs Project Prepare, a personnel preparation grant that prepares early childhood special educators to work in inclusive early childhood settings.

Howard P. Parette, Jr., Ed.D., is a professor in the College of Education at Southeast Missouri State University. He has published extensively regarding children with special needs. In recent years, he has focused particular attention on cross-cultural applications of assistive technology for children with disabilities and their families. He is currently Principal Investigator for a U.S. Department of Education Special Project designed to develop an interactive, bilingual CD-ROM that can be used with families across cultures, teachers, and related service personnel during augmentative and alternative communication (AAC) decision-making.